What Editors, Publishers and Writers are saying about
THE FREELANCE SUCCESS BOOK

"The most practical and entertaining book I've ever read on free-lance writing. A must for every writer's bookcase."
—*Mike Lafavore, Founding Editor,* Men's Health

"David Taylor is a master teacher, editor and writer. In THE FREE-LANCE SUCCESS BOOK he uses those talents to produce a work that will help writers earn paychecks and bylines. My strong advice: Buy this book before your competition does."
—*John Griffin, President, Magazine Group,*
National Geographic Society

"There is no better book on the art and commerce of freelance writing. As a writer, teacher, editor and publisher, David Taylor has worked all sides of the freelance street. Trust this man with your professional life. Rookies and dreamers: you may think you know how to get an assignment; you don't. Established pros: you may think you know it all already; you don't. From fair use to fair pay to cutting an edge with that strange new weapon known as the Internet, THE FREELANCE SUCCESS BOOK belongs in every writer's laptop case."
—*Michael Zimmerman, author,*
The Complete Idiot's Guide to Surviving Anything

"You can ride into the editorial process like a cowboy, six guns blazing, maybe hit the target every so often, or take David's advice and save your ammunition by carefully targeting the writing market. I handle a lot of copyright, trademark and even defamation legal matters, and only rarely have I found the information a writer needs put down so clearly and succinctly. THE FREELANCE

SUCCESS BOOK is a solid guide with important web addresses for reference."

—John Christopher Fine, author,
The Boy And the Dolphin, *former New York Chief Prosecutor*

"This book will absolutely improve your chances of selling your writing. It is more valuable than a writing course, and in a few hours will give you the insight of years of top-level experience."

—Barbara Newton, former Vice-President,
Managing Director, Prevention

"I plan on giving a copy of this book to every freelance writer I work with."

—Dave Zinczenko, Editor-in-Chief, Men's Health

"If you're serious about getting published or writing for real income, David Taylor will shorten the learning curve and help you skip the mistakes. THE FREELANCE SUCCESS BOOK provides the inside information and inspiration you'll need to make it in the 'really neat' career of freelance writing."

—Dana K. Cassell, freelancer, book author, and director of the
www.writers-editors.com *network.*

"This is the best book on the business of writing that I've ever seen. Fiction and nonfiction scribes alike will benefit from the well-researched, practical information on stuff that can be tricky and sticky: contracts, copyrights, and the conniption fits that editors sometimes have when freelancers don't follow the protocols and etiquette of the writing business. THE FREELANCE SUCCESS BOOK lets you avoid the unpleasantness and revel in the pay stubs. Buy it, use it, don't lose it."

—J.N. Williamson, editor,
How to Write Tales of Horror, Fantasy and Science Fiction

WANT TO SEE YOUR ARTICLES PUBLISHED IN THESE MAGAZINES?

Prevention

Outside

Men's Journal

Organic Style

Men's Health

Runner's World

Backpacker

Bicycling

Sci-Fi Channel Magazine

They're magazines at the publishing company where David Taylor served as executive editor for almost a decade, and magazines where he has sold his own features.

Let one of America's most respected magazine professionals take you inside an editor's office to learn some never-before-published techniques for getting all the freelance assignments you can handle. To become the kind of writer that editors dream of—and the kind they reward handsomely—all you need is:

THE FREELANCE SUCCESS BOOK

The
FREELANCE
SUCCESS
BOOK

WRITE IT, SELL IT!

The
FREELANCE
SUCCESS
BOOK

Insider
Secrets
For Selling
Every Word
You Write

DAVID TAYLOR

Foreword by **Bob Teufel, Magazine Publishers of America**

The Freelance Success Book
Insider Secrets for Selling Every Word You Write
By David Taylor

Other fine Peak Writing books available at local bookstores or online at
www.peakwriting.com.
Feedback to the author: david@freelancesuccessbook.com
Sales information: sales@peakwriting.com

Library of Congress Control Number: 2002095477

Interior design by Pneuma Books, LLC
For more information, visit www.pneumabooks.com

Cover by George Foster, www.fostercovers.com

Publisher's Cataloging-in-Publication
(*Provided by Quality Books, Inc.*)

Taylor, David, 1950-
   The freelance success book : insider secrets for
selling every word you write / by David Taylor.
     p. cm. -- (Write it, sell it ; 1)
   Includes bibliographical references and index.
   ISBN 0-9717330-4-X

   1. Authorship--Vocational guidance. 2. Freelance
journalism--Vocational guidance. I. Title.
PN153.T39 2003   808'.02
                  QBI02-200819

10 09 08 07 06 05 04 03   5 4 3 2 1

This book is dedicated to

Blake Ellis

for giving me the dream, the broadband and his unwavering belief
in Peak Writing and the revolution we call the Internet.

You were right, Blake:
"On the web, if you can think it, it can happen."

Same for our freelance dreams.

"The world is before you, and you need not take it or leave it as when you came in."
—James Baldwin

TABLE OF CONTENTS

"The profession of book writing makes horse racing seem like a solid, stable business."
—John Steinbeck

FOREWORD

Frankly I was surprised that David Taylor asked me to write a foreword to this wonderfully useful book. Although I have been in the magazine industry for nearly forty years, my career has been spent in the nasty business side. I'm from the world of P&Ls, circulation promotion, ad sales and production. What most writers would consider "the dark side."

But when I read *The Freelance Success Book* I had another view. Of course it's fitting I comment because this is, first and foremost, a business book—the business of writing and selling a desperately needed and fervently desired product: your words. Your words and articles are the product that publishers depend on to drive renewals, zip single copies off newsstands and move readers to action. And right now that editorial product—the articles, columns, interviews and features that David tells you how to create and sell—is needed more than ever.

Today, magazine revenues are stressed by higher postal rates, newsstand drop-off and a stagnated advertising market. Consumers are holding the line on paying higher magazine prices, with many subscription rates boldly advanced only to be timidly pushed back the following month.

The outcome is predictable. If a publisher can't increase revenue, he or she must consider the next option: reducing costs. And while publishers can lower paper quality, cut basis weight and perhaps negotiate with a printer, they cannot outsource postal costs—one of the greatest costs of publishing a magazine.

That leaves publishers staring coldly at the editorial expense line with another predictable outcome: wanting to outsource a substantial portion of that editorial cost by using you, freelancers.

Congratulations: You're finally at the right place at the right time. The magazine industry needs you and your services right now more than we have in a long, long time. I highly recommend that you read this book, get writing, and start marketing your wares. And do not be namby-pamby about it!

Magazines spend hundreds of thousands of dollars a year on their own public relations. They hire high-priced PR folks to pitch their story, their successes and their vitality to the media trade press and general media. Magazines know how to pitch, and good editors appreciate it when someone is professional in pitching to them. Editors know how the game is played. Read this book and you will, too.

—Bob Teufel
Chairman Emeritus,
Magazine Publishers of America

"You have to know how to accept rejection and reject acceptance."
—Ray Bradbury

PREFACE

Harsh fact—When it comes to the freelancing game, editors hold the trump card: the power to choose which writers to hire. This book helps freelancers deal successfully with that powerful fact. The method is simple: To whisper and sometimes shout to freelance writers about the things they've never heard before regarding editors, publishers, publishing companies and other insiders who inhabit the world that freelancers, by definition, are shut out of.

While serving nine years as an executive editor at Rodale Press (now Rodale, Inc.), I wish I had a Mac laptop for every time I said about freelancers: "If only they knew!" Everyone's life would've been a lot richer if only freelancers knew more about how to give editors what they want, if only freelancers had a foolproof way to figure out what editors want, if only freelancers understood more about the sometimes Planet Pluto-like world that editors and publishers live in.

Editors need and want good freelance writers. You give our magazines variety. You save us money and time. You don't demand medical benefits or a 401(k) plan—and labor costs are always an editorial expense budget's fattest line. We don't have to take a hard-working department editor away from daily duties for a story needed right away from a source in Iowa.

You're also what nonfiction writing is all about: Independence. Unique viewpoint. Digging. Getting the stories no one else can get, especially harried staffers. Writing nobody's stories but your own. It takes guts and determination to make it as a freelancer. That's another fact.

My hope is that this book of "insider stuff" will provide gutsy, determined freelance writers a bridge into the offices of editors, agents, publishing company lawyers (brrr!), prepress houses, printers and fact-checkers. When you get there, set the goods on the table, ready to be laid out and dummied up. That's when you'll get a friend for life—an appreciative editor.

—David Taylor

"Writers and ax murderers have little choice about their calling."

CHAPTER ONE

THE WRITING ITCH AND WHAT TO DO ABOUT IT

- Self Test: Do I Have What It Takes to Be a Freelance Writer?
- Self Test: Am I Ready to Go Full-Time as a Freelancer?
- What's It Like to Be a Full-Time Writer and Editor?
- Should I Quit My Daytime Job and Write?
- Is a College Degree Necessary for Success?
- How Do I Prepare for a Writing Job Interview?

Permit me to answer a question that likely dwells in the back of your mind, hidden like an intruder in the dark, ready to pounce: "Do I have what it takes to be a writer?" It is my absolute pleasure to assure you that, yes, by virtue of being a person of normal intelligence, ambition and drive, you do indeed have what it takes. I base that knowledge on 24 years of teaching aspiring writers and supervising professional ones.

It's true: If you want it, you can have it. You don't have to be born into a literary family, to have attended college (indeed, college can hurt your writing in several ways), or to have had a traumatic childhood that turned you inward. You just have to want it—then go out and get the knowledge and skills that let you do it.

And, by the way, that question about having what it takes? It's also my experience that only those who do indeed have what it takes ever ask the question in the first place.

SELF TEST: DO I HAVE WHAT IT TAKES TO BE A FREELANCE WRITER?

What's in a name? In this case, it's about 10 things that successful freelance writers have in common. How do you stack up? Note: This is not a timed test and the results will not appear on your permanent record.

Please answer "yes," "no" or "coming soon" to each of the following questions.

1. I own a computer, printer (laser or ink-jet, not dot-matrix) and professional word processing program.
    - ○ yes
    - ○ no
    - ○ coming soon

2. I own a market book for my genre (*Writer's Market, Novel and Short Story Writer's Market, Online Market,* etc.)
    - ○ yes
    - ○ no
    - ○ coming soon

3. I have identified the publications I want to write for, subscribe to them, own recent back issues, or visit them regularly online.
    - ○ yes
    - ○ no
    - ○ coming soon

4. I have designated a specific time during which I write at least five days a week.
   ○ yes
   ○ no
   ○ coming soon

5. I write in a workplace that I have set up especially for writing.
   ○ yes
   ○ no
   ○ coming soon

6. I frequently use the Internet as a research tool.
   ○ yes
   ○ no
   ○ coming soon

7. I have my own letterhead and business cards.
   ○ yes
   ○ no
   ○ coming soon

8. When writing, I regularly use my own dictionary, synonym finder, grammar and usage guides specific to my genre.
   ○ yes
   ○ no
   ○ coming soon

9. I have discussed my writing ambitions with my significant others.
   ○ yes
   ○ no
   ○ coming soon

10. My goal is to write, not just to see my name in print.
   - ○ yes
   - ○ no
   - ○ coming soon

Scoring Guide

- 8-10 yes. You have overcome the basic obstacles to freelance success: finding time, making a clear commitment, getting organized and getting wired. Put on some coffee. Crank up the tunes. And tell editors to watch their in-boxes.

- 4 to 7 yes. How does it feel, sitting on that fence? Just testing the waters? That's fine. Take your time. But at some point know that a commitment must come. At some point, a reckoning with the heart must take place. Use the tools in this book to make a firm decision, yea or nay. And remember: the key to making any decision work is what you do after you make it. Be firm, be committed to the direction you've taken, never look back.

- 0 to 3 yes. You're just starting out. That's fine, too. Hopefully it's clearer now that there are important differences between writing as a hobby and writing as a profession.

Comments

1. Deduct a half point if you share your computer with family or others. If you're going to write professionally, you need your own tools, not borrowed ones.

2. The first time you buy one of these books you quickly realize that you must find your niche in the freelance world. That means two things: (a) identifying and nurturing your areas

of expertise and interest; (b) immersing yourself in that specific world.

3. Understanding and writing for specific publications is the key to success. Although we all start with the dream of "being a writer," that grand dream can quickly turn into a grand illusion unless we learn to shape our writing for a specific outlet—whether a group of similar magazines, a book genre or TV show format. Each has its own "code" that you must break before publishing in it successfully.

4. and 5. Discipline. All writers struggle with it to some extent, and the struggle is never over. But it does become more of a nuisance than a roadblock. Like the urge some mornings to skip brushing your teeth. You may be tempted, but you know the outcome of your laziness will stink.

6. As an ad for the *Washington Post* says, "If you don't get it, you don't get it." The Internet is the most important advance for freelance writers since postage stamps.

7. At some point, you're really gonna wish you had these, although they may seem vain and superfluous to you now. I promise that some day you will be embarrassed that you don't have them, and then you will go out and get them immediately after.

8. Again, every profession has its tools. Your toolbox must include these and more. And forget Roget's. Use J.I. Rodale's *Synonym Finder*.

9. Same goes for getting on a weight-loss diet: It's not real until

the world knows about it. You need to identify who supports you and who doesn't. Don't be surprised at who ends up in the second category.

10. The thrill of seeing your name in print wears off after it happens a few times. What will replace that motivation when it does? Hopefully the answer has something to do with the satisfaction of practicing your craft and the importance of using writing to help make sense of the world, yourself, and your place in it.

SELF TEST: AM I READY TO GO FULL-TIME AS A FREELANCER?

Tired of being a wage slave? Ready to spread your wings and fly free? Without medical benefits and guaranteed paydays, it can be a long way back down to earth.

I forget the exact moment I suffered an entrepreneurial seizure and decided that, for now and forever, I wanted to own the products of my labor, set my own hours, write what I wanted to write and answer to the only boss who mattered—the one inside my heart.

It must've been during one of those blurry, post-Ayn Rand moments late at night or early in the morning, because giving up tenure, retirement plan, paid vacations, family-emergency leave, tuition assistance, expense account and a sabbatical every few years was definitely a decision that came from the gut, not my certified financial planner.

Oh well. What's done is done, and if you don't believe me, just look at my bank account.

But here I am, writing what I want to write, free of that spiritual jail called a corporate office. Is it worth it?

Without a peso of doubt.

Only one regret: I wish someone had made me complete the following checklist first.

Full-Timer Self Test

Please note: The results of this test will definitely appear on your permanent record.

Please answer "yes" or "no" to each of the following questions.

1. I write five or more days every week, without prompting, without fuss, and I find doing it significantly more rewarding than my current job.
   ○ yes   ○ no

2. I can write at least one feature article, one book chapter or one well-researched query letter per week.
   ○ yes   ○ no

3. Currently, my work is being accepted at least as often as it is being rejected.
   ○ yes   ○ no

4. I work regularly with at least one editor.
   ○ yes   ○ no

5. At least one editor has called me to initiate an assignment.
   ○ yes   ○ no

6. Last year as a writer, I earned at least one-third of my present salary, or $6,000, whichever is higher.
   ○ yes   ○ no

7. I have set up a writing business that includes an accounting system, office equipment, tax filing and business stationery.
   ○ yes   ○ no

8. As liquid financial reserve, I have saved at least one year's salary that is not invested in a tax-exempt retirement account.
   ○ yes   ○ no

9. I have written a one-year business plan that includes a full accounting of projected expenses, revenues and contingency plans.
   ○ yes   ○ no

10. My family/significant others are fully aware of my desires to work full-time as a freelancer and have pledged to provide their moral and emotional support.
    ○ yes   ○ no

Scoring Guide

If you answered "no" to any items other than 7, 9 or 10, it is my opinion that you are not yet ready to go full-time as a freelancer. Here's why:

Comments

1. If you're squeezing in time during a hectic schedule to write, that's wonderful; it shows discipline and commitment. But doing it full-time is going to mean sitting in front of a computer screen researching, composing and editing for 8 to 12 hours a day, often more. You had better find it not just rewarding, but the very lifestyle you wish to lead.

   I knew I was ready to go full-time when I started stealing time from my job obligations to write, when I would rather write than work out, when I would rather write than, well, almost anything. If writing is something that you're having to force yourself to do, you should wait and see how that situation resolves itself. It's probably just a matter of time before you hit your stride, get some bylines and all the confidence that comes with them.

2. This item is about productivity. A cruel calculus is at work: When you first begin, if you take the number of hours you need to produce a finished piece and market it, then divide that number by your payment, you'll get your new hourly wage. Don't be surprised if it's $15 per hour or less. When you're working at those rates, you had better be able to crank out copious amounts of copy. One feature article, chapter or query per week is probably a minimum if you're going to be financially self-sufficient.

3. Rejections will always be a part of freelancing. There will forever be reasons beyond your control why your work was not selected by that particular editor, on that particular day. But before you go full-time, your rejections should be well within the acceptable range: For most full-time freelancers, the rejection rate is lower than 50 percent. The reason why is contained in the next two items.

4. Before making the leap, you need to have at least one foot planted firmly inside an editor's door. Working regularly with an editor means you've found a home for your expertise, your style, your personality. You fit. You belong. You've got everything it takes. And if you can do it with one editor, you can do it with others. Also, by not sending in cold queries and manuscripts, you will lower your rejection rate significantly.

5. Of course, one sure-fire way to reduce rejections is to get an assignment directly from an editor. And that's exactly what

happens once your name begins appearing regularly in print within a specific genre—one more argument to focus on being a specialist when you're starting out.

6. If you're making this much money doing it part-time, you've got the skills and the contacts that will enable you to take your business to the next level. Don't cheat on this number. There are going to be good years and lean years. Be ready for one, surprised by the other.

7. OK, so you're a sloppy accountant and you don't have business cards. That doesn't bother me because I know that once you start writing as a full-time professional you'll treat it as a business, not a hobby—or you won't be doing it for long.

8. Plans and promises—When you're a self-sufficient businessperson you'll be shocked by how empty the promises of others can be. If you're like me, it's going to take a few hard lessons before you learn to tell the frauds from the real thing, and to develop the hard edge it takes to be an independent businessperson. In the meantime, I bet you'll count on projects and people who fail to come through for you. Guess what? Your mortgage company doesn't take excuses or sob stories.

9. Same as 7. I highly recommend the free resources offered by the Small Business Association and on the Internet (see toolbox).

10. I debated whether or not to make this a requirement. If I had written this while still a corporate slave, it would've been required. But now—hey, if you gotta do it, you gotta do it. In the meantime, hope for their acceptance, praise and sup-

WRITER'S TOOLBOX
ONLINE BUSINESS RESOURCES FOR FREELANCERS

- *www.allbusiness.com* — The self-styled "Champions of Small Business" provide 10 info-rich sections of articles, tools and forms—all for free.

- *www.bizmove.com/starting.htm* — Their "Small Business Knowledge Base" is a comprehensive free resource of small business information with guides, tools and techniques.

- *www.homeofficemag.com* — Articles from the company's HomeOffice magazine.

- *www.officedepot.com/BusinessTools/sbh/* — As if you needed another reason to shop there, OD's "Small Business Handbook" is a treasure.

- *www.smallbusinessbc.ca/ibp/index.html* — Don't miss this interactive workshop on preparing your business plan. A service from the experts at the British Columbia Business Services Society. Free, eh?

- *www.soho.org* — Another rich collection of freely accessed article archives, from the Small Office Home Office advocacy group. Good stuff.

port—sure does make things easier. Bottom line: nice but not essential.

WHAT'S IT LIKE TO BE A FULL-TIME WRITER AND EDITOR?

"I'm interested in preparing for a career in journalism, and I'd like to ask you a few questions. What are the greatest rewards and disadvantages? What's the best way to prepare for a writing career? What is the most important trait one needs to be successful? What do you do when you get writer's block? What influenced

you to become a writer? What is your weekly salary? What are the most important workplace skills? What related skills should I learn? Will writers be in demand when I graduate from college in 2006?"

Thanks for your many and varied questions. They provided a chance for me to stop and reflect about big-picture things that are important and that we sometimes lose sight of.

Greatest Rewards

Reveling in words. Seeing their effects on others. Making a positive difference in a reader's life. Feeling the rewards of being a professional. Fulfilling one of the most ancient roles in any culture: scribe for the tribe.

Greatest Difficulty

Overcoming the growing disrespect and cynicism generated by the shameless pandering of some mass media.

Best Way to Prepare for a Writing Career

At the academic level, the answer is easy:

1. Take the most difficult English track your school has to offer.

2. Commit to a personal reading enrichment program that includes a good newspaper, news magazine, popular fiction, great works, history and biography.

3. Write something every day without thought to style or grammar. Listen to your inner voice and capture the free flow of thought on paper or computer screen. Write as fast as you can without stopping for 15 minutes. Every day.

4. Seek out internships at newspapers, magazines or anywhere professionals writers are practicing their craft. Do ANYTHING to be there with working professionals.

5. Become the editor of your school newspaper or yearbook. Don't be satisfied with writing for them.

6. Go to the best liberal arts college you can get into. Don't go to J-School unless it's for a graduate degree.

Essential Trait for Success

An unquenchable desire to discover the truth and tell others about it, no matter what.

Writer's Block

Professional writers don't get the emotional type of block. They've learned to prepare properly, to control their writing environment, and they've developed tricks that allow them to plow through the rough patches.

Motivation to Become a Writer

I don't believe writers have any more choice about what they do than a sociopathic ax murderer does. I truly believe genetics and early experiences determine whether or not you get saddled with the compulsion to write. Sure, technique must be taught or gained through trial and error. But if you're going to write, nothing stops you. Not even the idiosyncratic advice from people like me.

Salary

The magazine *Folio:* publishes annual salary averages for all magazine positions by circulation size and geographic location. That would be more helpful to you. Pay rates for freelance writers can be found on the web site of the National Writer's Union (*www.nwu.org*) and in the book *Writer's Market* (Writer's Digest Books).

Workplace Skills

Respect and courtesy at all times, in all situations. Don't dwell on the negative. Assume the best about others, until proven otherwise. Focus only on those things in the workplace that make a positive difference. The rest is a waste of time and energy—and usually hurt your chances of getting ahead.

Important Related Skills

Ultimately, success is about marketing. And that is being done more and more via the Internet. Computer skills—Quark, Word, Adobe Photoshop and Acrobat, Excel, scripting in html, Perl, cgi, php, etc.—are becoming mainstream for today's writers and editors.

Demand for Writers in 2006

The Internet is already exerting a powerful influence on every aspect of publishing. It is creating more, not less, work for writers and editors, online and offline. Understand the Internet and web, know how to write for them, know how to research on them, know how to use them to market yourself and your writing.

SHOULD I QUIT MY DAYTIME JOB AND WRITE?

"I am one year out of undergrad and have been working in the financial services industry since graduation. But I hate it and am looking for a major career change. All I've ever consistently enjoyed has been writing. I would like to break into a career in publishing or editing, but I don't know how well received I'd be with so little experience. What would be the best way for me to get a foot in? I am very confident about my writing abilities, but I have

nothing to show for it (aside from dozens and dozens of poems I've written and a few short stories). Thanks!"

One of your statements makes me believe that you will find what you're looking for—a job where writing earns you a living: "All I've ever consistently enjoyed has been writing." Whenever I've heard a student say that, almost invariably it has meant that person was born to write and probably won't be happy until he or she is doing it in a serious way.

I am not kidding you. I taught fiction and creative nonfiction for 15 years to, literally, 1,000s of students. I came to the conclusion that, yes, there are people who, for some reason, have to write or they won't be happy. Understanding that about yourself, honoring it, giving in to it—that's the hard part. The rest is standard practical advice.

The only other thing I would add is this: Find a mentor. Shorten the learning curve by working with a professional coach or trainer. He or she will more than likely tell you:

- What you need is practical training and clips, lots of clips.

- Be prepared to spend time learning the basics of the type of writing you want to specialize in.

- Gradually build your clips (bylines) from better and better magazines, newspapers, copywriting projects and so forth.

- Once you're making approximately one-third of your present income as a freelancer, you'll have the skills and contacts to make the jump to full-time.

IS A COLLEGE DEGREE NECESSARY FOR SUCCESS?

"I'm a 25-year-old car enthusiast living near Houston,

TX. I would love to make a living writing articles for automobile magazines. I'm college educated and I think I have a great knack for writing. But, I'm not formally educated in writing or journalism (I have a business degree). How can I break into this industry? Would going back to school and getting a journalism degree be the only way?"

First, forget going back for a second degree in journalism. Higher education is highly overrated. Second, some good news: You've spent time and energy developing an expertise in a specialty, and the trend in today's magazine market (online and offline) is more and more toward vertical titles, sometimes called niche markets, and away from the general interest magazine.

Moreover, these vertical titles (focused on a narrow interest) are often for the enthusiast market. I used to make my living writing and editing for one such market: recreational scuba divers. I bet there are just as many car enthusiasts with just as much passion.

So, you've got expertise, you've got intelligence, you've got average to above-average language skills (which is all it takes to be a working pro). You've got everything you need to be a successful writer except one thing: craftsmanship.

This simply means the nuts and bolts. How to take an engine apart and put it back together. Except in this case the engine is the article and your marketing of it.

My advice: Again, don't waste your time going back to school. Most professors (I was one for 15 years) have never made a living doing anything other than talking to 18-year-olds. Professors are usually pretty clueless about the real world. Instead:

Consult the pros. We offer apprenticeship courses at *www.peak writing.com*, where we work with you until you get published. There are plenty of courses available on the Internet by solid pros like

Moira Allen (*www.writing-world.com*) and Dana Cassell (*www.writers-editors.com*).

Whichever you choose, make sure the course is taught by a working professional. Make sure that the goal of the course is to create a marketable manuscript and to help you get it in print.

Final word of advice: By all means, turn your enthusiasm into a living. But be prepared to have a different attitude toward your hobby once it becomes your livelihood. I won't say anymore about that. You'll see what I mean.

HOW DO I PREPARE FOR A WRITING JOB INTERVIEW?

> *"I am in the UK and have an interview in a few days at a newspaper as a marketing and promotions writer. Can you give me some information on the job and how to get on at the interview. Any help would be most appreciated."*

The specific duties of that position—or just about any other corporate writing job—can vary widely from company to company. I highly recommend that you contact the newspaper before your interview and ask for a detailed job description. What sort of projects will you be working on? The newspaper should either have a printed job description or be able to give you one verbally. If they can't, what does that say about their organization and their ability to define your job duties in order to measure your success or failure?

Once you've got the job description, you can brainstorm and research by looking at similar work being done at competing publications, then be prepared to offer some exciting ideas/enhancements or at least be able to speak to your expertise in each area of responsibility the new job entails.

Good luck. Be yourself. Don't put on a show. Know the dress

code for that office. Don't underdress; try not to overdress. When interviewing potential employees, the key things I look for are:

- Someone who listens and tries to understand before speaking.

- Someone with good social skills (we'll be working with him/her up to 60 hours a week) because respect and courtesy are so important to maintaining a positive work environment.

- Someone with a well-rounded education and good overall intelligence. The technical stuff can be taught. Also, job descriptions change over time, so it's important to have a flexible employee with a sound intellectual background who is open to change.

- Someone with ambitions and plans to make them come true. My favorite interview question: "Describe yourself and what you'll be doing 10 years from now."

- I notice you have some typing/spelling errors. They're a red flag. Be sure that whatever self-prepared documents you take into the interview are 100 percent error free. Hire a proofreader if you have to. Consult web sites like *www.writers-editors.com*. You can send in your work, have it proofed and returned within a very short time frame. In a situation such as a job application, using a pro can be a wise investment.

*"The best cure for writer's block
is writer's cramp."*

CHAPTER TWO

GETTING COMFORTABLE IN THE HARNESS

- Finding the Time: Balancing Writing with the Rest of Your Life
- Go Away! Avoiding Interruptions at Work and Home
- Productivity Boosters: How to Maximize Your Writing Time
- Can I Combine Writing and Motherhood?
- Can I Freelance Successfully While Holding Down a Full-Time Job?
- Generalist or Specialist? A Key Early Decision
- How Do I Get Started as a Professional Writer?
- What Should I Write About?
- $100,000 of Free Reader Research
- Roger Clemens' Deep Thoughts on Rejection

I freely admit having, er, borrowed this chapter's title from the first book I ever read on freelance writing by one of my mentors and heroes: Hayes Jacobs. The book is *Writing to Sell*, and it used to be the required text in the Writer's Digest School's magazine course back in the..., well, a good while back.

Jacobs was a pro from the old school: He came up through the newsroom with ink stains on his elbows. Most of all, the voice of his prose was crisp, rich and wise.

When first reading *Writing to Sell*, I wondered how Jacobs had developed such an authentic, comfortable voice and how I could do so myself. About three years and a half-million words later, I realized how he had done it:

By getting comfortable in the harness and staying there, no matter what.

FINDING THE TIME: BALANCING WRITING WITH THE REST OF YOUR LIFE

When starting out, few problems are more difficult or important for a writer to face than making space in life for this new, demanding thing called writing for publication. Finding time to write can be difficult for three reasons:

- It requires us and others to change, yet we are creatures of comfortable habits.

- It requires giving up some things so that we can have another thing—this dream of a writing life.

- It requires commitment and discipline, forcing us to look inside and come to terms with what we really want and to decide if we're willing to sacrifice to have it.

So, never underestimate the struggle you'll sometimes undergo when transitioning from the nonwriting you to the new you. It's a struggle we all continue to share.

Now for the good news: At some point you're going to look around and realize that there is a "new normal" in your life, and at the center of this stasis that everyone has adjusted to (well, more or less) will be a professional writer—you.

Timely Tips for Achieving Balance
Beware of False Choices
You'll always be able to conjure up things to do instead of write. Important things: laundry, weeds, groceries, trapping vermin under the house (editors can fit into the smallest spaces). But don't fall into the trap of believing you must choose between writing and your other duties. That's your guilt and fear working on you. Your goal is to make room for writing, not to let it take you away from your responsibilities. There will be plenty of other reasons not to write besides guilt and fear.

Question Routine
With this new thing in your life, it's important that you evaluate daily routines like the morning paper, evening news, laid-back lunches, bunco clubs and other consumers of your non-obligated time. A one-hour lunch can translate into a solid 45 minutes of speed writing the first draft of an article you gathered material for instead of watching TV the night before.

Think Small Time
To be successful as a beginning freelancer, all you need is an hour a day, which usually translates into 45 minutes of actual work. The key isn't the amount; it's the frequency. Tell yourself that if you simply sit down often enough, whether for one hour or for half that, eventually you will produce a finished something. And then another. And another.

Hemingway used to aim for two pages of useable copy per day. And he wrote very short sentences. Two pages a day, 10 pages a week (if you bullfight on weekends), 40 pages a month, and [reaching for calculator] a novel about every 7 to 8 months—if you want it.

Not into novels? Writing two pages a day, you could also produce a major feature per month in the following realistic scenario:

one week for research; one week for drafts and revisions; one week for a final draft proofed, polished and fact checked; then one week as a buffer and for mailing.

An article per month, 12 articles per year at an average sale of $500, and [calculator, please], you've now got $6,000 of extra income by devoting one hour per day to writing. As Woody Allen is quoted as saying, "80 percent of life is just showing up." I firmly believe that 80 percent of writing success is simply being in the routine of writing. The rest is marketing (19 percent) and talent (1 percent).

Speed Write

See the article in the next chapter on "Speed Writing" for a full discussion of this technique. Right here I want you to remember school writing, especially the night before the paper was due. No more putting it off. No more phone chat or trips to the library. You plunked butt in chair and wrote, watching the clock, writing fast, not worrying about quality but only about getting it done. After it was done, as the rosy fingers of dawn reached into your room, you would think two things: (1) Next time I swear I won't put it off to the last moment; (2) If I had more time to work on this, it could have been a lot better.

Let's put those lessons to use: You wrote best when a deadline forced you to overcome your fear and your self editing. You couldn't stop to rephrase the sentence; it was 3:00 a.m. and you weren't even halfway done yet. And the "If I had more time..." is now called the revising and editing stages that are built into your overall process of creation as a professional.

Point: one of the most important things you can do during your regular composing time—when not researching, marketing or polishing—is to write fast. Use speed writing liberally during the composing stage: to think through a problem, to get a grip on a nebulous idea, to make a list of character names. Then use the revising and editing stages to shape and polish.

As a writer, use speed; it is your friend.

Prewrite

You can make your writing time more productive by thinking about what you're going to do during your next scheduled writing block—in other words, if you prewrite the session. Then you can hit the keyboard with fingers flying. Just be sure to carry a notepad and pen with you at all times and never be tempted to believe: "No need to write that down; I'll remember it." Famous last words.

GO AWAY! AVOIDING INTERRUPTIONS AT WORK AND HOME

How do you get your work done and maintain civil relations with everyone but your in-laws? Tough one. There's a distinct Jekyll and Hyde feeling when your work is going well and in pops a colleague, child or spouse. Dr. Jekyll looks up from the keyboard with a smile, while Mr. Hyde wants to snarl and spit. You need a plan before somebody gets hurt.

Physician, Heal Thyself

Generally, people in your life want to please you. But they can't do so unless they know what you want. Announce your writing schedule and your desires to others along with a simple, business-like request to avoid interrupting you during that time, except in the case of emergency. You will be pleasantly shocked by their willingness to help. You must first establish boundaries in order to have them respected.

Create a Message Center

To fulfill your side of the don't-bother-me bargain, you need to provide convenient, effective ways for others to contact you: email, voice mail, post-its or a clipboard on your office or home-office door. The easier it is for others to use these (and the more habitual their use becomes), the less you will be interrupted.

Slay the Email Dragon

After nine years of managing a staff of 12 to 14 people, I've come to believe that the single greatest hindrance to workplace productivity today is the Internet, and I don't mean surfing eBay. Email. Be honest—how many times a day do you check it? Reading and responding to emails provides us the wonderful illusion of being productive. Computers are fun. We love to chat. And the Internet is insidious in the way it promotes chatting.

As a recovering email addict (now living life one email at a time), I now designate specific times of the day during which I open email and respond to it, with a time limitation on the "email break." And while you're at it, turn off that little bell on Outlook Express that signals new mail arriving in your box.

Use the Phone as a Business Tool

William Faulkner's father, the registrar at the University of Mississippi, once made the mistake of giving his son "Count No-Count" (as the locals called him) a job in the university post office. Business at Ole Miss soon ground to a halt. No one was getting their mail, U.S. or intercampus. An investigation revealed six-weeks of mail stacked in bags in a back room, where Faulkner used his time at work to write. When asked years later about his postal experience, Faulkner replied, "I refused to be at the beck and call of every sum bitch with five cents for a stamp."

The Count has a point. There is no requirement for you to be at the beck and call of every, uh, life form with an index finger who can count. As a professional writer, you hereby have permission to take phone calls at your convenience and, further, to return messages at your convenience.

Get Wired X2

One of the best investments my wife ever talked me into was a second phone line. If you are maintaining a home office, consider the few extra dollars per month a sound business investment (and it's tax deductible, if you itemize). You will more than likely make up the expense in continuous uptime on your computer and by not angering everyone in your life because you keep the phone line constantly busy. A second phone line also gives you fax capability, which a pro writer should have.

Stay in the Zone

It goes without saying that, as a writer, you should set up a comfortable writing area that insulates you and helps you be productive. Here's another tip: Make that zone self-sufficient. Once you're there to work, don't leave until your work period (however long it may be) is over.

If you're a coffee hound, that means having a coffee machine or a full carafe *in loco*. Same for snacks. Same for a printer. Same for anything you need while in that zone to do your work. Get there and stay there.

PRODUCTIVITY BOOSTERS: HOW TO MAXIMIZE YOUR WRITING TIME

Personal productivity guru David Allen offers some great pointers on how to organize your workday. Allen has been called "one of the world's most influential thinkers on personal productivity" by *Fast Company*, and with a magazine title like that, you figure those folks get lots done. Allen's clients include Microsoft, Oracle, Fidelity Investments and now—you.

Psychic RAM

One of Allen's theories is that human beings, like computers, have a limited amount of RAM, or Random Access Memory, which is what your computer uses to run its programs and what your mind uses to run your life. Allen advises doing a daily download of your psychic RAM—all the "woulds, coulds, shoulds, need tos, ought-tos and might want tos" that take up available memory. This downloading takes the form of a daily inventory of projects that helps close the "open loops," frees up our heads and prevents that nagging, vaguely panicky sense of incompletion that dogs us during our waking hours.

Aren't You Talking about a "To-Do" List?

No. Most "to-do" lists are what get you into trouble in the first place. They fail to separate three very different things: goals, projects and action steps. This confusion in our planning often leads to confusion in our execution.

In Allen's "Getting Things Done" system, your ability to distinguish a project from overall goals and individual action steps is one of the keys to boosting productivity.

- A project is more than a simple action step; a project entails several steps.

- A project describes a positive, concrete change in your world. "Finalize taxes," and "Complete contract proposal to editor" describe something that, when completed, will constitute a positive change in your reality.

- A project is not a mission statement, personal vision statement or other grand objective. A project is something that can be completed in a few weeks, not years. "Increase my profit margin by 25%" is a long-term goal that would require multiple projects over the course of an entire year in order to be attained.

• A project is something that should be evaluated on a weekly basis, at least.

The Stunning Weekly Review

When you sit down to write your project list, prepare to be stunned. As Allen predicts, most of us have between 30 to 100 projects in our lives at once, whether we realize it or not.

Also expect resistance: "Big Idea" folks don't like to get concrete, and frenetic workers don't like to be reminded how frazzled their lives really are. Making the project list will help you distinguish between big goals, weekly projects, and the individual action steps that lead to finishing a project.

The Weekly Review ties the elements of this three-level hierarchy together, charting progress on each tier: vision, project, action step. Your purpose during the Weekly Review is to identify and capture necessary actions for the upcoming week's projects, which lead to achieving your overall vision. The Weekly Review may also require you to take a few steps back and revisit missing action steps in order to keep a project on track.

More Tips for the Project List
Define Independently Attainable Projects

Another common problem occurs when setting goals that are dependent upon the actions of others in order to be achieved. True projects are those you can complete regardless of what others do or don't do. "Sell my Belize adventure story to *National Geographic*" makes you dependent upon others for success. But "polish and mail my Belize travel story to *National Geographic*" can be a win for you, as can "study *National Geographic* and revise my Belize travel story accordingly."

Use the Right Verb

Begin each project with a carefully chosen and appropriate verb. "Research the article on e-rights" has a much different outcome than "Submit the article on e-rights." The first is an action step; the second describes the overall project, of which researching is merely a part. Verb choice is also important in maintaining the independence of your projects: "Create a co-author project with Philip" relies upon Philip, whereas "Explore co-author project with Philip" is independent of Philip's mood and other commitments.

Provide Personal end Points

End points are important when you are part of a project involving others. Allen advises framing the project with a personal deadline for handing it off to the next member of the team: "Provide director shooting script by Thursday," as opposed to "Begin shooting on schedule."

Workflow Management

Perhaps the tip that has made the most difference for me is based on a simple principle: When something lands on your desk, touch it only once. How is that possible? By answering a single question—"Is it actionable?"

If the answer is no, the thing goes into one of three places: (1) the trash; (2) a "someday maybe" file; (3) a reference/research file. If the answer is yes, you again have three options: (1) do it—goes into project file; (2) delegate it—goes to someone else; or (3) defer it—goes on your calendar.

The key is to make a yes/no decision once and only once, getting it out of the in-basket on your desk and into the appropriate place.

WRITER'S TOOLBOX
DAVID ALLEN RESOURCES

• David Allen's home page: *www.davidco.com*

• Free productivity newsletter sign up
  www.davidco.com/productivity_principles.php?newsletter

CAN I COMBINE WRITING AND MOTHERHOOD?

"I'm a thirty-something mother of two young boys, co-owner of a business with my husband, and recent college grad (BA in English). After pondering my career options, I've decided to write. For a while, I considered writing fiction, but feel I'm more in my element as a nonfiction writer. I'm a former editor of several magazines and KNOW I do not want to be an editor again.

"My question: How do I get started in the nonfiction market? I would like to write articles that deal with important social issues, but I'm not a certified expert in sociology, you know what I mean?

"I'm also considering compiling an anthology of essays about a specific social issue—I know a few people that would probably be very willing to contribute—how do I go about approaching them? Should I be trying to get an agent or publisher?"

I'm delighted to answer your questions and to be part of this exciting change in your life. First, congrats on making a decision to follow your true desires for a career in writing. It takes courage to do so. Your statements make me believe that you will find what you're looking for—success. Now for the practical advice:

Writing Fiction vs. Nonfiction

Writers of nonfiction are in great demand right now, and the proliferation of the web and email will continue that trend, not shorten it. For better or for worse, our need for fiction continues to dwindle. For every fiction book published there are over 300 nonfiction books and that many more web sites. Same for magazines—we've transitioned from a prevalence of fiction in magazines to a prevalence of nonfiction service journalism.

Getting Started in the Nonfiction Market

You get started the same way every freelancer without clips gets started: by acquiring clips however you can, then working your way up the ladder of those magazines in your field until you're writing for the best 'zines and editors at the highest rates. The best per-word rates are $1.00 to $3.00. Many of the top writers charge a flat fee of $5,000 to $12,000 per article, depending on length.

At first there will be rejection slips and low pay, but over a period of a year or two your career should grow until you are making at least one-third of your present salary as a freelancer. At that point, go full-time with full confidence. But you first must be willing to pay your dues as a freelancer, to learn the basics of the type of writing you want to specialize in, to start low and gradually build your clips from better and better magazines, newspapers, etc.

Not a Certified Expert

You've just made one of the most important decisions you'll be faced with: whether to be a generalist or a specialist. Also, it's common for journalistic specialists NOT to hold field-specific academic degrees. As a journalist, you will be judged by the quality of your research, your reporting and your language abilities—not your academic degrees. Your job is to report on professions, people and issues, not to be a practicing member of them. That's an important distinction that speaks to the need for journalistic distance from the things and people you report on.

Making a Book Proposal

If your former position as an editor gives you contacts in the book publishing world, you could do a book proposal to a publisher on your own with credibility. Otherwise, target your book proposal to agents who have that content area as one of their specialties.

Questions to You

- What special knowledge and experiences come to you by virtue of your present job?

- How can they be leveraged into nonfiction works?

CAN I FREELANCE SUCCESSFULLY WHILE HOLDING DOWN A FULL-TIME JOB?

"I would like to thank you, truly, for your advice. You are the first person, in a long time, that has not made me feel like a career in writing is silly. I have memories of loving writing since before the third grade and it is wonderfully encouraging to think that my greatest passion in life is not completely useless and that I can be building an enjoyable career.

"Here's a follow up question for you. I currently work in corporate finance which places unruly demands on all of my time. I'd love to start somewhere, anywhere, when it comes to breaking into journalism, but I, literally, never see the light of day. I am uncertain about mak-

ing a move from my current job simply because it is pretty secure and it more than pays my bills. I wouldn't mind taking a leap if I thought I would be able to maintain some financial security.

"So the question is, with no formal writing experience, is there a way, aside from attempting to freelance, that I can write and put food in my fridge?

"And, if freelancing is, in your opinion, my best option right now, can you give me an idea of how I'd go about writing my first freelance article? Do I choose to write about something I'm interested in and find a paper/magazine that will take it, or do I find the paper/magazine first and then think of something that I think they may be interested in hearing about?

"I don't mean to bombard you with questions...I just want to find the best route to bliss (in my case, writing professionally)...Thanks a gazillion for your help!"

Your question shows what's really in your heart. And your admission that you've been belittled in the past for wanting a perfectly attainable and respectable career as a writer is sad and maddening. I'm sorry you've had to endure that, but it's part of the myth that surrounds writers and the writing profession. Like most of the popular knowledge about writing, it is almost totally false.

Time crunch—No easy answers here. Heard of J.K. Rowling of the Harry Potter series? She was a mother of an infant living on welfare and wrote during her child's naps, on subways on the way to work, and when she was exhausted.

When I was teaching and wanted to be a full-time writer instead, I used to get up at 4:00 a.m., make coffee, rub my eyes, turn on the computer and make myself type SOMETHING for two hours every morning. I did that for three years until I had the clips, contacts and skills to go full-time. Point: there is always time for the things you really want to do, for the things you have to do.

Where to start: I highly recommend a mentoring and apprenticeship program like the ones offered at *www.peakwriting.com*. Why learn things the hard way? Let a professional mentor shorten that learning curve for you. Find an apprenticeship that is thorough, self-paced, one-on-one, and will result in the submission of a professional manuscript to a publication you have targeted. You should also expect follow-up help until your work gets published.

To answer your marketing question: at your stage (starting out) you need to target a magazine first, study it, really get inside the head of the editor and the formats being used, then write something that fits. Being able to conduct that analysis, then apply it to your own writing, are essential skills for any writer, not just nonfiction freelancers.

If I were you, I'd:

- Sign up for a freelance nonfiction feature course taught by a working professional via the web. Ask for a teacher with experience in writing or editing for financial publications.

- Work through the course every day: in the mornings before work, on your lunch break, at night instead of watching TV—anytime you have 30 minutes.

- Use your expertise and current position to give you credentials (important in nonfiction) to write and sell a series of finance-related how-to articles to newspapers and magazines.

- Leverage those bylines into something bigger. Remember, today's nonfiction writers must see themselves as information providers and information packagers. Your readers/customers expect to receive information in a variety of formats:

books, CDs, audio cassettes, web sites, live workshops, email courses, phone conferences, seminars and more. Establish an expertise and learn to market yourself as an information provider in all media, not just print.

Those are my suggestions. But go with your gut. That's where the truth is.

GENERALIST OR SPECIALIST? A KEY EARLY DECISION

Strong arguments exist on both sides. Consider them carefully, make the decision that's right for you, then feel free to change your mind. Here's why. On the one hand is the familiar admonition, "Write what you know." On the other is commonsense, "Why limit yourself?"

What does reality say? Basically it says, "Be both." Of course, no one wants to close off lucrative markets. Yet, in this age of specialization, with the number of general-interest magazines shriveling faster than appendages in cold water, writing nonfiction usually means being a specialist. Listen to these arguments and see if you agree.

Be a Generalist!

- "As a generalist, I'm constantly learning new things, constantly being challenged."

- "Diversification opens up more markets for my writing."

- "By publishing in a variety of fields, I demonstrate my versatility as a writer, my ability to handle whatever an editor throws at me."

- "I'm able to enrich what I write with a variety of perspectives."

Be a Specialist!

- "Specialization allows me to write about what I really know, the prime directive of freelance success."

- "My current expertise is a natural place to begin and will provide the shortest path to a byline."

- "Specialization provides a foundation on which I can build."

- "Since I'm writing about what I have experience in, I have pre-established contacts, credentials and I will be seen as an expert by editors."

- "As a specialist, I am already familiar with many of the publications I want to write for."

- "Writing nonfiction today almost always requires special knowledge. Why start from scratch with each article?"

- "The research I do for one project can often be carried over to the next, saving me time and resources."

- "As a specialist, I can combine a number of separate articles on a single subject into a book, or they could become the basis of a regular column."

False Either/Or

Like most dichotomies, this one is also an either/or fallacy. You don't have to be either a specialist or a generalist. There are no Freelance Police who will arrest you for doing both. And, in truth, you'll most likely end up with several areas of expertise, making you a...TA DA!...generalist who specializes! Don't you love it when a plan comes together?

HOW DO I GET STARTED AS A PROFESSIONAL WRITER?

> *"Traveling and writing are my passions. I have always longed to find a way to merge them and believe that there IS a way! I just don't know it! Can you help me with some tips on how to get started? Also, are there any books, web pages, etc. that you can refer me to? Thanks for your help!"*

There's absolutely no reason why you can't merge your two passions. Many have before you. All it takes is ambition, perseverance and an average facility for words. Here are what I believe to be the keys to success for any freelance writer:

Key 1: Target a Publication and Internalize It

Either go to the library or purchase one of the market books: the *Writer's Market* book from Writer's Digest books; *Bacon's Directory of Magazines* (library); *Internet Media Directory* (library), etc. Once you have access to current market materials:

- Identify the genre of magazines or publications you want to write your first piece for.

- Select one publication that would seem most receptive to you at this point in your career.

- Collect samples of your target pub.

Key 2: Crack the Code

When you've done that, DEVOUR the publication. Your goal is to decode its editorial formula. Know exactly what the editor wants in features: the formats, slant, voice, paragraphing, number of words, use of quotations, descriptive level of the language—everything.

Key 3: Transmit the Code

Now write an article based upon your analysis of what this editor wants. Your goal is to produce a manuscript that the editor doesn't have to touch in order to use in his/her publication.

Key 4: Know the Ropes

Freelancing is a profession, and like any profession it has its rules of conduct, from how to submit a query to how to ask for a reply. What I'm saying is, they don't let brain surgeons in the operating room until they've learned their craft and served an apprenticeship. Same is true of editors: they don't let you in the magazine until they believe you are dependable and honest (that last one is more important than you might think).

I highly recommend that you find a published author or an expert to mentor you. Don't try to reinvent the wheel on your own. That road can lead to a LOT of frustration, even failure.

Key 5: Read the Greats

And not just the writers who've done books. In your case (travel writing), some of the best writers today are found in magazines like *Condé Nast Traveler, Travel + Leisure, Islands, Natl. Geo Traveler.* If your goal is to publish in those magazines (and make the kind of money they offer), then read these writers, study them, emulate them. Then add your own twist and personality. Virginia Woolf studied Joseph Conrad. William Faulkner studied James Joyce. Should we be any different?

Key 6: Be Committed

Getting your first byline is going to be hard. Bylines aren't merit

WRITER'S TOOLBOX
ONLINE AND PRINT RESOURCES FOR TRAVEL WRITERS

- American Society of Travel Writers: *www.satw.org*

- *The Best American Travel Writing.* An annual anthology from Houghton Mifflin Co.

- Freelance Travel Writer: *www.freelancetravelwriter.com*

- *How to Make a Living as a Travel Writer.* Susan Farewell

- *Teach Yourself Travel Writing.* Cynthia Dial

- Travelwriter Marketletter: *www.travelwriterml.com*

- *Travel Writer's Guide.* Gordon Burgett

- *Travel Writing.* Louisa Peat O'Neil

badges; they're emblems of significant professional achievement. Expect rejection. But remember: *The only difference between a published writer and an unpublished writer is that one has given up.*

WHAT SHOULD I WRITE ABOUT?

> *"How does a writer know what topics are hot and what are not? I want to write articles out of Japan, mainly on culture and natural elements there. But I wonder if there is interest in Japan (specifically) in U.S. and Australian magazines."*

I like this question. It gives me a chance to say six things I believe strongly:

Editors are Starved for Good Stuff

A good article—one filled with solid, interesting material slanted toward a specific audience and publication—will always find a home. During my years as an editor, we were always starved for good freelance stories. Here's why: *There are plenty of freelancers who want to get published. But there is a tremendous shortage of freelancers who know how to do it for specific publications. When it comes to the latter, you have little competition.*

Good work from freelancers saves production time and usually expenses. The only problem: most freelancers don't take the time to study the publication closely and smartly enough to understand the formats the magazine is using, topics that are desired and those that aren't, and the specific needs of the readers the publication is trying to serve. As a result, most freelancers in my experience send in something that may be well written, but simply isn't useable. It doesn't fit.

The point: If you do your job as a freelancer—which is to target your writing for a specific audience and publication—you can sell what you write about Japan or anything else.

There Are No New Topics, Only Fresh Writing

Again, it's my experience that readers and editors are always interested in the unique and the well-written. If you have something fresh to say from your own observations and perceptions, there will be interest in it. There are no new topics, only new writers. All of Shakespeare's themes are hackneyed—revenge, ambition, loyalty—but the perceptions and writing rarely are.

You Got to Read

To offer something fresh, you have to know what's already been said and how it's been said. Select 10 publications in the field where you want to publish. Read them voraciously. Identify the topics that appear most often. Now choose one of those topics and write about it in a way you haven't seen in any of the publications you studied. No, this isn't cheating or being a hack. It's being market savvy.

Know the Difference between Form and Formula

Form is structure, which everything in the universe has. A water glass gives form to water. The shape of the glass can vary from ornate to practical, but some form is always there. A formula, on the other hand, is designed to fabricate things in cookie-cutter, assembly-line style, like Beanie Babies and pecan logs. Editors don't want formulaic writing, but they do want the forms or patterns that they are required to use in their magazines. Find the patterns that your editor needs: the article types and slants they take.

Target

Go to the library and use the most current issue of *Bacon's Directory of Magazines, Consumer Magazine Advertising Source* (from Standard Rate and Data Service) or buy a copy of the latest *Writer's Market* (print or online at www.writersmarket.com). Use these resources to find periodicals most likely to be receptive to your article. Shape your writing accordingly. Start with publications appropriate for your level of experience. That usually means smaller: in size, circulation and reimbursement.

Don't Give Up

Take rejection slips and throw them into the furnace of your writing to put steel in your prose. In 1957 Jack Kerouac was down and out in New York City; his *On the Road* manuscript had been rejected by 25 publishers. His girlfriend tried number 26 and an American classic was born. There are several morals in that story.

$100,000 OF FREE READER RESEARCH—
HOW TO USE ADS TO ANALYZE A TARGET MAGAZINE

The price is certainly right. So is the information. Each year print advertisers and publishers spend millions of dollars for syndicated research to study readers (they call them "consumers") of a magazine. Their goal is to understand everything they can about these readers/consumers in order to slant their marketing and editorial directly to that set of demographics and psychographics.

As a result, the advertisements in a magazine provide the freelancer, literally, direct access to research that you would otherwise pay $30,000 to $100,000 per study for. At Rodale, Inc., we did these studies on a regular basis, often annually. At the large magazines like *Prevention* and *Men's Health*, which have their own research staffs, the studies were even more frequent.

How to Analyze a Print Advertisement

Create a table with five columns, one each for:

1. Name of advertiser

2. Description of the ad (what is happening in it)

3. Important sell lines

4. What the ad tells you about the reader

5. On a scale of 1 to 5, a rating of how interested these readers would be in your article. How will you slant your article to appeal to the readers that the advertisement is trying to reach? How does the ad help you answer the most important question asked by all readers—"What's in it for me?" In other words, what strong reader benefit must your article offer in order to be of interest to this reader?

Example

Let's say you're preparing a story on "How to Get the Most from Your Interns." Your target magazine is *Inc., The Magazine for Growing Businesses.* Using this technique, you take several recent issues of *Inc.* and use your grid to study the advertisements in order to find out as much as you can about the magazine's readers. The first full-page ad you come across is from the fine folks at Office Depot. You fill in your grid (see page 45).

Conducting this exercise with a variety of ads from the same magazine will supply you with a clear picture of the readership— and its primary needs—that the editor must satisfy each issue. Armed with these insights and a working knowledge of the article formats the editor must use (*Inc.* loves profiles), you can shape your materials into that magic bullet: a submission that makes the editor sigh in relief that a freelancer finally "gets it." Soon after that sigh, you will receive a phone call or an email that will make your day.

ROGER CLEMENS' DEEP THOUGHTS ON REJECTION

Roger would spit a wad on rejection slips because he knows the cosmic law of averages. Here it is. I'm writing this in September. If you're a baseball fan, no more need be said. This is the season of hope and glory, defeat and bitterness, heroes and bums. Hey, sounds a lot like the writing. We can experience all of those things in a single day. Don't need no series.

Ever try to imagine the pressure Roger Clemens must feel when pitching in the ninth inning of a series-deciding game? What elation he must feel when he gets the K, what wretched dejection when he watches some scrappy Angel slug one over Babe Ruth's head?

Elation and dejection. Again, writers can get their daily dose at the mailbox, without half the world watching. So, what does Roger Clemens do if he's the bum, not the hero? Leaving out the personal stuff, you know exactly what he does: He does it again. He goes back

READERSHIP PROFILE: INC. MAGAZINE

Advertiser	Description	Sell Lines	Reader Profile	Interest Level
Office Depot	Three people stand in full profile, staring into camera, holding something.	"No one knows your office needs like the experts at Office Depot."	Office Depot has spent lots of research dollars to determine *Inc.* has the kind of readers who'd be interested in OD's goods and services. Who are they?	4.5
				Would readers of this ad want to read my article?
	A beer-bellied white guy in polyester holds a fist-sized diamond. A smocked and goateed Generation Y'er holds a pair of scissors. A 30-something black woman in Office Depot uniform holds a ream of paper.	"We not only have what business needs—we have what business needs to know."	What do these entrepreneurs have in common: the need for knowledge and tools from OD to make their businesses successful.	Yes!
				These entrepreneurs want nuts and bolts tools and information to make their businesses better.
	They are labeled, respectively, "Rock Expert," "Scissors Expert," "Paper Expert."	Who's their copywriter? Should be:	In its ad, OD positions itself as an outfit that can fulfill that practical need in a down-home, "just folks" kind of way.	I must focus on how an intern adds directly to several sample business' bottom lines and is an asset.
	Ha, ha.	"We have what business needs—and what business needs to know."	Office Depot knows that *Inc.* readers want practical advice and tools—what works.	I will add sidebars of resources on how to find free interns.
	The ad is trying very hard to establish a broad, democratic stance: young and old, black and white, male and female.	A negative statement takes 10% longer to read than a positive one.	*Inc.* is not *Forbes* or *Fast Company*. It's not the *Wall St. Journal.* *Inc.* is Main Street, America.	Select example businesses to appeal to small and medium business leaders/entrepreneurs.
	A larger version of this ad would contain an Asian and Hispanic.		OD knew that and used an ad that fit.	Profile businesses led by people of different races and ages, just like the ad.

to the mound when it's his turn in the rotation, chew stuffed in his cheek like a ping-pong ball, spittin' and diggin', going for the dubyah.

Because Roger knows that some days he'll win and some days he'll lose. Over the course of a season, pitchers try to win more than they lose. But, here's the key: Pitchers know—and accept— that they will win AND lose. Both are part of their chosen profession. Again, sounds suspiciously like writing.

What about batters? The greatest batters hope to achieve a lifetime average of around .400. In other words, less than half the time do they plan on "winning" by getting safely on base. They consider themselves a success even though they are "rejected" six times for every four times they are "accepted" on base. Batting is hard. Hitting a little round ball going 90 miles an hour with a wooden stick with any precision is just a damn hard thing to do. So is writing.

Putting words together with thought is one of the great triumphs of human evolution. Putting them down in writing is one of the great triumphs of human will. We're dealing with the fickle hand of creativity, the soft underbelly of thought and the infinitely nuanced world of symbolic language.

And then there's editors. Talk about fickle. We've all heard the stories of masterpieces being rejected umpteen times, with the future Nobel Prize winner barely rescued from the abyss of destitution and despair. Those stories are true. Whether by James Joyce or J.D. Salinger, a frightening number of works enshrined as masterpieces in our literary canon were once considered crap by at least 20 editors before somebody got a clue.

So here's what we got so far:

1. You will inevitably be rejected as a writer, probably more often than you are accepted.

2. You've chosen a difficult craft because of the nature of language and thought.

3. Few editors like to take chances.

Should you take solace in those cold realities? Yes, you should. Here's why.

Acceptance Is Inevitable

You sit down. You write. You submit your stuff. Do that enough and the law of averages dictates that it will all come together (the ideas, the words, the editor) successfully at a rate determined by variables like your experience, work habits, chosen market, etc.

What is the rate of acceptance vs. rejection? What are the odds, to put it in gambling terms? According to my calculations based on my own experience and that of freelance students, about 1 in 8 is the average. In other words, on average, a manuscript from a competent freelancer submitted to appropriate magazines will be rejected 7 times and accepted on the 8th.

This is why you should always have 6 to 8 different stories circulating at once. You increase your odds of acceptance. A roulette wheel has 50 numbers. Place one bet and you have a 1 in 50 chance of winning. Place 50 bets, you have a 100 percent chance of winning. If you have 8 stories on editors' desks, the "Law of 8" says that one will be accepted. Lots of variables, of course. But the point is clear:

If you submit a single story to three magazines, get three quick rejections, then give up, you have failed to understand the rules of the game. If you want to drop out of the game, fine. But do so knowing the rules: One acceptance for every 8 submissions—on average.

Rejection Is an Invitation

To what? To learn and to revise, thereby improving your odds on the next submission. This learning—and the willingness to revise in light of it—is the key to getting and keeping legs in the profession of writing. However, too many of us, too often, continue to be bedeviled by two great American myths:

- "The Natural"—the person who can do it perfectly without even trying.

- "The Discovery"—the person who suddenly finds out they have this perfect gift or is discovered to have it by some expert.

Guilty as charged? Hey, who isn't. We all enjoy fantasy. But the key is knowing that "The Natural" and "The Discovery" don't exist. What does exist is our hard work, our commitment to being writers, and the peace that comes from knowing that rejections and acceptances conform to cosmic laws at work in our lives, in the offices of editors—and even at home plate.

More Tips for Rejecting Rejection
Separate Yourself
From the work. Remember, it was the work that was rejected, not you as a person or as a writer. Separate yourself from the business of writing and the work produced during the course of business.

Go Postal
When rejected, mail the piece back out. The same day, if no revisions are needed. Have a list of 15 to 20 submission names and addresses ready. Enjoy the act of getting another story in the mail to a fresh pair of eyes—and needs.

Switch Editors
If one editor at a publication didn't like it, try another at the same pub who has different responsibilities. *Warning*: Don't do this more than once at the same publication.

Build a Brag Board

Hang a bulletin board above your computer and tack up your acceptance letters, assignment letters, pay stubs. Obviously, the editor who just rejected your work needs to get a clue from these other, more enlightened colleagues.

Learn the Zen of Patience

Robert Pirsig had plenty of it with his book *Zen and the Art of Motorcycle Maintenance*, which was rejected over 100 times before finding a home on the official list of American classics. *Chicken Soup for the Soul* was shown to 111 publishers before a small Florida publisher named Health Communications took a chance: 65 million copies and counting.

Understand Rejection vs. Nonselection

Unfortunately, the wrong word has been adopted to describe not having something chosen for publication. "Not selected" or "not chosen" is more accurate. "Rejection" most often refers to disapproval, disdain, mockery, even expulsion. The fact that an article was "not selected" by a given editor on a given day does not imply any of the highly negative denotations of "rejected."

Because an article was "not selected" does not necessarily mean it has any major failings. It's also unfortunate that publications usually don't have the time or resources to be specific about why an article was not selected. Nonetheless, if you have confidence in your writing, you should see a rejection slip for what it is: shorthand for "not for this market at this time," and feel free to continue to find a home for your well-done piece.

Consider the Source

If you received a form rejection slip, you've now got some valuable information about how that publication deals with new freelancers.

If the response was a rude kiss-off, you've got even more valuable information about that market: Don't waste your time there.

Consider Any Personalization as Encouragement

If you receive any written comments from an editor, this is a good sign for several reasons: (1) your work was read and considered; (2) a professional is taking the time to help you hone your writing for this market because he or she sees promise. You should assume this editor will be open to future submissions from you and is reaching out to establish a working relationship. Go for it.

"Write fast and let your heart breathe upon the page."

 **CHAPTER THREE**

YOUR WRITING PROCESS: THE NEED FOR SPEED

- Writer's Block: The Four Real Causes
- Top Seven Block Busters
- Get It Done—Now! A No-Fret, No-Sweat Plan
- Speed Writing: How to Master the Blank Page
- "Chained Mercury": Sample Speed Draft

Like many writers, I suffer from writing anxiety. For years it had a predictable effect: I wrote little or not at all for publication. When I did finally finish something, I didn't like it, always feeling the piece didn't reflect what I was truly capable of.

Then, as I worked one-on-one with young writers at Moravian College's writing center, I began to see myself in them: a welter of confusing and conflicting notions about writing and the writing process. Most of all, like my students, I was addicted to "headwriting"—trying to compose and edit sentences in my mind before putting them on paper.

I've come to believe that headwriting is the one of the most significant and unaddressed problems that beginning and intermediate writers—whether in college or in the kitchen—encounter and are held back by. So, at Moravian, we cranked up the volume and the speed. And it worked.

WRITER'S BLOCK: THE FOUR REAL CAUSES

I don't believe in writer's block. It's like "dyslexia" and "backache"—terms so general as to be almost useless when it comes to trying to help someone. A dyslexic can have problems with short-term memory or visual discrimination. A backache can be either muscle or nerve related—or both. The first thing a doctor has to do is get past the wastebasket terms and find out what's really going on. Same with "writer's block." Here's what I do believe: The persistent inability to begin or finish writing projects has at least four origins, all of which are remediable.

The Causes
Cause 1: Writers Are Sometimes Not Ready to Write

Perhaps the hardest thing about writing is not knowing what to write. This condition accounts for most instances of writer's block as I've come to understand it. The key to knowing what to write is knowing the format of the thing you're writing.

Imagine trying to make a chair without any concept of what one looks like or what its purpose is. Yet everyday I work with writers attempting to do just that: to create a how-to article, novel, short story, essay, business letter or even screenplay without knowing it has a seat, legs and back designed to support the weight placed on it.

I'm not talking about formula writing. A formula is used to produce identical items in quantity: rubber duckies and romance novels. I'm talking about form: the underlying structure that gives shape to writing in the same way that a glass gives shape to the water it holds.

Many experts tell you to "research and plan thoroughly." Good advice. But often the real problem occurs prior to researching or planning/outlining. That problem is: Not knowing the underlying pattern for the kind of thing you're about to write. Without that pattern (also called a "template"), the writing problem may present itself as a lack of research or planning, but those are merely symptoms of something else.

For *students*, not being ready to write can mean: not knowing how to decode the writing assignment and identify an appropriate template that will supply what the teacher wants; or not knowing how to write a controlling statement that predicts the chosen pattern. During my 15 years of teaching college writing, almost without exception, once I helped a student to understand the underlying pattern of what the teacher wanted and we came up with a solid controlling idea that fit the pattern, the student was miraculously "cured."

Applying this same analysis to *freelance writers*, "not being ready to write" can mean: not knowing the project's format well enough, whether a roundup article, profile piece, advertising slim jim, or infomercial TV script; or not knowing how that format is being adapted to the target magazine or outlet.

Now, before you start lifting nostrils into air upon reading the word "form" or "template" in connection with your writing, recall Shakespeare's sonnets: 14 lines of rhymed iambic pentameter. Bill wrote some pretty good stuff within that rigid form. All writing has patterns, even post-modern "plotless stories." It's what you put in the pattern that counts.

For *business writers*, "not being ready to write" can mean not having identified the specific type of letter, memo or email that is required for the communication to be made. Business writing is one of the most highly formatted of all genres. The formats are a type of business etiquette that must be understood and followed.

Cause 2: Writers Are Sometimes Afraid to Write

The fear of writing can come from as many places as there are individual neuroses. Here's a general list that applies to most of us low-grade neurotics:

- *Favorite writers sitting on the shoulder saying you'll never write like them.* And they're right. By definition, you'll never write like Faulkner, Woolf, Bellow, or Beattie. They are them, you are you. And you should never try to write like them, unless it's an exercise. You have to write your own stories in your own voice. They did their thing, now it's time to do yours.

- *Confusing the fear of failure with the likelihood of failure.* This is addressed in more detail in "Get it Done—Now!" in this chapter. The main point is that when we sit down in front of the blank page, we often have an irrational fear of not being able to duplicate our successful writing efforts of the past. And that's silly, because our prior success was gained through skill and work, not magic or luck. Your skills haven't gone anywhere. All you need to do is put in your normal time and effort.

- *Being confused and humiliated by poor teachers who are themselves poor writers.* This used to drive me nuts when I was teaching. My most important work was salvaging egos and undoing the harm these teachers had done and myths they had promulgated. Not intentionally. But when nonwriters try to teach writing, it can get pretty ugly.

Cause 3: Writers Often Try to Compose in Their Heads

Headwriters fail to distinguish between editing and composing. They try to come up with the right thought and its correct expression at the same time in their heads. Ouch. There is a time to create and a time to evaluate. Both are legitimate parts of writing, but they are best done at separate times. Otherwise, the normal writing process becomes an exercise in task overload and frustration.

What is the normal writing process? Individuals differ, thank goodness, but generally writers go through the following stages, sometimes looping back to them as the work moves toward its final form.

1. Prewriting: This is everything you do before you sit down to write: read, surf the web, take notes, talk it over with others, do interviews, daydream about it, scribble on napkins, whatever. The subject, slant and materials are being stuffed into your mind and tumbled together.

2. Planning: Sitting down and making a list, drawing a schematic, writing a summary or treatment, maybe even the dreaded outline. "Speed zero drafts" (discussed later in this chapter) fit in this stage when used to explore possible structures.

3. Composing: Your attempt to match thought with words as you explore the soft underbelly of thought and try to use writing to discover what you really think and feel. Initial drafts should be seen as experimental works, written quickly and considered disposable—in whole or part.

4. Editing: This is where the shaping begins. You shape the work's overall structure, its paragraphs and its sentences so that they form a unified whole and march toward the effect you want them to have. You delete stuff, add stuff, move stuff around. You fret over sentences and the nuances of individual words. You make it sing.

5. Proofing: OK, time for the grammar police. Pull out the dic-

tionary and style book. Apply polish to your punctuation. Make it shine.

I hope you took time to read about each of those steps. If you did, you couldn't help but notice how very different and even conflicting they are. How on earth can you "explore the soft underbelly of thought" and worry about the grammar police at the same time? If you're trying to do so, review your ingrained writing process with an eye to separating writing tasks that should be kept discrete.

Make no mistake about it: Changing your writing habits will be hard and will require discipline. Things might even get worse before they get better. But, man, is the change worth it. If you continue to sit and try to craft the perfect sentence in your head before daring to put it on paper, you will likely:

- require more time to write than you would otherwise;

- become frustrated and a victim of writer's block;

- miss many of the important thought connections that could be there if you weren't trying to put ideas into words and edit those words in your head at the same time; and

- never enjoy writing or find it a powerful tool for analysis and self-expression.

Cause 4: Writers Often Start in the Wrong Place

We know how important the first paragraph is in an evaluation of our work. Yet it's often difficult to write a final version of this crucial paragraph until the rest of the piece is done or close to it. That's because the first paragraph must set the stage with just enough suggestion without giving it all away. It must set the tone for the entire piece and compel the reader to continue on.

Sure, it's imperative to get the first paragraph just right. And, I promise, you'll have plenty of time to do so. But instead of sitting with pencil or fingernail stuck in your mouth, trying to write the first paragraph before anything else is written, maybe you could just start somewhere else. Anywhere will do. If you're stuck on the first paragraph, bag it. Write down, "First paragraph goes here," leave a space, then write "Second Paragraph" and start there. Be prepared to skip over anything that tries to keep you stuck. Save that part until later. The answer will likely become obvious later on when you've done more writing and know more about the thing you're creating. Or, at the very least, write a first paragraph and be prepared to throw it away or substantially revise it. Again, approach writing in stages, not under the gun to produce a polished first draft.

Confession: There are times when I spend more time writing the first paragraph than any other part of the piece. Writers who do this are, I think, actually using the first paragraph as a time to think through the piece they are about to write. The inordinate amount of time spent there isn't wasted if you're productively working out a slant, tone, and organizational structure. Just be conscious that this is your method and don't get so frustrated that you end up "blocked."

Top Seven Block Busters

Chances are, even if you follow the above advice, there will be times when the words aren't flowing well or at all. You're stuck. Don't panic and don't let the negative tapes start playing in your head ("Oh, I knew this would happen. I'm just not a good writer. Never have been. Even my kids think so."). That's usually when "stuck" turns into "block." When stickiness comes your way, here are some tricks that I've relied on in the past to get the motor running and the words flowing. Some are hokey, some are based on writing habits we should foster for the long term.

Bust It: Freewrite

Popularized by one of my heroes, Peter Elbow, freewriting forces you to set an arbitrary amount of time, start the timer, then begin writing as quickly as you can without stopping for anything until the time period is over. The writing can focus on a specific problem or remain unfocused, its purpose being merely to generate thought. Regardless, once you set pen to paper or fingers to keyboard, you cannot stop for ANY reason: not spelling, not grammar, not embarrassment, not lack of words. If the words aren't there, you type/write, "OK, words aren't here, I'm trying to get them back, here they come..." and keep up the flow for the entire period of time you've set for yourself.

When teaching, I make all students (regardless of their level) keep freewriting journals and turn them in once a week. More than anything else, this exercise helps students over their fear of writing and puts them in touch with the inner voice that gives writing its authenticity. Freewriting also helps to clean out the synaptic junctions that lie between brain and fingers, junctions that tend to rust over when writing isn't a habit.

Use freewriting to get started on a first draft, to talk through problems, to record daily observations for use in your work or just as a way to let off steam. The key is to write fast, because then you will write without fear.

Bust It: Copy and Write

Sometimes I take out a favorite author's work, read a paragraph or sentence, then try to recreate it on the page. You can get inside that writer's language and its rhythms when you do. My juices are sure to start flowing when typing, "I refuse to accept the end of man. I believe that man will not only endure, he will prevail, that when that last ding-dong of doom sounds from the red and resounding shore, there will still be one tiny, inexhaustible voice crying out in the wilderness..." (William Faulkner, Nobel Prize acceptance speech). But be careful that old drunk isn't perched on your shoulder when you start your own ding-donging.

Bust It: Reread and Notate

Put your research materials beside your keyboard. Read through them with your fingers on the keys. As you read, react to the materials—explain, speculate, relate, add to, explicate, argue with, rant. In other words, use writing to explore the materials. At the end, you'll have a huge mess on screen or on paper. But some good stuff will have been made concrete, and you'll be raring to get started.

Bust It: Write to Someone

Thank goodness for caring, understanding friends, students and family. There have been times when the best way for me to get started on something was as a letter to someone. The someone represented in some fundamental way the actual audience I needed to address in the piece.

This works because we're so familiar and comfortable with letter writing, and especially because we have internalized the trick of matching our materials to the person we're writing to. As a result, letter writing provides an easy way to get our voice into our materials with a slant that is right for the audience. The trick is to know whether to mail it or not.

Bust It: Write Dialogue

Set up a conversation on your screen between yourself and some person who's asking you about your topic. Make it someone you have a strong reaction to. As you answer his or her questions, you'll discover the reasons you're sitting there and also the words you need to get started.

Bust It: Write Invisibly

This will be disorienting at first, but is definitely worth it. You can't edit and correct what you can't see. Ha, ha. So, make your computer screen go black by turning down the brightness control or some other trick. Not using a computer? No problem. Stick a sheet of carbon paper between two blank pages and write on the top with an empty ballpoint pen. It's amazing what cutting yourself off from visual reinforcement will tell you about how much you have been relying on headwriting and hypercorrectivity.

Bust It: Write about Writing

When you're totally stuck, you still have this outlet: describe your feelings about writing. Use writing to vent about your blockage. Rail against Mrs. Grumpy in the fifth grade who always criticized your handwriting and made you feel hopeless and hapless. Write about what you think is blocking you. Write about how the writing went yesterday. Write about what you hope to write tomorrow. Pretty soon, you're putting enough words on the page that the dialogue between it and your head is back on track. Writing about writing will teach you something about yourself as a writer, too, and you may want to keep a writing log about these concerns on a daily basis. Such a "Writing Progress Log," when kept over a period of time, can help you pinpoint what factors cause the writing to go well, poorly, or not at all.

But Don't Do This

1. Don't reread stuff you've already published. Doing so encourages the fearful reaction: "But ... but can I do it again?" It also allows you to procrastinate and allows you to rely on previous writing tricks instead of challenging yourself to grow beyond them.

2. Don't spend time editing what you wrote the day before. Rereading it to get back into the flow is fine. But remember, there's a time to write and a time to edit. If it's not time for the latter (when the draft is done), get your butt in gear and stop procrastinating.

3. Don't talk to others about what you're writing. Yes, I know a lot of advice-givers disagree with this one. But here's my experience, especially with fiction and screenplays: You can talk the life right out of your story. You can also get opinions and ideas that will get in the way of your own. And you can also end up putting more pressure on yourself because now others have specific expectations of you. There are times to seek input: but I don't think it's during the gestation stage when you're in the middle of those first few critical drafts.

Get It Done—Now! Your No-Fret, No-Sweat Plan

Here's a technique that can help you develop the discipline to stay in the harness and get the job done. I call it "block writing," and it can save you time and help you overcome self-doubt and procrastination. If you're like me, chances are you'll need tricks like this one at some point. Here's why.

Other than an empty mailbox, perhaps the most frightening sight for a freelance writer is the blank page. Its terrors have driven many of our brethren to strong drink, greatness, or both. Sometimes I even hate finishing a page because I know another is waiting, its vastness daring me to fill it with my puny thoughts, meager vocabulary and—by the way—how could I produce anything worthy of the writers who have gone before me? I used to make C's in high school English! And so goes the constant babble of recrimination spewed by the monster of self-doubt lurking behind every blank page, which often becomes a mirror for our deepest insecurities.

The Monster's Source

The source of the monster's power is not merely the risk of humiliation we take every time we write, when we reveal parts of ourselves as personal as our underwear. There's also the mystery of the creative act. Although humans have explored deep space and the mysteries of DNA, we still know frighteningly little about creativity except that some of us have more of it than others, and that if we study our craft and work real hard, maybe, just maybe, the magic will happen—but maybe not. It's that possibility of not measuring up, of Monster Doubt's voice drowning out our own, that makes some of us write not at all, others of us write less than we would like, and many of us write at a lower level than we could if sitting down and doing it were not so anxiety-ridden, so unpleasant, so *frightening.*

When I left my job as a teacher of writing in order to freelance full-time, I was forced to deal seriously and quickly with these issues of self-doubt, procrastination and their effect on my daily output. I developed a technique I call "block writing" that helped me overcome three common mistakes that self-doubting writers make, especially when the writing clock strikes high noon and it's time to create that crucial first draft.

Mistakes Writers Make
Mistake 1: Writing Too Slowly

Ever watch a painter or sculptor work? They rarely pause after each brushstroke or chisel strike. But I know writers who cannot pen more than a sentence without stopping to reread and revise it, as if perfect prose should flow from them like birdsong and the final product should take shape sentence by perfect sentence. *Au contraire.*

On a first draft, the writer must probe the amorphous cosmos of thought where words and vision, form and intuition come together. Taking that inward journey means a commitment to writing in an uncensored way, and that usually means writing quickly and without stopping to second guess. By writing quickly, we can finally silence the critical monitor, the little devil who sits on our shoulder interrupting the creative process: "Is that the best word?" "This is probably a dead end." "Will the reviewer think that's stupid?" The devil gets his turn in the revision and polishing stages, not now.

Writing quickly also gets us in sync with our internal voice, which gives writing its authenticity and resonance. The bottom line is that there is a time to create and a time to evaluate. Although both are legitimate parts of writing, they are best done at separate times.

Mistake 2: Not Distinguishing between Fear of Failure and Possibility of Failure

It amazes me that every time I sit down to write, I still get that panicky fear in my gut that makes me want to wash dishes, sharpen pencils and walk the cat—anything to procrastinate. I still have to remind myself of the important difference between the fear of failure and the likelihood of failure.

Rooted in our insecurities, fear of failure usually has little connection to its actual possibility. The reality is that if I've done good research, know the format and market I'm writing in, and I'm willing to put in the time, then failure is unlikely. Although I've learned to accept my irrational fear of failure as a part of my writing personality, even to welcome it because it makes me try harder and keeps me humble, I've also learned to trust reality: I recall all the other times I've sat down to perform this same act and been successful. Why should it be any different this time? The strong likelihood is, I tell myself, it won't be.

Mistake 3: Focusing on the Final Product

While fox hunting and occasionally teaching writing at the University of Virginia, William Faulkner talked of the difference between "those who want to write and those who want only to have written." I think he meant that we are better off focusing on the challenges of writing, the potential it offers us for personal artistic growth, the satisfaction of creating something—rather than the by-products of our work, whether ego or money. Books and articles are mere things. Their completion offers only momentary fulfillment. In the end they will be read by few, remembered by fewer. What's left to sustain us? The doing.

Over the years, block writing has taught me the following four simple but important lessons, without which I don't think I could make a living doing this:

1. To write, no matter my mood or level of fear.

2. To focus on discrete steps and problems as they arrive in predictable sequence, not the final outcome.

3. To keep my head down and butt in chair, ignoring the long, arduous road I must travel to produce final copy.

4. To derive primary satisfaction from the actual process of creating, not its outcome. While I always hope that the final product will be one of my best, I know that there will always be successes and failures and things in between, but the satisfaction and joy of my craft will never abandon me.

How to Block Write

To begin block writing you need a timer, preferably with an alarm, to divide your writing day into 45-minute or one-hour blocks, each followed by a short break. The goal is simple: to sit derriere in chair and not get up during that time period. Eventually, doing this will become automatic. You'll give it no more thought than you do to brushing your teeth. You just do it—without the complaining, the hesitation, the extra push of will. And when things aren't going well, when the demons of doubt snarl their loudest, when the writing chair seems a green mile away—you'll have a simple ploy: "Well, I guess I could sit down for at least *one* block."

The Law of Regularity

Tell yourself: "If I sit down for enough writing blocks, eventually the work WILL get done. All I have to do is show up." Avoid commitments like, "During each block I will produce two pages of copy." It doesn't work that way. You never know what's going to happen once you sit down. You could produce 20 pages or 2 or none at all. Each outcome will have occurred for a legitimate reason. All you know is this: Spend enough time in the chair and, eventually, it will get done.

The Need for Commitment

Like any regimen, whether a weight-loss diet, exercise program or good dental hygiene, block writing will work only if you give yourself to it and play by the rules. That means that no matter how much you dread writing that day, no matter how unprepared you feel, no matter how frightened of failure you may be, no matter how sleepy you are, the simple act of putting your tush in a chair and starting the timer becomes the most important thing you can do to ensure your eventual success. It means you are acquiring a writer's discipline.

The Need for Trust

You must know and believe that during each block something will get done. Even an hour of false starts is important. Sometimes you have to write stuff you won't use in order to clear the way for stuff you will, or say things the wrong way in order to find the right way. But, most of all, you must trust that if you simply sit down for your time in the harness, block after block, eventually the work will get done. At the end of each writing period, you are always one block closer to success.

The Five Benefits of Block Writing

To understand the benefits of block writing, it's important to understand why it works: Although imposing artificial structure on the creative act of writing may seem counterproductive, I remind you of the formula for classical Greek tragedies, from Sophocles to Euripides: the fall of a flawed protagonist in a high position and use of dramatic irony to evoke pity and fear. Structure and pattern, it seems, have the power to free our creativity, whether it's the perfection of *Oedipus Rex*, the symmetry of a sonnet, or the timed bursts of block writing. With the structure of block writing come important benefits:

Benefit 1: Defined Limits

For writers plagued by doubt, simply sitting down isn't enough. Without a tight seat belt, it's too easy to spring back up at the first itch of doubt, the first wretched paragraph or unyielding problem. By allowing yourself to arise in frustration, you reinforce failure— not success. On the other hand, successful writers learn to stay in the chair and write through the problems, to get the work done one way or another. Learning to do that on a daily basis is, I believe, the defining characteristic of a professional writer.

Benefit 2: Artificial Pressure

Freelancing on a part-time basis is psychologically more difficult than full-time. For a full-time writer, the sheer fact of having to sit down and write every day makes doing it as normal as going to the loo. Motivation is also important. Full-time writers have no problem being motivated. No write, no eat. Simple enough. But as a part-time freelancer with a full-time paycheck, you have little to lose besides pride (doesn't that goeth before the fall?). Sometimes we need the motivation that real-world pressure provides—whether a mortgage payment or an editor's deadline. Writing blocks apply a helpful jolt of pressure that feels familiar, especially to the procrastinator in us who often depends on outside pressure to finally get things done.

Benefit 3: Sharper Focus

I used to watch college students make this mistake every day: "I'm going to the library to study for three hours!" Well intended, but few students knew how to break long study periods into effective blocks with specific, achievable goals for each block. The result was usually sadly predictable—wasted time despite honest effort, ending in frustration and disappointment. But writing is like a construction project, and from foundation to rooftop we must constantly ask, "What comes next?" Writing blocks encourage focus on one thing at a time: an effective lead; a main character's back story; a bridge section between main points. If the specific goal is achieved in one block, great! If not, what the heck—have another block on me.

Benefit 4: Required Rest

How long you can sustain concentration and remain efficient is an individual call. But one truth applies: going beyond your productive limit eventually leads to frustration, which can become its own problem. I have found 45-minute to one-hour blocks to be the most comfortable work period for me. For you it could be more, could be less. The key is to be disciplined and to give up romantic notions of working furiously while in the breathless grip of inspiration, losing all sense of self and time, emerging with masterpiece in hand. On some days that may happen; when it does, feel blessed and know it was possible because you treated the other 364 days like a job, complete with coffee and chit-chat (why do you think God gave us email?) during breaks.

Benefit 5: Concrete Goals

Vague dreams lack the juice to sustain us through the tough work that a writing project requires. "I want to be published!" Fine, but as a binding contract with yourself that's a little soft around the edges, exclamation point notwithstanding. Writing blocks are a series of concrete obligations reinforced by timers, beeps, up and down movements, specific goals for each block. All of these things help bind us to the ultimate writing contract: To write our best, to grow from the challenges we've set for ourselves, and to be proud that we're doing it—not merely dreaming it.

SPEED WRITING: HOW TO MASTER THE BLANK PAGE

Speed writing is a way of thinking as well as a way of composing. Most of all, it's a state of being when you sit in front of the computer. When sitting down to write, I am convinced the very worst thing we can do is to let our hands be idle. In other words, to head-write—fingers awaiting the thoughts to form themselves into acceptable sentences in our head, then transcribing them onto the screen. Ding dong, that's wrong. At least for me.

During the process of creation, our mind and fingers should work as one to produce the rough shape of the artistic vision. Our goal should be to initiate a flowing stream of thought and expression, to connect word and thought in a simultaneous oneness. Om.

But this isn't New Agey at all. Like a painter's brush, a keyboard is a tool for creating. Like a painter, we need a process that helps us immerse our creative selves into that passionate moment of creation. Later, we can change colors (revise). Later, we can get out the smallest brush and, like a painter, work up close until the details are in sharp relief (edit/proof). But first comes creation. Speed writing is a way of inserting into your writing process a time when passionate creation can take place.

How Speed Writing Works

Speed writing works very much like freewriting, but you focus on getting from the beginning to the end of something: a paragraph, a section, an article, a chapter, perhaps an entire book. You set a time frame, you begin writing, then you do not stop until you come to the end of the entire thing you want to write: whether a sentence, or a novel. Yes, your novel will be reduced to six pages, your feature article will be nasty lump of clay, your screenplay absent most of its dialogue. But its flaws aren't the point. After a speed draft is done, you've got something you can either work with or throw away—that's a choice you didn't have before. Other rules include:

- You must not interrupt the flow of words upon the screen, even if it means making up quotes and facts, or taking up space with things like "OK, I've run out of something to say, I really don't know where to go next, let me think, what if I tried..."

- You must not stop to reread or edit what you've written until the speed session is over.

Some writers, including Stephen King, like to listen to loud rock music when speed writing. Some do it standing up. Some like the feel of a number two pencil; some love the sight of a yellow legal pad. Some drink coffee; some drink that miracle of modern marketing: bottled water. Whatever. Suck on a pacifier, if you wish. Just start writing and don't stop. Don't edit. Don't second guess. Don't evaluate. Don't do anything but listen to that little voice inside your head and write down everything it says.

Beyond Zero Draft

Speed writing can be useful in just about every stage of the writing process: planning, drafting, revising—any time you need to figure something out, whether it's a sentence or a book plan. But between the end of the material gathering stage and before the completion of the first draft, writers dwell in a place I call the "zero draft." That's when this technique can be important.

The fear of beginning a first draft is legitimate. Until it is complete, we have no way of knowing for sure that the right connections will be made and salient points brought out, or how many dead ends we'll hit and "do overs" we'll have to perform. The traditional answer to this dilemma is the outline, which can be helpful, especially in highly formatted articles. But outlines have the tendency to dissolve like toilet tissue in the rain once the real writing begins and each sentence must build on the one before it.

Another solution: the speed draft. During a speed-draft session, your goal is to get from the beginning of the entire piece to its end in a single block of timed writing. No matter what short cuts you must take—summarize entire sections in a sentence, put in XXX's to substitute for blocks of narration or main points—your goal is to get from beginning to end *in some form* without stopping.

Do this for an entire screenplay, and you've got your first stab at a treatment. Do it for an entire novel and you've got your first stab at chapter summaries. Do it for an article, short story, scene or a book chapter, and you've got a first draft. Very rough, but very important. This speed draft serves three distinct purposes:

1. It lets ideas connect to each other where it counts—on the page in actual sentences and paragraphs.

2. Because several speed drafts can be done in one morning, you can play around with different organizational structures without committing serious composing time to any one.

3. With the work's overall structure in front of you, albeit in rough form, you have slain the monster of the blank page and the work now exists at least in some form. All you have to do now is to refine it and have fun playing with it.

Speed Writing's Other Uses

When I compose, my computer's screen has two windows open on it. In one large window is the actual piece in whatever form it happens to be at the time. The other window contains a "Speed Pad," which provides me a place to speed write. Any time I need to think about how to do something, instead of pausing to stare at the computer screen, I put the cursor on the Speed Pad and think by typing, whether it's to:

• flesh out an idea;

• plan a dramatic scene;

• find out what should come next;

• talk through what bothers me about what I've written;

• write different versions of a sentence to see which works better; and

• anything else that would make me stare at the screen instead of write.

Once the speed writing is done, there are two choices: (1) cut and paste if it's good enough—and sometimes it is; or (2) print it out, set the hard copy by the computer and refer to it. Regardless, the goal has been achieved: Think with writing. Writing is our way of thinking. It's also our way of relating to the world. Our way of being. Don't let anything get between you and the words and the world you are exploring with them.

"CHAINED MERCURY": SAMPLE SPEED DRAFT

This is an example from a speed-writing session for the screenplay "Chained Mercury: The Jerrie Cobb Story." My goal was to plot a sequence of scenes that follow the main character (Jerrie Cobb) as she prepares to fight a government decision to ban women from the Mercury space program in the 1960s. The scenes lead up to Congressional hearings to reconsider that action. During the sequence she interacts with the media in a montage sequence and then meets with NASA and other government officials to garner support for her position.

The speed-writing session took about 25 minutes. I had read plenty of research materials for the scene, and I knew its purpose in the plot. My goal was to get past the zero-draft stage (nothing on the page) and work out a sequence of scenes. All of the typos are real and not some printing or proofreading problem. Speed writing means moving your fingers as fast as you can and ignoring EVERY-THING but the flow of thought. You can compare this speed draft to the finished portion of the screenplay that follows it.

Chained Mercury Speed Session
by David Taylor

ok we'll start wsith another media frenzy but this has a much diff tone the hedlines start turning it into one of America's mfirst wars of sexisms, inflamig passions on both sides one interview frm researach:

rrepotere
why do you want to compete with men

jerrie
I don't think of this as a competition. we're all pilots, we're qualified
for the space program

reporter
what do you hope to accomplish here in washington

jerrie
to help America in the space race, to contibute what we can as. I
hope we can do that.

then after a dose of headlines and the above interview, we start sitting jerrie down in front on washington officials

got to come up with two new types

how bout a young one with pocked mark face:

his excuse:
no pressure suits for women
well, where did you get the pressure suit for the men? Perhaps they
could make a few more?

next:
political type with appropriations
this is really a funding issue, miss cobb I hope you understand that.

jerrie
tests show we're lighter. you could save money on fuel, we eat less
too

politoco
oh my my not quite that simple, take your bathrooms for instance.
now if we let women go, we'd have to have separate bathrooms.

jerarie
then send either an all male crew or all female crew. keep the one
head.

politico
I'm afreaid you
re not ffollowing me. you see, if we let women go, then other mi-
noriies would want to go. and now we've still got to build extra
bathrooms. don't you see

finally, she's with crew cut severed pinky finger

this scene is a little longer so slow down expand and use CUs

crew caut
I'll be frank. I've been told to see you.

jerrie
thank you for being frank

crew cut
let's heear it.

jerrie

in yhour position in NASA you have the ability to help get out the truth to Congress and the nation about our qualifications

crew cut
whose we

jerrie
the mercury 13 women

crw ut
look miss cobb. here's what I think about you m 13 women. you're unamerican.

jerrie
sir

cerw cut
whyu are you endangering this program. this is a war yuou know. do you understand war? in a war you fight, you fight for what you bleive in, you protect everyintg that holy and you dodn't let anyting or anyone get in your way

war isn't pretty. war isn't for women

jerrie
id on't see how we're endangering the war

crew cut
crhist you libbers

ok, let's say we put one of you in the program. let's sayu it's yuou. blond hair, pretty, from okalhoma. singlel a sexy gal.

now lets say something happens youu get hurt. the prety little gal fdrom okklahoma screws the poouch.

you know what thay meas

jerrie
of course

crew ut
now we got one little dead bitch on our hands, the pride of merica womanhood.

who's balls you think tahe prress is going to come after

your's

janey harts, her wimply llittle senator husband

oh that's right. yuou don't have them, I bet he doesn't edither.

jerrie
I think I get your point

I bet you do nd here's one more little thing you're gonna get

jerrie
what's that.

a surprise in tomorrow hearing. we've got it all laid out.

your finished and your buddies too.

Cut to: his severed pinky fintger curing the intercom

recptionis
yes sir?

crew tut
please show miss cobb out. her work here is done.

Excerpt from Chained Mercury: The Jerrie Cobb Story
Original screenplay by David Taylor


```
MONTAGE - MEDIA FRENZY


--This montage contrasts sharply with the quaint
headlines of the previous media montage. This woman is no
longer an amusing sideshow to the space race: she flies
military fighter jets and she wants her place with men. A
nation's sexism button has been punched. Headlines flash
across the screen:
"Lady in Space? Ha-Ha"
"Now Women Try to Invade Last Male Frontier—Space" (Miami
Herald)
"No Space for Women" (accompanied by a cartoon of a
rocket firing into space with its side covered by a sign:
"Men Only")


--Jackie Gleason gets in the act on TV. Cut in footage
from the skit that includes a reference to the
controversy. Ralph warns: "We better get a woman in space
before the Russians. Otherwise, we'll NEVER hear the end
of it!"
```

--Montage ends with recreation of a famous TV interview:

> REPORTER
>
> So, tell us, Jerrie. Why do you want to
> compete with the men?

> JERRIE
>
> Well, I don't think of it as a
> competition. We're all pilots,
> we've all qualified for the
> space program.

> REPORTER
>
> What do you girls hope to
> accomplish here in Washington?

> JERRIE
>
> We're here to contribute what
> we can. We want to help America
> win the space race.

INT. GOVERNMENT OFFICE — DAY

Jerrie sits in front of RODGERS, a young, pock-marked
campaign worker recently rewarded by Kennedy's election
victory with a bureaucratic position.

> RODGERS
>
> Sorry we can't help you. It really comes
> down to something pretty simple.

                    JERRIE

          What's that?

                    RODGERS

          When the previous administration
          funded the program, they only
          requested pressure suits
          be fabricated for men.

Jerrie looks puzzled.

                    RODGERS

          Don't you see? We just don't
          have any suits for women!

INT. GOVERNMENT OFFICE — DAY

Jerrie sits before yet another bureaucrat, this one a
florid POLITICO, far more wise in Washington-speak.

                    POLITICO

          Strictly an appropriations issue,
          Miss Cobb. The tyranny of budgets,
          I'm afraid.

                    JERRIE

          Well, women are lighter. You could save
          on fuel costs.

                    POLITICO
              (not getting the humor)

Interesting thought. But there's a
larger funding problem that will
take some thought and hard work.

                    JERRIE
What's the problem?

                    POLITICO
Well, just to give you one example:
restrooms.

                    JERRIE
Restrooms?

                    POLITICO
Yes, as of now, all of our
facilities, including the
spacecraft themselves, have
only male lavatories.

He raises his hands as if everything
is now perfectly clear.

                    POLITICO
Can you imagine the expense and
delay of adding facilities for
women, especially in something
as complex and small as a spacecraft?

                    JERRIE
Send up an all-male crew or
an all-female crew.

                    POLITICO
              (chuckles condescendingly)
        I'm afraid you're not following
        me, Miss Cobb. If we let women
        in, then all the other minorities
        will want in, too. Now we've got
        a real toilet issue on our hands. See?

INT. GOVERNMENT OFFICE — DAY

Jerrie is with a high-level NASA official, a military
officer with his jacket off, in white shirt behind an
imposing desk. A gruff, CREW CUT warrior who has learned
to scowl at the civilian world.

                    CREW CUT
        I'll do you the honor of being frank.
        You're here because I was ordered to
        see you.

He lets that sink in, studying Jerrie for weakness.

                    JERRIE
        I appreciate your frankness, sir. I'll try to
        be brief. As you know, the hearings begin
        tomorrow and--

                    CREW CUT
        Cut to the chase, Miss Cobb.

                    JERRIE

We want you to use your position in NASA
to get the truth out to Congress and to the
nation about our true qualifications.

                    CREW CUT

Who's we?

                    JERRIE

The Mercury 13.

                    CREW CUT

The Mercury 13. Uh huh. Miss Cobb,
let me tell you what I think about
your so-called Mercury 13. You're
un-American. You're a threat to the
security of our nation. You deserve
exactly what you're gonna get tomorrow.

                    JERRIE

Sir?

                    CREW CUT

Let me ask you a question, a serious one:
Why are you endangering America's
space program? What's your motive,
Miss Cobb? Who are you really working
for?

                    JERRIE

Sir? How am I endangering the space
program? What are you talking about?

                    CREW CUT

          I'm talking about war, Miss Cobb. You
          were a snot-nosed, barefoot brat in the
          last one, so let me educate you: in a war you
          fight. You fight for your country, you fight for
          what you believe in. You're willing to kill
          and be killed. And you don't let anything—or
          anyone—get in your way.

                    JERRIE

          I still don't see how we—

                    CREW CUT

          Okay, let's say we put one of you women in the
          program. The real program, not just tests like
          you've been doing. Let's say it's you: blond
          hair, pretty, real sexy gal from Oklahoma.

He leans forward, arms on desk, enjoying it.

                    CREW CUT

          Now let's say that you're a bona fide
          astronaut. We sit you on top of the rocket.
          We light it. Something happens. The pretty
          little thang from Oklahoma screws the pooch.
          You know what "screw the pooch" means?

                    JERRIE

          Yes, of course.

                    CREW CUT

          Now we got one dead little Okie on our hands,

pride of American womanhood, deader than
a piece of road kill.

He leans back into his chair.

> CREW CUT
> Now who you think the press is gonna come
> after, huh? The Mercury 13?

> JERRIE
> I get your point.

> CREW CUT
> Good. America isn't ready for its women to die
> as warriors, Miss Cobb. Not today. You screw
> the pooch on top of one of those rockets,
> NASA'll be shut down faster...

Crew Cut pauses, gives sly smile.

> CREW CUT
> Why, faster than a speeding car on a hot,
> Florida night.

> JERRIE
> I think I understand now.

> CREW CUT
> I bet you do. Enjoy your moment in front of
> the cameras tomorrow. We've got a little
> something prepared for you. I'm sure you of
> all the gals will appreciate it.

                                                    CUT TO:

His severed index finger stabs the intercom.

                          RECEPTIONIST (V.O.)
          Yes sir?

                          CREW CUT
          Please show Miss Cobb out. She's finished here.

*"Certain words can put your
readers into a trance."*

 **CHAPTER FOUR**

QUERY LETTERS, TITLES, AND OTHER MYTHS

- A New Query Letter Strategy
- Magic Titles: 27 Secrets Guaranteed to Sell
- Straight From the Source's Mouth: 11 Interviewing Tips
- Can I Use Fiction Techniques in Nonfiction?
- How to Write a Regular Column
- Hidden Freelance Market: Newspaper Weeklies & Dailies
- How Do I Get Press Credentials?
- Hidden Freelance Market: Publication Rights Clearinghouse

One of the biggest myths is that writers aren't marketers. Just the opposite. Our articles are our wares. We're door-to-door salesmen, peddling our works to editors and their readers. As book salesmen, we close the deal when the reader puts our title and a plastic card on the checkout counter at Barnes and Noble. Cha-ching. Like competing sales reps going after the same account, we compete with each other for the reader's attention and time—even more important than money

And editors? They're marketers, too. Newsstand sales are a

boss's favorite way of evaluating an edit package's ability to attract an audience: On a newsstand an editor is head-to-head with her competition and readers are paying premium airport prices. It's no accident that editors call cover lines, "sell lines."

Query letters, headlines and titles—they're also marketing tools. Why not explore the techniques that professional marketers and copywriters use, then adapt them judiciously for our literary marketing needs? Emphasis on "judicious," please.

QUERY LETTERS: MYTHS AND STRATEGIES

Few topics in freelance writing have received more ink than the query letter—and deserve it less. New freelancers in particular seemed fascinated by the query letter. Maybe it's the obscure, insider name: query letter. Surely that's something only writers know about. Maybe it's the promise of a quick payoff—heck, anybody can write one or two pages. Maybe it's the fact that writing queries can easily substitute for the harder work of writing articles.

No surprise: I believe far too much has been written about query letter strategies, query letter models, query letter workshops, query letter dos and don'ts. Far too many writers spend time on queries when they should be researching and writing manuscripts. Novelist and freelancer Bob Sassone calls it the "query letter trap." Maybe it's also a "query letter pit" filled with procrastinators and the terminally timid.

Are You Telling Me Never to Write Queries?

There's no doubt query letters can serve a legitimate purpose:
- By gauging an editor's interest before slanting your material for that publication, you keep yourself from getting overdrawn at the Psychic Reserve Bank, whose currency is used for dealing with rejections.

- Queries certainly can prevent the inanity of "blind submissions," where you add to slush piles with unsolicited stories that haven't been asked for, probably haven't been slanted, and end up making you look like an amateur.

However, let me hasten to add that there are times when blind, multiple submissions make a lot of sense: See "Hidden Freelance Market: Newspaper Dailies and Weeklies" later in this chapter. Other times: shorties, fillers and humor columns.

Big Old Hoary Query Letter Myths
Myth 1: A Well-Written Query Proves to the Editor That You Are Qualified to Write the Piece.
The only things that prove you can write the piece are (a) the piece itself; (b) closely related clips, and I mean really closely related. Don't send a terrific travel story clip if you're proposing to write a how-to. It'll have just the opposite effect: "Oh, this writer has never published a how-to before; otherwise, she would've sent it."

Myth 2: A Formal, Detailed Query Gives You the Opportunity to Do Preliminary Research for a Piece That Can Be Quickly Converted into an Article.
Ah, perfect example of the query letter trap: If you've done enough research for a "formal, detailed query," you probably should write the piece and not waste time on the formal query process, which can take a month or more.

Myth #3: Short Informal Queries Will Often Not Be Read or May Be Given Less Weight by an Editor If the Editor Is a Stickler for the Formal Process.
Huh? Editors don't judge query letters by their length. If the query gets the job done, length is not an issue. The only time I know when length, not content, becomes an issue: if the query letter is too long.

Myth 4: A Good Query Letter Often Begins with the Article's Actual Lead in Order to Give the Flavor of Your Writing and the Article.

Writers who do this are in the query pit and need to get a life and a manuscript. If you're spending time polishing a lead for a story that hasn't been written or fully researched, you're wasting time. If the story is written, polish its lead and send it to an appropriate market, pronto.

Query letters with the article lead as the first paragraph often seem laughably out of place to me. You're writing a letter, for crying out loud. Make it sound like a letter. The lead-as-letter opener delays getting to the point: What story are you pitching? Is it right for this magazine?

New Query Strategy: Short 'n' Sweet

If you've got a good idea for an article but haven't written it yet (or it's been written for another market and you're considering repurposing it), then write a query letter that is:

Highly Targeted

Not only should you read and study back issues of the publication you wish to write for. You should also target a specific feature or department type:

No: I'd like to write a feature for your magazine.
Yes: I'd like to write one of your popular make-over how-to's.

No: I have an idea for a short piece for your magazine.
Yes: I want to write a 500-word piece for your "Seaviews" department.

Show the editor you are writing for that specific magazine and that you've studied it.

Addressed Properly

Find the specific editor on the masthead who handles freelancers or, better yet, handles freelance submissions for the kind of feature or department story you're writing. (For instructions on how to do this, see chapter 5: "How to Find the Right Editor for You.")

Pitched in the First Paragraph

Don't monkey around. Get to the point in two to three sentences, max:

No: "As Richard did his giant stride off the back of the dive boat and splashed into the popsicle blue Caribbean, little did he know that the dive buddy coming in behind him was a lawsuit waiting to happen. When the dive started going bad, his buddy didn't have a clue. Richard had to provide help he wasn't qualified to give but, as he found out too late, he was legally obligated to perform."

Yes: "Dear David: Several of your recent 'Scuba Law' columns have focused on the legal obligations of dive operators. As a divemaster and lawyer I see something just as bad every weekend: Divers who have no idea that agreeing to be a dive buddy implies serious legal risks. I want to write a 750-word article for your 'Scuba Law' department that details for divers what those risks are and how they can be managed."

Short

Both of the above examples have the same number of words (73). After the descriptive loveliness of the first one, I still have no clue what the writer is proposing. After the second one, I have everything I need to give an assignment, including the writer's qualifications.

Attached to Clips

But make sure they're relevant. Otherwise they signal that you've never written this kind of article before, thereby inserting a significant question mark in the editor's mind at a time when you really don't want to. If you don't have relevant clips, mention previous publications your work has appeared in. If you don't have clips, simply talk about your other qualifications and experience for writing this piece. Don't try to fake it.

Presented Professionally

That means a proofread letter that conforms to business-letter format and includes a SASE, if it's not an email query. Now, get back to work! Write more articles, fewer queries.

More Query Letter Faux Pas

- Mentioning how long and hard you've worked on this piece.

- Crowing about others who have liked the idea you're proposing.

- Asking for feedback and making clear your "willingness" to revise.

- Hoping that the editor will like the idea because you'd be thrilled to be in their magazine. Editors rarely care about a freelancer's hopes or other feelings.

- Discussing pay rates and rights. You don't have the assignment yet!

- Pitching too many articles in one letter. Two or three is the max, I think.

• Including qualifications that aren't. The only ones that count are related directly to your subject matter and your experience as a writer.

WHAT'S THE BEST WAY TO SUBMIT A QUERY?

"What's the best way to submit a query by mail? How soon after submitting should I follow up to see if the editor liked it?"

The best way to submit a written query is to observe the etiquette for making your letter look and sound professional. At this stage, when an editor is asking himself/herself if you're an amateur or a pro, trustworthy or not, appearances count. Make sure your letter is:

• Printed on your own unpretentious letterhead.

• Addressed to a named editor on the masthead.

• Addressed to the right editor. Make sure you have researched the publication and found the appropriate editor for your query.

• Folded neatly in thirds.

• Accompanied by a SASE (self-addressed, stamped envelope) if the query is made by surface mail .

• Supported by relevant clips, if you have them for the type of article you're proposing.

Then wait up to two weeks. Then wait some more. Don't phone unless it's a timely story that needs a timely response. If an editor hasn't responded in a month, send a brief follow-up, wait a bit more, then forget it if there's no response. Obviously, he/she wasn't interested. Don't take it personally. Move on.

More Tips

- Many editors consider fax queries unappealing—cheap substitutes for a professionally done letter.

- On the other hand, email queries are becoming popular. I love email queries. They can be efficiently dealt with in a few keyboard strokes. No paper cuts are a plus, too.

- Resist querying by phone unless you've been invited to.

- Query only one publication at a time with your story idea. If you ever send out simultaneous queries selling exclusive rights and receive two acceptances, you've got a problem. If the two editors find out what you did, you'll likely not get that assignment or any others from them. An editor's willingness to trust you is more important than your writing skills.

- Keep it short. A half page is better than a full page. Editors value compression in writing and love freelancers who can say things in as few words as possible without a lot of "gee whiz" attitude and breathless prose.

HOW MUCH SHOULD I RESEARCH BEFORE QUERYING?

"How much research should I do before sending in my query? A lot? Just enough?"

Ideally, you should do just enough preliminary research to ensure that you can deliver the story you promise, no more. If you get the assignment and begin the research only to discover the story isn't there or has changed substantially, you've got some "s'plaining" to do, putting yourself at risk of losing the editor's faith and trust. Good research is never a waste of time. It's money and facts in the bank, ready to be withdrawn for that story and possibly others.

DO I ALWAYS HAVE TO QUERY FIRST?

"Should I query an editor first or just send in the completed manuscript?"

No, you don't have to query first, but if you're just starting out, it's probably a good idea to try a short query letter after a thorough study of the magazine and the editor's needs. Two reasons:

1. Doing so signals your professionalism. Editors know that, in most instances, professional freelancers don't write stories and send them to people they don't know and who may not be interested. It's a waste of everyone's valuable time.

2. Querying first shows a respect for the editor and an understanding of his/her job. An editor needs only a moment to read a query letter and make a decision. With a full manuscript, the editor must spend time to figure out what's going on, then worry about whether or not the manuscript was requested (we forget!), if there is a legal obligation to return it and any artwork accompanying it. In other words, a pain in the hard drive.

During nine years as an executive editor, I can count on one hand the number of times I read an unsolicited manuscript and decided I could use it. Both times, it was luck.

MAGIC TITLES: 27 SECRETS GUARANTEED TO MAKE YOUR HEADLINES SELL

Time to write your title? Please remove your writer's hat and put on this marketer's beanie. The job of a title is to rescue readers from a chaotic world and put them into a reading trance as they stand in the bookstore aisle or at a magazine rack. A title must have the power to transport readers from the concrete reality of their lives into that quiet, cozy world inhabited only by your voice, your words and them.

In other words, a title must do more than get attention. It must hold attention. This feat of hypnosis is tough to accomplish in the brief moments a reader spends scanning your title, but it's what advertising and marketing folks have honed to an art. "But I'm a writer, not an ad flak!" you exclaim. Hey, I believe you. But you don't have to morph yourself into Dale Carnegie or P.T. Barnum to write headlines that will help your work gain attention and readers. You don't have to sell out in order to sell. What do you need?

The Most Important Words of Your Life

Titles matter, a lot. They can mean the difference between your work selling or languishing. Titles also matter to your first reader: an editor, agent or publisher. These folks are responsible for the successful financial relationship between your creative product and the buying public. And they know the importance of titles to motivate potential readers to buy and, after they buy, to actually pick it up and read—then want more.

Here's another point about titles: It's not just your main title that's important. You should also put effort into the internal titles (subheads, teaser decks, chapter headings, etc.) that can make your work more compelling than all the other magazines and books lying on the coffee table or in the bathroom begging to be picked up and read.

Article Titles That Make You Rich

That could be one of them, but it's more appropriate for the hyped-up world of Internet marketers than, say, advice columns for troubled teens. That's why if you're searching for hard and fast rules about titles, you're likely to find only one: *Whatever works*. Finding what works is a combination of knowing: (1) a few marketing basics, (2) the reader benefits of what you're writing, and (3) what would be appropriate or inappropriate for your audience.

Strong Benefits: The Basis of Marketing

Time to tune in to that worldwide radio station, WRIT-FM: "What's Really In It-For Me." This is why attracting attention isn't enough. Strong headlines in nonfiction today also need to communicate a strong benefit. Promising a strong benefit is not only the safest and most widely used type of headline; it is also the basis for most other headline styles, which convey what that benefit is with a variety of different language patterns and rhetorical devices.

This point cannot be emphasized enough: *People don't just read whatever is put in front of them. They read (and buy) what interests and benefits them in a directly personal way.* As a nonfiction writer, you are selling results, from weight loss to new riches, popularity to inner peace. This is why most how-to articles about writing titles, headlines and book-cover copy start with having you sit down and write out the reader benefits of your work—one benefit/headline per index card.

Together, the benefits add up to your USP: Unique Selling Proposition, the thing that a reader can get from your work and not anywhere else. The clearer and more direct the USP is, the better chance you have of being read and of being purchased by your first and most important reader—the editor.

How to Crack the Secret Code: Title Patterns

One trick to writing headlines and titles is to find those that have historically worked best in your field, then use their underlying patterns to write your own version. It's these underlying patterns that make up the genetic code of what works for your audience in your particular market.

One of the best-known examples is Dale Carnegie's title "How to Win Friends and Influence People." The power of this phrase isn't simply word choice. Although "How to Remember People's Names and Keep Them from Arguing with You" contains clumsy phrasing, the underlying pattern of the famous original still resonates beneath:

How to _____ and _____

This pattern has become an archetype in today's service journalism, which attempts to improve our lives through the application of information:

- How to Eat More and Lose Weight

- How to Make Money and Stay at Home

- How to Speak Up and Be Heard

- How to Stay Fit and Be a Mom

Let's Apply It
- How to Write Titles and Sell Your Books

In service journalism, the power of "how to" stands alone, although it makes a lousy book title because in alphabetic listings like Bowker's *Books In Print* your title will appear under the "H's" along with thousands of other books that don't relate to your subject. But for articles and other headings, the how-to variations are legion:

How to get	How to conquer	How to market
How to keep	How to end	How to burn
How to begin	How to get the	How to get rid of
How to improve	most out of	How to save
How you can	How to develop	How to laugh
How to avoid	How to start	
How to enjoy	How to become	
How to improve	How to have	

Let's Apply It

- How to Write Titles that Make Editors Beg for More

One More Example of Pattern Divination

As editor of a scuba diving magazine, I knew one of my readers' primary concerns was safety, especially of the life-support equipment their lives depended on. We lab tested and ocean tested this equipment, then reported the results in a *Consumer Reports* format. When we found some poorly designed, dangerous regulators (the things that deliver air under water), we adapted the pattern of one of the most successful product review headlines of all times. Our title was: "Unsafe at Any Depth: The Truth about Mail-Order Regulators."

Today, "Unsafe at _____" and its variations are used so often that few remember its origin: Ralph Nader's 1965 book that savaged one of the first turbo-charged production automobiles, the Chevrolet Corvair. Nader killed the Corvair but gave birth to an archetype for titles.

Let's Apply It

- Safe at Any Length: The Truth about Headlines and Rejection Slips

Title/Subtitle Pattern

This pattern packs a one-two punch. The short main title grabs attention with one of advertising's power words, then the subtitle compels reading with the promise of benefits:

• Computer Breakthrough: New Circuit Design Triples Laptop Speeds

• Internet Secret Revealed: How You're Being Hacked and Don't Know It

"Breakthrough," "secret," and "revealed" are part of advertising's set of "magic words" that have proven their attention-getting power over and over. When writing titles, it's helpful to have a list of these words handy. Taken together in a list like the one below, they seem hokey and slick, like tossing down a shot of snake oil. But used judiciously and appropriately in your market, they can be, well, magic.

New	Today	Powerful
Free	Latest	Limited offer
First	Guaranteed	Time sensitive
Best	Acclaimed	Proven
Improved	Endorsed	Striking
Special	Recommended	Sale
Successful	Famous	Classic
Introducing	Surprising	Handy
Convenient	Unusual	Reliable
Bargain	Popular	Fantastic
Sensational	Astonishing	Magic
Startling	You can	Certified
Easy	First	Wealth
Revolutionary	First-rate	Money
Remarkable	Genuine	Marvelous

Tested	Exclusive	Wonderful
Stunning	Rare	Incredible
Provocative	Superior	Uncommon
Revealing	Exciting	Overwhelming
Fascinating	Announcing	Wonderful
Discount	Fantastic	Love
Lowest	Super	Miracle
Highest	Unique	Useful
Phenomenal	Urgent	Versatile

Let's Apply It *Also "shocking"*

- Magic Titles: 27 Secrets Guaranteed to Make Yours Work

- Easy Titles: Surprising Secrets for First-Rate Headlines

- Fantastic Titles: 18 Ways to Make Yours Instant Classics

- Power Up Your Titles: Secrets of Successful Headlines

- Complete Guide to Titles: Proven Techniques to Boost Your Sales

Titles with an Open-Ended Question

This is a favorite of marketing whiz Joe "Mr. Fire" Vitale: Engage readers and make them curious by asking an open-ended question:

- What If You Went Sailing and Never Came Home?

- Think You've Seen Outrageous? Take a Look at This!

Let's Apply It
- What If Writing Titles Made You Rich?

Titles That Offer a Solution to a Problem

This is a service journalism favorite in our stress-filled, health-conscious, success-driven world: a title that provides answers and solutions to the problems that plague your readership.

- Now You Can Melt 3 Inches of Fat from Your Waist in 30 Days or Less—Guaranteed!

Notice that the headline presents a real solution to a real problem, not just a milquetoast possible prevention:

- Alone Again at 50: How to Keep from Going Nuts

Instead, go for the jugular with specific numbers, specific problems and solutions to them:

- 7 Reasons Your Management Staff Could Be Better

- 22 Ways to Increase Profits in Your Internet Business

Let's Apply It

- Banish Lame Titles: 19 Power Principles of Writing Headlines You Won't Learn in School!

- Win Editors with These 27 Secrets of Writing Titles—Guaranteed to Get You Out of the Slush Pile

Titles with Flags > *Woman's World (!)*

A flag is a phrase (some say gimmick) that hails the attention of the reader:

- ***Attention Students!*** This Reading Technique Cuts Your Study Time in Half—Guaranteed!

A flag can also be at the end of a headline:

- Your Internet Business Depends on Up Time, Fast Time, All the Time—*Join Our Free Hosting Plan Today!*

The flag can also be phrased as a question:
- *Got Herpes?* Don't Worry, So Does Everyone Else

Let's Apply It
- *Writers—Look!* Don't Miss These 27 Secrets to Writing Killer Headlines

Titles with Warnings
This is a variation of the flag technique that plays upon fear in order to motivate the reader:
- ***Warning: Dieters***
  Don't Take Another Pill Until You Read This Startling Message about Heart Attacks!

Let's Apply It
- ***Warning: Freelancers***
  Don't Write Another Headline Until You Learn These 12 Techniques!

Titles with Magic Pills
Westerners seek the one thing that can quickly, painlessly, effortlessly take care of all our woes, concerns and needs. And could I get fries with that?
- 1001 Ways to Market Your Books

- How to Easily Make Your Book an Amazon Bestseller

- Create Your Own Profitable E-Book in One Hour!

Let's Apply It
- 27 Easy Ways to Write Titles That Grab—And Don't Let Go

- How to Create Great Titles Without Scratching Your Head

Titles with Puns and Allusions
Here you play upon the familiarity of a famous title, word or phrase by integrating it into your own. Caution: humor is great when it works, death when it doesn't.
- National Velveeta: Elizabeth Taylor's Middle Years

- We're Growing Fonda of Jane: The Video Abs Revolution

- Tongue Fu: How to Defuse Verbal Conflict

- Car Pool Tunnel Syndrome: Confessions of a Soccer Mom

- In Vino Vomitas: Why I Love Cheap Wine

Let's Apply It
- Giving Headlines: Titles That Don't Suck

- Title Match: How to Win the Headline Game in 5 Minutes or Less

- Title Heirs: Crowning Achievements in Headline Writing

[(En)titled Kids: How to Avoid Raising One"]

Titles That Contain a Testimonial
Quotes placed around a satisfied customer's words automatically draw attention and make the headline's claim seem more believable:
- "I Lost 37 Pounds in 37 Days"—How Richard Matlock Rediscovered His Waistline

Specific numbers are the key to making these testimonial claims believable.

Let's Apply It
- "I Made 17 Sales with 17 Great Headlines"—Mike Donner Did It, So Can You

Titles That State a Position
These are effective for writing reviews and other opinion pieces. By declaring a clear position, you stir emotions in those who agree with you, as well as those who don't.
- If You Can Read Only One Newspaper, *USA Today* Should Be It

- Daycare Is Ruining Our Children

- Rush Limbaugh Is a Big, Fat Idiot

Let's Apply It
- Your Titles Are Wimpy and Here's the Reason Why

Titles That Shock
Big caution: What follows the shocking title had better justify the flag you just waved.
- You Name It, I Vomited It

- Like a Cold Gun Up Your Behind

Let's Apply It
- Do Your Titles Smell Like Diapers? How to Take the Stink Out of Headline Writing

Warnings and Don'ts

These titling techniques must be used carefully when writing web copy. The microcontent of web prose (headlines, page titles, subject lines) needs to be, in the words of Jakob Nielsen, "pearls of clarity": 40–60 characters that explain the macrocontent. Here's why:

Unless the title or subject make it absolutely clear what the web page or email is about, users will likely not read it or open it. Remember that online headlines are often displayed out of context: as part of a list of articles, in an email program's list of incoming messages, in a search engine hit list, or in a browser's bookmark menu or other navigation aid. Even when a headline is displayed together with related content, the difficulty of reading online and the reduced amount of information that can be seen at a glance make it harder for users to learn enough from the surrounding data. In print, a headline is associated with photos, cutlines, decks, subheads and the full body of the article, all of which can be interpreted in a single glance. Online, a much smaller amount of information will be visible in the window, and even that information is harder and more unpleasant to read, so people often don't do so.

That's why, online, headlines must stand on their own and make sense when the rest of the content is not available. If the choice is to be clear or be clever, always opt for clarity, especially online.

STRAIGHT FROM THE SOURCE'S MOUTH— INTERVIEW TIPS

Interviews are a nonfiction writer's bread-and-butter. Getting great interviews is both an art and a science. I've been fortunate to have the chance to interview the late Jacques Cousteau, Gene Hackman, Jimmy Johnson, Derek Jeter and a host of other kind, generous sources who spent time to share their knowledge and their lives. I will always be indebted to them. As you will be with your sources. During these experiences, I've learned the hard way some definite

WRITER'S TOOLBOX
WORDS THAT SELL

Find a copy of Richard Bayan's *Words That Sell: A Thesaurus to Help You Promote Your Products, Services and Ideas*, and keep it on your desk next to your *Synonym Finder* by J.I. Rodale.

If you haven't discovered these two invaluable reference books yet, just think how great your headlines and text will be now that you'll be using what other insiders have learned to use.

Roget's Thesaurus? One word: Ha!

dos and don'ts. Beyond all the tricks and techniques, the most important "do" for any interview is very simple: Be yourself. Focus on the story, not your ego. Be relaxed. Oh—and do it a lot. In the meantime, consider these pointers.

Don't Be Impressed   *Don't gush.*
Do not under any circumstances act like a fan or let on that you are impressed by a subject's status. Sources hate that, especially the celebrity types. Act cool and professional. All you're doing is a job. Treat celebrities as you would anyone else you're interviewing: "Good day. So nice to meet you. Thanks for taking the time to sit down and talk . . . etc." Act NORMAL.

Research. Research. Research.
You absolutely cannot read enough, listen enough or watch enough about a public figure. Their own works, other interviews, critical reviews, biographies, all their artistic output, etc. The better prepared you are, the better you will come off as a professional inter-

viewer, the better job you will do, and the more likely you'll be asked to do it again.

Prepare Your Questions, Then Feel Free to Ignore Them

It's good to write your questions ahead of time. But then try not to look at them again until the end of the interview. Seriously. The biggest mistake you can make is to let a series of pre-fab questions prevent you from engaging in genuine give-and-take with your subject. Listen and respond as if you are simply having a conversation with someone interesting. And if you don't find them interesting, if you can't at least in your mind during the period of the interview believe your subject is the most fascinating person on earth, then you might never realize your full potential as an interviewer.

At the end of the interview, take a moment to review your notes and questions to see if there's anything else you need to touch upon. Don't be afraid of the pause when you do that. Don't be afraid of any pause. Pauses are actually much shorter and more important than you think. They give you and the subject a chance to reflect and to move ahead with confidence. I actually believe handling a pause with confidence puts you in more command and control. And one more secret: the "Mike Wallace Uncomfortable Silence Technique"—some of the best stuff will come when a source tries to fill the silence.

Let Your Readers Do the Interview

You can't prepare good questions unless you get into the minds of your readers and know the questions they would most want to hear the answers to. You are their proxy in that interview. You must be their mouth and brains and smile. Know your readers inside out, represent them honestly, and you can't go wrong.

Start Lite

Know some recent facts about your subject and start with softball questions that are really just chit-chat, but signal your interest in this person and your research about them: "You just finished a gig with Greg Allman—how did it turn out?" "I hear you just returned from Hawaii—do any hula dancing?"

Climb the Pyramid

I try to keep in mind a pyramid: Start with easy questions that evoke straightforward responses to build rapport. Ascend to the meaty questions that readers most want to know the answer to and that may even be a bit uncomfortable or challenging for your subject. Then wind down with some closing chit-chat—if you haven't overstayed your welcome or been kicked out yet.

Observe Time Limits

Make it clear at the outset that you know this person has set aside a certain number of minutes for the talk and you promise to get them out on time. Then, when time is up, find a place to say, "Thank you again for chatting. I know the readers of XYZ publication are going to enjoy hearing this conversation." Shake hands and get gone. Don't linger. Don't ask for autographs.

Take Notes and Use a Tape Recorder

Place your recorder in an unobtrusive place and simply say, when you are ready to begin, "OK, I'm going to start recording now, if you don't mind." Don't make a big deal out of it. The proper etiquette for recording a phone conversation, no matter what state you live in or its laws, is to ask permission first.

Make Eye Contact, Listen Intently, Respond Appropriately

Don't continually look down at your notes, the tape recorder or your list of questions. Not making eye contact makes it seem like you're more interested in something else than in them. And celebs are used to commanding complete attention. Most will accept nothing less.

Enjoy

Interviews are a rare treat to get to know the real person behind the persona. This is a privilege. Recognize that, respect it and enjoy it.

Bonus Tip: Do the Truman Capote

Don't worry; it won't get you arrested. During the six years he spent researching and interviewing subjects for *In Cold Blood*, Capote developed a unique method that he swore worked like magic on murderers and politicians: Begin the interview by telling the subject *everything* you know about them, *everything* you've discovered about them. Now, what's left to talk about? Ah, the stuff you don't know. Maybe even the stuff they've never told anyone else.

CAN I USE FICTION TECHNIQUES IN NONFICTION?

> *"Can you use fiction in nonfiction writing? The reason I ask is an editor told me that my writing is too dry and I should spice it up."*

Fascinating question. In the not-too-distant past, the answer was a resounding NO! Most journalism back then read like a "Dragnet" rerun. One of the most important events in changing that attitude was 1965's serialization in *The New Yorker* of Truman Capote's *In Cold Blood*, subsequently published in book form in 1966. Capote believed *In Cold Blood* to be a new art form, the "nonfiction novel," which combines the factual accuracy of journalism with the emotive impact of fiction.

There has always been a strain of personal journalism in English letters, from Addison and Steele to Defoe and Mark Twain. But in the 1960s and 70s, "New Journalism" champions such as Truman Capote, Tom Wolfe, Norman Mailer, Hunter S. Thompson, Gay Talese and others helped to develop a type of "creative nonfiction" that still wins most of the magazine writing awards today. It is characterized by:

1. Detailed characterization. By closely observing subjects and giving them breath and life as the fiction writer does (including telling habits, dress, movement and speech patterns), they have more impact as they come alive on the page.

2. Dialogue. By arranging quotations as dialogue in the manner of fiction writers, nonfiction writers create the sense of slice-of-life realism and the immediacy of storytelling.

3. Plotting. Long-form magazine features are often structured so that a dramatic conflict is established, rises to a peak, then is resolved.

4. Creative writing. Including the use of literary devices like similes, metaphors, personification, hyperbole and other types of language that at times can approach the precision and beauty of poetry.

5. Detailed scene setting. The selection of key details that evoke a specific sense of time and place that is usually associated with the close observation of mainstream realistic fiction.

Each year the American Society of Magazine Editors (ASME, www.asme.magazine.org) conducts the National Magazine Awards. The winners are listed on ASME's web site and their works are collected in an annual anthology, *The Best American*

Magazine Writing, which contains some of the best creative non-fiction being written today.

HOW TO WRITE A REGULAR COLUMN

If you've got the knack, the voice and the discipline, a regular column can be one of writing's sweet pleasures. For seven years I wrote a regular monthly column in a consumer magazine, which translates into about 84 pieces of writing, all entitled "Behind the Lines." The column was short (600 words), but it was also some of the writing I enjoyed the most. Being a columnist offers a set of pleasures and challenges rarely found together in other formats.

Please, Come In

One of the best pieces of advice given to me when I started was by an old hand named Phil Trupp, who said that when writing a column, "You can never be too personal or too controversial." He was right. A column really must become your living room, bedroom and bathroom into which you don't mind inviting readers. In a column, readers want to spend time with a person, not an AP reporter. Column readers are seeking someone with a distinct voice and point of view. Most of all, a columnist often must be willing to talk about the things he or she feels deeply about on a personal level.

It's this unique personal take on the world, as well as the authentic and passionate voice, that builds a column's audience. However, "personal" in this context only occasionally means the actual details of your life. When building the personality of the column, you are actually building a persona for yourself, an alter ego who becomes a fictional character you create for readers: William Safire, the prissy linguist; Studs Terkel, the gruff sentimentalist; Dave Barry, the hapless baby boomer. Threads of those traits are in all those men; but the real Dave Barry cannot be found in his humor column, only the persona he has created.

Stand for Something or Fall for Anything

One way to see a column is in direct contrast to the publication it appears in. The main purpose of a newspaper or magazine is to present information and news, while the column provides analysis and opinion of it. Indeed, one of the conventions of column writing is its sometimes idiosyncratic point of view. Returning to that column means that readers are seeking out its specific point of view: George Will's conservative take on the latest development in the Middle East; Ann Landers' middle-class orthodoxy on the latest outrage committed by in-laws.

As a columnist, you must clearly establish your personal take on the world and filter experience through it for your readers. That filtering becomes the take-away for the column. It sets up a clear expectation in the reader's mind: "I want to know what my columnist thinks about this." Creating and fulfilling that expectation satisfactorily over and over is the essence of successful column writing. The point of view can be humorous, serious, sentimental, moralistic, conservative, liberal, hectoring or polite. The only thing it can't be is weak or unclear.

The Role of Research

Only inexperienced or unemployed columnists believe that the short, personal format of a column provides an excuse not to do research and develop sources. One of the duties of the column is to provide research, behind-the-scenes access and other non-mainstream details not easily found elsewhere. Washington-based political columnists are known for their "insider sources" and their own research staffs. Their proprietary info may be presented in a highly slanted or even personal way, but it is often the bedrock and jumping off point for the column.

The overall slant for my column in the scuba diving magazine was the unvarnished "truth"—about equipment, marine environment, dive operators, destinations and the industry itself. One of my goals each month was to find some information that would not be printed elsewhere in the magazine or even in the industry. (According to the magazine's sales reps, I succeeded far too often.) With that proprietary research, I could give readers another reason to return regularly: to get not only my unique point of view, but also unique information—sometimes even behind-the-scenes stuff they could not find elsewhere: thus the column's title, "Behind the Lines."

Getting to Know "Your" People

Another of your goals as a columnist is to build a loyal following. The larger the better, of course. Loyalty is what gives a column legs, enabling it to outlast changes in editors and publishers. Creating that loyalty requires one more important element: identification of your core.

Your core is that group of people, often not even a majority of a publication's readers, who identify most strongly with the column, who will read it even if they read nothing else. As a columnist, you expect and hope that your point of view is strong enough that it will rule some readers in and some out.

Knowing who those readers are—their demographics and psychographics—is part of your job as a columnist. Only if you can see the color of their underwear can you hone your topic selection, research, even style. Whatever you do, hang on to your core readership; let the other folks come and go. Only by writing to the core can you fulfill the column's most important convention: the need for a distinctive voice and point of view.

Example: At *Scuba*, we knew from research that the magazine's overall readership was 75% male, average age of 39, average income of $81,000, college-educated professionals who went on 2.5 overseas dive vacations per year. But the core who read my column was shown by additional research to be those who had as one of their primary diving interests the preservation of the marine environment, were an even mix of males and females, younger than our average reader, and considered themselves advanced or professional divers. They, not the general readership, were my core: serious divers, males and females, concerned about the marine environment and about significant developments in the sport diving industry. No surprise: My column became known for its strong environmental slant and its serious take on industry issues like safety, truth in advertising and other "core" concerns. I did not speak to the beginning diver very often, and almost never to the casual diver. I stayed focused on the hard-core.

Stylistic Illusions

This last piece of advice seems oddly contradictory: Write in a personal but compressed style. Personal usually means breezy and chatty; compression just the opposite. It's this contradiction that makes the style of a column one of the hardest and slipperiest. Hard like Pete Sampras' backhand or Tiger's tee shot: Both seem effortless and simple. But both represent a level of achievement that belies their simplicity. Writing in a tight conversational style is similar to a good athlete's skill: there is the illusion of ease, but getting there is a matter of working your way there and being an unforgiving editor of your own prose. Tight and right. Rarely is compression in writing more important than in the column format with its constricted word length.

Tips for Your Own Column

1. Read, study and read some more. It's like getting down your chops in any genre: you first must master the basics and internalize the conventions and formats. That means collecting your favorite columnists and studying them. Chart every aspect: column length, topics, use of sources, typical struc-

ture, opening and closes, level of personal detail, etc.

2. Be specific. Research your targeted readership, their interests and, most of all, how your column will attract readers by fulfilling an essential need. Use that research to help sell your column to an editor. Convince him or her that you are meeting a significant need of a strong core of that publication's readers.

3. Provide a take-away. It's the thing—insight, information, laughter—that you want your reader to have after they put your column down and walk away. As a columnist, you have a contractual obligation to provide a specific take-away that fits your readers.

4. Write samples. After you've answered the basic questions about topic, point of view, readership, format and style, write the first five to eight pieces, not just one. Columns aren't like features: once and done. Columns are a series of pearls strung together. To get a sense of a columnist, your potential editor must see at least this many.

5. Syndicate. Besides self-publishing on the Internet, there are basically two steps to becoming a syndicated columnist in print:

   Self-syndication. First, be your own syndicate and market your column to non-competing magazines or newspapers. Do this for a small amount of pay or even for free, if you're comfortable doing so. Why? Your ultimate goal is mass syndication, not just one or two outlets. When your column is appearing in multiple outlets (at least two), you are ready for the next step.

WRITER'S TOOLBOX
SYNDICATE DIRECTORIES

• *Editor & Publisher Syndicate Directory*. The definitive directory of U.S. and Canadian syndicates and syndicated news, features and services. A subscription is $20. Can be ordered by phone: 1-888-612-7095. Published each August, so make sure you have the most up-to-date version. Read more on their web site: www.mediainfo.com/editorandpublisher/index.jsp

• *Writer's Market* (Writer's Digest Books) also contains a section of syndicate listings.

How-To Books

• *The Complete Guide to Syndication*. Barry Kipnis.

• *How to Syndicate Your Own Newspaper Column*. Lincoln B. Young.

• *You Can Write a Column*. Monica McCabe-Cardoza.

Syndicate submission. Prepare clips of at least five columns and begin the submission process to appropriate syndicates. You are looking for (a) the largest syndicates for obvious financial reasons; (b) syndicates open to new writers; (c) syndicates that handle your type of column.

HIDDEN FREELANCE MARKET: NEWSPAPER WEEKLIES AND DAILIES

They may be cheap, but they're plentiful. Here's how to leverage the plentitude and frequency of newspapers. But, first, that contradiction: how can something published so frequently and so ubiquitously be a "hidden market"? Because the potential of newspapers as a market for freelancers is often overlooked. The low pay rates (often one-tenth of what a magazine might pay for the same story) turn off most writers, but don't forget a key fact: Few newspapers have overlapping markets.

What this means for you is the magic of "multiple sales"—getting paid for the same article at different publications. And with the ease and low cost of today's electronic submissions, the ability to make a large number of simultaneous submissions can add up to some significant paydays.

Step-by-Step

1. Determine non-local coverage. Most of a local paper is, well, local. But articles, fillers, quizzes, syndicated columns and some features without a local slant are also an important part of most papers, especially travel and how-to features. You can usually determine non-local coverage via the newspaper's web archives and, of course, by buying copies.

2. Make a big list. Build a database of 100, 200, even 1,000 or more target newspapers. Include the proper editor's email address, the publication's web address and other pertinent fields to allow you to track and record your submissions and sales.

3. Submit *en masse*. Use desktop mail-merge tools or free Internet ListServs that allow you to send the same document and attachments to all the addresses you select from that database. Make sure the email is formatted so that the recipient cannot determine the email was sent to more than one person. Remember that volume is the key. Instead of selling your travel article (with digital photos) to a magazine for $500, you are trying to sell that same story for $25 to 20 newspapers. Sell it to 40 newspapers for $25, and you've

doubled what you would've made for a single magazine sale. Become a regular at those newspapers and you're making some serious bucks.

4. Sell it rights. To make this plan work, you must sell only one-time rights, also known as "simultaneous rights," giving you the ability to sell the article on a non-exclusive basis. Make it clear on the front of the manuscript that you are selling these limited rights.

WRITER'S TOOLBOX
NEWSPAPER DIRECTORIES

Online:
- Gebbie Press.
  www.gebbieinc.com/weekly1.htm
  www.gebbieinc.com/dailyint.htm
  You couldn't ask for more: a free, searchable database of all newspapers (weeklies and dailies are in separate databases) that have a web site. Let your fingers do the walkin' and the talkin'.

Print:
- *Editor & Publisher Market Guide.*
  Another remarkable directory, this one for 1,463 newspaper markets. But you'll pay: $145. Check your local library or, if you must, order by phone: 1-888-612-7095.

5. Are you telling me to skip the query? In most instances, yes. The pay rate for newspapers is too low, and the cost of submitting electronically is virtually the same for a query or full manuscript with digital photos attached. Need is also an issue: These editors have daily and weekly deadlines and

space to fill. The quaint game of thrust and parry during the query process usually doesn't fit in this world. If you've got something, send it in and let the editor look at it. They can hit the delete key. So can you.

HOW DO I GET PRESS CREDENTIALS?

"Do you know how one goes about getting press credentials? I've just started writing movie reviews for Cinescape *(prior to that I did book reviews for them) and they told me they could hire me as a stringer if I had press creds. I could also go to film screenings (they aren't particularly interested in after-the-fact reviews). I didn't want to seem stupid, so I refrained from asking the editor how... so I'll be stupid here! Care to educate me? Also, is it possible to make a living doing reviews, or is it just another coin in the freelancing kitty?"*

Press credentials, fortunately or unfortunately, are easier to get than a gun license. Naturally, you can order them over the Internet these days: *www.ifpo.net/pressclassic.html*. Don't let the name "International Freelance Photographers Organization" fool you. They'll be happy to sell you what you need for $60US. However, there is a *caveat emptor* that comes with them: A few reports from online discussion groups (alt.journalism.freelance) complain that these credentials are not as universally accepted as the sellers claim.

The more traditional way to get press credentials is through the publication you are working for. It's usually best to have an assignment first, not only for the usual reason (to ensure some editor will be interested in the fruits of your labor), but also so that you can acquire press credentials specific to the event and locale. Publications most likely get credentials through that particular city's public information office, usually a part of the mayor's office. Freelancers such as yourself can apply for credentials through a mayor's office, too, but you'll likely need clips or an assignment letter. No problem in your case. If you live in NYC, the web site for ordering press credentials online is: *www.ci.nyc.ny.us/html/nypd/html/dcpi/press-cred.html*.

Can you make a living writing reviews? George Bernard Shaw did. But then, he was George Bernard Shaw. After doing it myself and helping my students do it, my advice is this: You are ready to go full-time freelance once you are making no less than one-third of your present income via freelance assignments, whether it's writing reviews or obits—sometimes the same thing.

HIDDEN FREELANCE MARKET: PUBLICATION RIGHTS CLEARINGHOUSE

A landmark legal decision spearheaded by the National Writers Union puts some easy money in your electronic pocket. Here's how it works: Wouldn't you love to be Kid Rock? No, not because of Pamela Anderson or that great tour bus. Every time one of the American Bad-Ass' songs is played on the radio, the Kid gets a few cents. Maybe he'll be able to afford a shirt soon—or a new tattoo.

Because of the leadership of Jonathan Tasini, president of the National Writers Union, freelance writers can join the illustrious ranks of shirtless, tattooed musicians: getting paid additional usage royalties on an automatic basis.

Roe vs. Wade for Writers

As usual, it took a while for law and ethics to catch up with technology. In this case, publishing companies were (and many still are) buying print rights such as First North American Serial Rights and automatically assuming use of that work on the web and Internet, especially when selling to large electronic databases like Nexis/Lexis, University Microfilms and others. This is tantamount to Kid Rock getting paid for the CD he cuts, but not for the use of that CD's songs on the radio, in movies or TV commercials and so on. The Kid doesn't like that.

Moreover, when publishers sell articles to electronic databases, those publishers are getting paid, as are the databases who sell the works on an individual basis. Uh, excuse me, what about the people who created the work?

Jonathan Tasini felt that writers were being exploited unfairly. He and a group of freelance writers filed suit against the NY Times, Newsday, Inc.; Time, Inc.; Lexis/Nexis, and University Microfilms, Inc., charging copyright violation regarding the electronic reuse of work produced and sold on a freelance basis.

Tasini *et al.* prevailed, with the case ultimately being decided in the Supreme Court in June 2001.

Opening the E-Door: Publication Rights Clearinghouse

The Tasini case has been called a landmark decision for freelance writers, and it's hard to disagree. The stakes were high: Who, exactly, was to reap the benefits of republication of intellectual property on the Internet? Thanks to Tasini, the National Writers Union and other supporters, a writer's electronic copyright is now legally distinct from print rights.

The NWU has taken the next logical step by creating a process by which writers can profit from electronic republication of their work. It's called the "Publication Rights Clearinghouse," a collective licensing agency. It works like this: Writers register their work with the PRC, which in turn licenses non-exclusive electronic use of that work to its database partners, who at this writing include SIRS Mandarin, ingenta, and the Copyright Clearance Center. As PRC adds new partners, your work becomes available to them as well, if you wish.

How to Sign Up

Registering your work is a simple process. You complete three

WRITER'S TOOLBOX
COPYRIGHT LICENSING RESOURCES

- National Writers Union : *www.nwu.org*

- FAQ for the Publication Rights Clearinghouse Program: *www.nwu.org/prc/prcfaq.pdf*

- Collective rights agreement: *www.nwu.org/prc/prcjoin.pdf*

- Title Clearance form: *www.nwu.org/prc/prctitle.pdf*

- CCC Rightsholder Agreement form: *www.nwu.org/prc/prcccc.pdf*

forms offline and mail or fax them to the National Writers Union. The three forms are a "Collective Rights Agreement," "Title Clearance," and the Copyright Clearance Center's "Rightsholder Agreement." The forms are sent to:

Publication Rights Clearinghouse
National Writers Union
113 University Pl. 6th Fl.
New York, NY 10003
Fax: 212.254.0673
Phone 212.254.0279 ext. 21

To add new titles to your personal database, you simply complete an additional Title Clearance form.

What's the Payoff?
Currently, enrollees in PRC are earning between 75 to 90 percent of the sale of their work in this system. Authors set their own royal-

ty rates in most instances. During one year, the Copyright Clearance Center alone distributed over $41.6 million to authors through their system. Perhaps the biggest payoff, however, is knowing that you are participating in a program that helps secure a future for you and other writers of the Internet Age.

"Being an editor definitely broadened my mind a little and my butt a lot."

CHAPTER FIVE

HOW TO MAKE EDITORS BEG FOR IT

- Why Are Editors So Rude?
- How to Find the Right Editor Every Time
- Foot in Door: Landing Your First Assignment
- How Do Editors Acquire Stories?
- What's the Most Common Freelancer Mistake?
- Setting Project Fees and Word Rates
- How to Get Everything You Want in a Contract
- What to Do When You Don't Get Paid

Every editor hopes for good stuff to come in over the transom or pitched in a query. However, they are doomed to disappointment most of the time. I honestly believe there is a dearth of good freelancers, not a surplus. Why? It isn't their writing skills or laziness or ego-problems. It's being stuck on the outside of the magazine's office doors.

Once you're on the inside, you suddenly see the editorial formula that is at work—that must be at work—from issue to issue. Once inside, you suddenly and miraculously know what that group of editors wants and how to give it to them. Once inside, you suddenly have steady work. So, how do you get inside as a freelancer? You press the right buttons and avoid the others. You set a goal and worm, uh, work your way to it.

Heartfelt advice: Find a subject area where you do good work. Now, target a magazine in that field where you want to become a contributing editor: a freelancer who is so valuable, he or she gets an honorary title—and regular paychecks.

WHY ARE EDITORS SO RUDE? A FORMER BAD BOY REPENTS

Dealing with most editors is only slightly less painful than watching a Mariah Carey movie. Just close your eyes and wait for it to be over. For 15 years I was a kind, patient, gentle writing coach of college students. When I became an editor, I swore that I would never become one of the surly, impatient, arrogant A-holes that my freelance students and I had to deal with at times. I am proud to say that, as an editor, I was never arrogant.

Despite my promises and knowing better, as a managing editor I could be short with freelancers. As executive editor, I was downright rude. Excuses don't cut it: Everybody's busy, everybody's got deadlines, everybody's got pressure. I was bad, and *I'm sorry.* In my defense, the roots of rudeness came from specific behaviors that freelancers can and should avoid:

- **Asking for help**

  Once an assignment is made, dialogue between editor and writer is important. But before the editor-writer relationship is established, asking for help is out of place. Editors are business people, not writing coaches. Editors want freelancers who don't need help, who can supply ideas the editor wants by reading the magazine or writer's guidelines. Besides, put yourself in an editor's chair for a moment: An unknown freelancer asks for your help, then asks you for a paying assignment. What's wrong with that picture?

- **Wanting to be published**
  Nothing wrong with that *per se*. But when the eagerness to see one's name in print is the primary motivation, an editor can usually sniff it out with a highly evolved WEWS: "Wannabe Early Warning System." It's clear from the way these writers present themselves and their ideas that their primary goal is to use the magazine for ego gratification. As an editor, my livelihood depended on the business of the magazine. It offended me personally that someone wanted to use that business for something as crass as the bragging rights of a byline. Be serious. Be a pro. Most of all, be businesslike.

- **Not distinguishing between the target magazine and its competition**
  Editors tend to take it personally when a freelancer proposes a story for a department that only his competitor publishes. This *faux pas* is more than just a matter of misdirected mail. It's clear the writer hasn't bothered to look closely at the magazine—freelancing's original sin. The staff and I took pride in our work. The magazine was our creative lives. We poured ourselves into it, lived it, breathed it, worried over it, rode the waves of success and failure with it. Not bothering to read what we labored over was a form of disrespect we found pretty off-putting. Pitching us a competitor's department was like rubbing road salt in the wound.

How to Please an Editor

While the world of publishing will always have its share of arrogant grouches, with these tips at least you'll have a shot at making one smile, reach for the phone and start punching in your area code.

Target

Read and dissect the editor's magazine. Use the name of a specific column or feature type when pitching your idea. Make sure (by reading back issues) that the magazine hasn't written about your topic recently. Give your material a unique slant that the editor hasn't seen before. Before going on vacation, wannabes would call me up and say, "I'm heading to Belize next week. Need anything?" Talk about lack of a slant. I was often tempted to say, "Yeah, pick me up a quart of milk and a loaf of iguana."

Keep It Short

Seriously, an effective query can be done in few paragraphs. Keep it short. Get to the point. Real example:

"Hi, David:

In your 'Behind the Lines' column you've talked recently about diver impact on fragile coral reefs. At the dive operation I run on St. Lucia, we see exactly what you're talking about every day. And you're right—lack of buoyancy control is the usual culprit.

Our daily experience has allowed us to identify the diver most likely to be a reef wrecker: 'The Quarry Gorilla.' This is the macho diver who straps on 30 pounds of lead, wears a thick wetsuit or dry suit with hood, and mistakenly believes that his cold-water, quarry-diving skills from back home are appropriate for the bathtub called the Caribbean. Our reefs know the truth.

I want to write a 500-word self-test for your 'Dive Like a Pro' department that will alert your readers to the habits and attitudes of the 'Quarry Gorilla' so when they come down to dive with us, they leave the monkey business at home.

Thanks for your consideration."

He'd read the magazine and targeted a department, had thought out a unique slant on a frequently discussed issue (buoyancy control), established his credentials and even demonstrated magazine savvy by proposing the quiz format. All in 150 words. I paid him $500 for the story.

Get a Clue; They're Free

Find out how an editor likes to do business. Some prefer the phone, some email, some fax, some the entire manuscript. By the same token, some hate the phone, hate email, hate faxes, hate getting an entire manuscript. Why not find out first by asking? Doing so shows respect, an understanding of an editor's job and will put you ahead of the pack.

Be the Smartest

Convince the editor you're an expert on the topic you're proposing. Here's why: Trust is a significant issue when doing business with an editor. It's one of the reasons proper manuscript format and other matters of etiquette are so important: They are ways for you to signal that you're a pro who can be trusted. That trust is the basis of your relationship. An editor has to trust you to deliver the goods on time, to be honest, to get the facts right, to represent the magazine well when interviewing and conducting other on-assignment duties. If you go over budget, miss a deadline, get the facts wrong, or piss off an advertiser, who do you think is gonna get reamed? So, not only do you need to observe all the rules of etiquette, you also have to inspire trust by doing solid research on the topic so that you come across as authoritative. The first contact is the first opportunity to build or destroy trust.

Secret bonus tip: Most editors define "authoritative" as anyone they think knows more than they do.

Think Cover Lines

Another secret: When it comes to stories, editors often think in headlines. How will they pitch the story on the cover? A story with a great sell line can boost newsstand sales and subscription renewals; a great sell line also indicates the story is on target with that readership. So, study a magazine's cover lines and entitle your article accordingly.

Some Quick Don'ts

- Don't tell an editor how much you love the magazine. An editor wants a business relationship, not a fan club.

- Don't threaten: "If I don't hear from you in two weeks, I'll feel free to send my story to *Men's Fitness*." Gosh, don't want to hold you up. Please, go right ahead.

- Don't ask an editor to suggest another outlet, if rejected. Get your own agent and market book.

- Don't offer to rewrite, "if needed." Gee, talk about confidence! Also, pros know that rewriting is part of agreeing to any assignment.

Tips for Dealing with Editors on the Phone
Script It

Nothing labels you as a newbie faster than the inability to state your business and your needs in a succinct, professional way on the phone. You can't pre-script an entire conversation, but you can have a list of salient points and facts at hand.

Keep Voice Mails Brief

Scripting is especially important if you have to leave a voice mail. The most common sins are talking in circles (repetition), rhetorical fillers ("uh," "duh," "umm," etc.), and garbling the important stuff like the return phone number.

Forget the Schmooze

Don't confuse a business call with a social one. This is not the time for chit-chat. One ritualistic pleasantry is enough. Don't be brusque or antagonistic (you'd be surprised how many people use those to mask their nervousness and insecurity). Get down to business in a pleasant but direct way.

Put It Up Front

Just as you should in journalism's inverted pyramid, put key info up front. For voice mails, this means beginning with a clear statement of your name and phone number before the rest of the message. This prevents an editor from having to replay an entire message in case they miss or need to recheck a phone number or name.

Know When It's Over

Another common mistake is lingering and jabbering once business is taken care of. Once your questions have been answered and your request made, be the one to say, "Thanks for your time. Look forward to working with you. Bye." Then hang up!

Bonus Tip

When you're confident enough, take a second at the end of a long conversation to recap the major points. Doing so helps you both avoid miscommunications and unneeded call backs for clarification.

HOW TO FIND THE RIGHT EDITOR EVERY TIME

Time for the payoff: printing out a final copy of your story, sticking it in an envelope, and sealing it with a kiss. But wait—did you address it to the right editor? Getting your manuscript in receptive hands lies at the heart of the freelance game. Sending your article on the latest sex moves to ensure orgasm to a magazine's nutrition editor won't help your credibility. The best you can hope for is that the nutritionist will feel sorry for the hapless freelancer and pass the story on to the right desk. Don't count on it. It's just that kind of mistake that lights up any editor's WEWS. Take some time to investigate the staff and their jobs before submitting to that publication, publishing house or production company.

How to Read a Masthead

Newspapers, magazines and many newsletters have mastheads—a nautical term that found its way into journalism and refers to a section of the publication (usually up front) that lists the publication's employees, job titles, place of business, circulation and other business details. For larger publications, mastheads may be divided into the editorial masthead and the publishing masthead, which lists the business and marketing folks.

Hierarchy is one of the few things these mastheads have in common: the higher your level of responsibility, the higher up your name appears on the masthead. This bit of information is critical because job titles vary significantly from company to company. For instance, sometimes the top editorial person is the executive editor, sometimes editor-in-chief, sometimes just plain editor. Regardless of job title, the hierarchy will accurately display the pecking order.

Unless you have a prior working relationship with the top person, you will probably send your story to sub-editors down to the assistant-editor level. Below that level are editorial assistants, copy editors, production editors and manuscript editors who lack the

WHO SHOULD YOU SUBMIT TO?		
Title	**Probable Duties**	**Submit to?**
Acquisitions Editor	Seeks, develops, evaluates and likely buys manuscripts from freelancers	Yes
Assistant Editor	Duties range from gopher to copy editor, to department editor	Maybe
Associate Editor	Usually has significant editing responsibilities	Yes
Consulting Editor	Usually a freelancer hired for a specific project	No
Contributing Editor	A trusty freelancer who has been rewarded with this honorary title	No
Copy Editor	Responsible for proofing and editing stories in the prepublication stage	No
Department Editor	An assistant, associate or senior editor with overall responsibility for acquiring and developing stories for a specific section	Yes
Editor-at-large	Sometimes on the editorial staff to perform a variety of duties, but most often a freelancer	No
Editor-in-chief	Top editorial position	Maybe, if you're acquainted or it's a small pub
Editorial Assistant/ Editorial Associate	Usually will not have responsibility for interacting with freelancers	No
Executive Editor	Top editorial position when listed first on the masthead; otherwise functions as a sub-editor	Yes
Managing Editor	Responsible for the day-to-day editorial production process and copy flow; doesn't necessarily interact with freelancers.	Maybe
Production Editor	Focuses on the physical product as a liaison to ad folks, prepress house and printer	No
Senior Editor	A higher-level position, below managing and executive, usually with responsibility for working with freelancers	Yes
Supervising Editor	Often the same as managing editor	Maybe

power (or interest) to read your submission and make a recommendation on it. The larger the publication (usually indicated by the number of names on the masthead as well as the circulation figure given), the lower down you should stay. And vice versa for smaller publications.

A last clue is any specific information given in the editor's job title: training editor, book review editor, nutrition editor, features editor, departments editor. Look for information that will help you target the most appropriate person for your submission.

If you aren't comfortable with your ability to narrow the field from a masthead, call the magazine's general number. At large companies, you'll likely have to ask to speak to someone in the editorial department. When you reach someone in edit, describe the type of submission you wish to make ("a 500-word sidebar on new butt-firming scams") and ask who would be the most appropriate editor to send it to. Confirm spelling of the editor's name while on the phone in case it isn't on the masthead.

Resource Warning

Use print resources like the *Literary Market Place* and *Writer's Market* carefully. Even books that are updated yearly can lag behind personnel changes in the fluid job world of publishing. The most reliable books of listings are, by far, the various resource books by the Writer's Digest people, including market books for fiction, poetry, art, children's works, photography and more. However, since it's a book, the lag time between information collection and its publication can be a half year or more—plenty of time for some staffing musical chairs. Try to confirm names and positions via a web site or, better yet, a phone call.

FOOT IN DOOR: LANDING YOUR FIRST ASSIGNMENT

You've got the goods, now you've got to get an editor's attention and keep it until you land that coveted first assignment. Don't underestimate the difficulty of this task: Getting a first assignment from an editor is the hardest one. But do a gangbuster job on it, and you may not have to ask for more. Here are some tips.

Find a News Peg

A news peg is any current news item that gives immediacy and relevance to your story. Seasonal pegs are good for many consumer magazines: the subject of child safety in public places takes on an edge at Halloween. Local recycling efforts will generate more interest around Earth Day. The seasons for forest fires and floods get many people thinking about home insurance. But remember, seasonal material for magazines must be submitted six months or more in advance.

Polish Tomatoes

At Rodale Press, this was our expression for the need to freshen up perennial topics. "Tomatoes" referred to the company's oldest magazine, *Organic Gardening*, and the excruciating burden on its editors to make tomatoes fresh and exciting at least six times a year. Amby Burfoot, executive editor at *Runner's World*, has the same problem with "Running Your Best 10K." And the editors at *Men's Health* spend, literally, days brainstorming new versions of "Flat Belly—Now!" One of the greatest favors you can do for an editor is to read back issues and find those perennial topics. Then come up with fresh takes on the hoary old things that must be covered, whether the editors want to or not.

Create Cover Buzz

When measured per word, editors spend more time writing cover sell lines than anything else in the magazine. If you study the kind of cover lines that work in that genre, then come up with powerful headlines for your stories, you'll be getting paid in a matter of no time. I promise.

Keep It Pithy

Today, magazine editing is all about cramming maximum information into minimum space in order to save costs and provide more room for ads. So, in every contact with an editor, keep it short and pithy. Show compression. It's what today's editors are looking for. And while you're at it, avoid breathless, frothy prose. Such verbal inflation signals possible exaggeration when it comes to reporting. Keep it crisp and plain.

Cloak Praise

I advise against gushing over how much you love the editor's magazine, which is almost always seen as a transparent attempt at ingratiation. But there is a way to work it in invisibly: Speak specifically as a writer—"I thought the Honduras story in the last issue contained some solid reporting—very balanced." Now you're speaking as one pro to another.

HOW DO EDITORS ACQUIRE STORIES?

"Do editors mainly assign stories to staff writers instead of freelancers? I've been getting an awful lot of rejections and I've got the feeling the magazine just doesn't want freelance stuff."

You could be right. Check the publication's writer's guidelines (you may need to ask for a copy if you haven't already), check their market listing in one of the latest market books, or give a call and ask directly: "Do you accept freelance queries and submissions? If so, in what departments?"

To answer your larger question: Most story ideas are generated by the editorial staff and a cadre of outside freelancers writers called "contributing editors," who write regularly for the magazine. In a sense, you have to be an insider to know what story ideas work for this group, what stories have been done or are going to be done.

Now, the good news: There's a way to get inside. You purchase six or more of the most recent issues of your target magazine *and its competition*. Study them, because you darn well better believe that editors read every issue of a competitor's magazine. Now propose something new or an irresistible twist on a perennial topic. Mention your research in your query.

If you're just starting out, consider hiring a good writing coach. He or she will help you focus on a single market, analyze it, and write something that fits. Your goal is to signal to the editorial team that you are one of them. Two desirable things can then happen: They'll listen to your story idea attentively or they might even give you one of theirs to work on.

DO FREELANCERS REALLY HAVE A CHANCE AT THE BIG MAGAZINES?

"What percent of a newsstand magazine's stories are written by freelancers, what percent by staff writers? Do we freelancers really have a shot?"

Generally speaking, a newsstand magazine's contributions are predominantly by regulars, either staffers or regular freelance contractors. It's simply good business: With limited resources and deadlines, an editor can't afford to take too many chances on the ability of unknown writers to produce the goods on deadline and on budget. That doesn't mean you can't break in. You can. Editors are always in need of fresh ideas and writing. When you submit something that rings those two bells, you will get noticed. I guarantee it. But submitting a fresh idea that an editor can use in a specific section of the magazine requires study and intuition that are only gained through hard work.

The specific answer to your question can often be found in the latest edition of *Bacon's Directory of Magazines* (available at your library) or *Writer's Market* (Writer's Digest Books), where you'll find descriptions of thousands of magazines. Bacon's is for public relations professionals and contains almost double the number of titles as *Writer's Market*; however, *WM* is geared directly to writers and is more useful in some ways. Another source not to be overlooked is Standard Rate and Data Service's *Consumer Magazine Advertising Source* and *Business Publication Advertising Source* (trade publications) also available at many libraries. SRDS's publications are geared toward media planners, but contain a wealth of information useful to writers.

Many of the descriptions in *Writer's Market* clarify what departments and features are most open to freelancers and how much of the total magazine is contributed by freelancers. A magazine's own writer's guidelines often give this information, too. More quick tips for hitting the big time:

Create Buzz-Worthy Stories

Controversy sells, and editors know it. If you can handle a controversial subject delicately and effectively, it may be the kind of story that an editor is looking for to gain an edge over the competition. Also consider the media: It's a significant coup for an editor if a story from his/her magazine gets picked up by the broadcast media. What has been grabbing the media's attention lately in your subject area? Finding a story that piques the media's interest can create buzz for the magazine and paychecks for you.

Give Yourself a Reporting Edge

Again, don't forget that editors within a certain category of magazines are competing with each other for readers. What can you offer your target magazine's readers that its competing magazines don't: A unique approach to quizzes? A story with emotional resonance in a field that usually doesn't see that kind of treatment? How can you outdo the writers at the competing magazines? Writers in the men's service magazines go through this each issue with their ultimate guides: how to survive anything, how to get anything you want from a woman, how to fix anything. Set the bar high, vault over it and past your competition.

Write in a Distinctive Voice

Definitely one of those things easier said than done. But think about your favorite writers: more than likely you can hear each distinctive voice playing in your mind's speakers. A unique, confident voice is truly one of the defining characteristics of the best-paid writers: Bruce McCall's jazz riffs masquerading as car reviews; Tim Cahill's self-deprecating travelogues; Jon Krakauer's spiritual honesty. A distinctive voice is a commodity that can open the big doors. How do you acquire such a voice? By turning off the self-monitor in your head, letting the tiny voice living in there speak, then writing down everything it says. It may not always be grammatical, but it will be honest. The first you can fix, the second you can't buy.

WHAT'S THE MOST COMMON FREELANCER MISTAKE WHEN CONTACTING AN EDITOR?

"I want to write for a certain magazine. It's my dream magazine. I know I'm right for it and so I want to avoid blowing it on the first contact. What mistakes should I definitely avoid when contacting the big cheese?"

The most common mistake is, hands down, laziness. Here's what I mean: Most often the writer has not thoroughly studied the magazine and taken the time to hone a story idea that fits it exactly. Most editors find it pretty insulting to be contacted about a story that clearly shows the writer has never actually read past the magazine's cover or didn't do so attentively. This point cannot be emphasized enough: To break into a magazine, you must write something that fits. It must fit the magazine's philosophy and slant on its subject matter, its voice, its department and feature formats, its everything. Show the big cheese that you're not a mouse. You know the magazine as well as he does, and you're ready to roar.

DOES SELF-PUBLISHING COME AFTER REJECTION AND FRUSTRATION?

"Thanks for getting back to me. Since the time I posed my question regarding publishing I have had an essay published in the National Woman Writers Association's monthly publication, and I was just told by a metaphysical publication in North Carolina that they are interested in publishing one of my articles in their January issue. So things are looking up. Thanks for your invaluable help.

"Now I have a book manuscript that is ready for publication and I'm looking around for a possible publisher. The manuscript is metaphysically based and consists of short stories, letters and essays that I have written regarding my own personal spiritual journey. I have contacted a number of publishers. As you warned me, if you are not already an established author, they are not interested and the rejections are mounting. My question is how do you get that establishment if nobody is willing to give you a chance??? What am I supposed to do— publish it myself? Just a little venting on my part."

Wow, you've been busy. Congrats on your byline in the women's writers group! I think you are smart to focus your writing on this one area and explore various publishing possibilities in it. You're on your way to positioning yourself as an expert in this genre, and that's really the key to success in nonfiction. Good going. Sorry about the publisher rejections. Part of the process. Welcome to the club. To answer your specific questions about your book manuscript:

First, Make Sure Your Mail Is Addressed Correctly

Remember that 90 percent of all freelancer mail in America is sent to the wrong address. Editors, publishers and agents receive many good ideas and stories, but often the material just isn't what that publishing house or agent specializes in. Before submitting, use the Internet, a market book or the phone to make sure your book topic fits what they do.

Here's an important lesson: There's rarely anything generic in magazine or book publishing. You have to write a specific work, at a specific length and slant, for a specific magazine or book market. For example, if you wanted to publish a feature on "Spirituality in Modern Marriage" in *Cosmo* and *Oprah*, each article would have to be substantially different to fit the magazine where it is being sent—even though both those magazines are in the same genre. Imagine the difference between how *Cosmo* and *Oprah* would treat the same topic of spirituality in love relationships! In one it would be a quiz or dirty story, and in the other it would be a life-altering experience guaranteed to make you weep. Same topic, different reader expectations, therefore different treatments.

Second, What Should You Do with Your Book Manuscript?

1. Write a kick-butt nonfiction book proposal, and send it to an appropriate agent or publisher whom you have researched and ensured that they represent your category. Most nonfiction today is published by small presses (less than 10 titles),

university presses and independent publishers. I urge you to focus your search in those categories. Example: Health Communications, Inc., a small publisher in South Florida, has always specialized in books for the self-recovery movement—*Adult Children of Alcoholics* was an important success for HCI. Two beginning writers felt they had a book that fit HCI's specialty and pitched it to them. The name of the book was *Chicken Soup for the Soul.* The right book, the right publisher, the right market.

2. Divide your manuscript into magazine articles and try to sell them.

3. Self-publish your book and learn to market it yourself. If you attempt the last option, you had better be ready for what it entails: becoming an independent businessperson called a publisher. The work is hard and your ambition must burn intensely. Nonetheless, given the economics facing today's big publishers and the proliferation of information about self-publishing, it's an option many nonfiction writers are looking at closely. Consider the comparison on page 147 by one of the leaders of the self-publishing movement, Dan Poynter (reprinted with permission from Poynter's web site, *www.parapublishing.com*).

Given those comparisons, it's no surprise that, according to Poynter, a "New Model" of book publishing is emerging. Currently, New York-based publishers account for less than 10 percent of published nonfiction. Will you reduce that by another fraction? I'll share with you my favorite quote from Dan Poynter's *The Self-Publishing Manual*:

> *Have you ever heard anyone say, "Simon & Schuster, I*

IS SELF–PUBLISHING FOR YOU?	
Traditional Royalty Publishing	**Self–Publishing**
Must draft proposal	No wasted time
Must find agent	No wasted time
18 months to get off press	5 weeks to print the book
Advance	No advance
$3,000+ for promotion	$1,000-$3,000 for printing and promotion
No royalties for 2-3 years	Money flows in 30 days
Little promotion by publisher	You control promotion
Lose control of book	Keep control of your book
Make less money	Make more money
In stores for 4 months only	Book sells forever
No revisions allowed	Always up-to-date
Fewer tax deductions	More tax deductions
Possible rejection	No rejection
You focus on writing	You focus on writing and running a business

love their books, I buy everything they publish?" Of course not. People want to know what the book is about. Is this something I need to know? Who is the author? Is she a credible person? No one ever asks, "Who is the publisher?

For a fuller discussion of this issue and a list of self-publisher resources, see Chapter Eight's "Catch the Wave: Is Self-Publishing the New Model for the Book Industry?"

WHAT'S A SLUSH PILE? HOW DO I GET OUT?

"I have written my first feature article for a national

magazine and got a call from the editor who said the article was in the consideration pile. That's not the same as the infamous slush pile is it? What do the odds look like for this, and is there any way to increase the odds of them buying it?"

Congratulations on a significant achievement: a feature submission to a national magazine and a call from an editor! Because of the call, I don't think you're in a slush pile. A slush pile is usually a messy heap of unsolicited manuscripts lying on a junior editor's floor. If the mess gets confused with the trash and thrown away, no one will mind—except the authors. Nobody asked to see them in the first place.

Odds of getting out of a slush pile? Not good. But that's probably not your problem: the editor said "consideration pile." Can you improve the odds of having your manuscript accepted? Yes, you can: By not being a pest to the editor. Give her several weeks, then pen a short note asking about the story's status. If there's still no response, forget about it and send the manuscript elsewhere. Since the editor initiated the call to you, you should be hopeful. It's probably the pile on her desk, not the floor. You should take any personal contact from an editor as a positive sign.

WILL AN EDITOR STEAL MY IDEAS?

"Have you ever had the feeling when talking with an editor that she or he may have called to fish for information? This happened to me recently. She asked an awful lot of questions, yet never said anything about giving me the assignment. Said she'd get back to me. Am I paranoid?"

Paranoid that the editor may steal your idea? Rest easy. Only rarely does anything like that happen. It's hard to imagine that anyone with such an obvious lack of ethics could make it to the middle- or upper-levels of publishing. I'd say that the editor was doing her job by probing your idea for a possible fit in her lineup. She was probably trying to get to the meat of the story and find an angle on it that would work for her readership. That's my guess, and it is certainly what I'd do, especially if the query letter was tempting but lacked sufficient detail. If you want to email it to me, I'll critique it, too. Writing a good query is an art by itself: not too much or too little, not too aggressive or shy, not too gimmicky or plain. The best way to get a handle on what would be a good query letter for a specific pub is to devour that pub: its style, subject range, slants, voice, attitude toward readers, etc. That'll put you in the editor's mind, and that's where the deal is closed.

SETTING PROJECT FEES AND WORD RATES

What are you worth as a writer? Hopefully, it's something between "a penny for your thoughts" and "the moon." Determining how much you should charge is one of the most important exercises you will ever perform as a freelance writer. It causes you to think deeply about your personal financial plan and commit to an annual salary target. Like it or not, as a freelancer you're no longer just a writer. You're also a businessperson. Businesses succeed or fail based upon how well they are managed. The very essence of good management includes a realistic analysis and a conscious setting of clear, attainable financial goals—the proverbial bottom line.

A financial spreadsheet has a top line (revenue), a middle line (expenses), and a bottom line (net income). The number on the bottom line is either black (a positive financial result) or is in parentheses and sometimes red (a negative result). Just because you are no longer a wage-slave and corporate 'ho, don't think you can escape the tyranny of the bottom line. Matter of fact, you're now the one responsible for it. You're the boss. How does it feel so far?

"How much should I charge?" is really another way of asking, "What are my financial goals as an independent businessperson who is responsible for the profit of this company?" That's a serious question which deserves your careful thought and analysis.

Writing for Periodicals

Normally, if you're writing for a magazine or newspaper, you'll find fixed pay rates that vary somewhat according to what you're writing, your status (first-time contributor, regular, etc.) and your reputation in that field (credentialed authority, national-level clips in prestigious pubs, etc.). You can usually find out what these pay ranges are from market books, the publication's own writer guidelines, and by asking. The National Writer's Union also maintains a members-only database of pay rates of many periodicals. And don't forget your ability to negotiate those rates.

Contract Writer

Depending on the field you're writing in, you may be asked to set an hourly rate or quote a project fee. This is true in a number of fields open to freelancers: advertising and PR copywriting, TV scripts, business and technical writing, and a number of jobs related to book publishing (proofing, indexing, ghost writing, etc.). When determining what to charge as a contract writer, consider these four factors:
- Overhead

- Experience/clips

- Client attributes

- Project requirements

Overhead refers to all expenses related to running your freelance business and includes: rent and utilities (if any); connection charges (phone, fax, Internet); office supplies; equipment purchases and maintenance; travel; postage and shipping materials; subscriptions to professional associations, publications and books. The total of these expenses comprises your fixed overhead. To break even, you must earn at least this amount.

Calculating Hourly Rates and Net Income

The overhead figure provides a starting point for determining your hourly rate. If you are writing for a periodical and receiving a per-word rate or set article fee, you should also perform these calculations to determine the pay you require in order to accept or reject an offered assignment.

The next factor is your net annual income, which is your gross income minus expenses and 35 percent for taxes and benefits: health, life, dental and disability insurance, retirement fund contribution, etc.

Example:
If you have fixed expenses of $8,000 per year, and you want to net $50,000 a year via freelance work, you must gross $78,300:

$78,300
− $8,000 (overhead)
− $20,300 (35% taxes/benefits)
= $50,000

Now comes the calculation of how much you should charge per hour to achieve that goal of $50,000 net. Consider basing your calculation on a typical, Monday to Friday, 40-hour work week, giving yourself 12 weeks of non-writing to account for holidays, sick days, bank and bookkeeping days, marketing and other non-writing days, family emergencies, etc.:

40 hours per week x 40 writing weeks = 1,600 billable hours

$78,300 ÷ 1,600 hours = $50/hour (rounded up)

Keep in mind the overall economics of freelancing: $50,000 per year is definitely a lofty goal, since the National Writer's Union reports that only 15 percent of freelancers make more than $30,000 per year. And now for the good news: The NWU also reports that pay rates are either stagnant or declining!

Other Hourly Formulas

In her article "An Inside Look at Consulting," Anne Wallingford provides a valuable way to see yourself from an employer's perspective. This example is created by comparing a freelancer's rate to that of a corporate employee earning $50,000 annually.

1. **Determine daily labor rate**

   Step 1: Multiply your desired annual net compensation by 1.5 to account for life, health, dental, disability and retirement benefits. This reflects the real cost to a company of an employee.

   Example: $50,000 x 1.5 = $75,000 annual labor rate

   Step 2: Divide the annual labor rate by 180. This is the standard number of billable days in a year once 365 is subtracted by a total of 185 non-work days (104 weekend days, 8 holidays, 10 vacation days, 5 sick days, 24 days for administrative tasks, 34 days to market yourself and your business).

Daily Labor rate:
$75,000 ÷ 180 = $417 daily labor rate

2. Determine Expenses

Statistics show that overhead for a self-employed consultant averages 44 percent of labor.

Example: $417 × 44% = $183 daily overhead expenses

3. Factor in Profit Margin

As a business, you are taking risks and providing service and/or products the same as any other business. Each consultant must determine a reasonable profit margin; this can range from 15% to 40%, with 20% being considered fair in most markets.

Example: $417 × 20% = $84 daily profit

4. Determine daily billing rate

Add daily labor rate + daily overhead expenses + daily profit

Example:
```
     $417 daily labor rate
 +   $165 daily overhead expenses
 +    $84 daily profit
     $684
```

Divide by 8, the typical number of hours in a business work day
$684 ÷ 8 = $85 hour

Best Source for Fee Info

The yearly edition of *Writer's Market* includes a report on current hourly rates and flat-fee rates for a variety of industries and publishing formats. It is the best source of information I've found on current practices in the freelance industry. *2002 Writer's Market* also includes its own simple formula for figuring an hourly rate that results in the same $50 per hour rate as mine:

Required annual income + 30% expenses + 30% benefits ÷ annual billable hours = hourly rate

Thus:
$50,000 + $15,000 + $15,000 ÷ 1,600 hours = $50/hour

Experience & Talent

The more of each that you have (and can prove you have), the more you can charge. One of the best ways of getting a handle on where you fit is to talk to other freelancers, locally, nationally, and internationally. The online forum at www.freelanceonline.com provides one of the most active congregations of fellow scribes. You can also check your local yellow pages for writing consultants, writing groups, PR and advertising consultants and firms.

The Client

Several factors come into play:
- Client location

  In general, clients on the two coasts (especially in the big cities) expect to pay more than clients in Rocky Top, Tennessee.

- Client size

  Larger and more affluent clients usually pay more, and if you try to charge noticeably less than what they normally pay, you will raise their suspicions.

- Client regularity
A client who gives you steady work deserves a lower rate than a one-timer.

- Client special needs
The most common is a client who needs a job done on a "rush" basis—one that will require you to work "overtime" or otherwise alter your normal schedule to accommodate the request. The Code of Fair Practice from the Editorial Free-lance Association recommends a 20 to 50 percent surcharge be added to your normal hourly rate.

- Client dependability
This raises the question of "kill fees" and "cancellation fees." These come into play when a client engages your services, you begin work, but the job is cancelled prior to delivery. To account for this scenario, it is recommended that your contract include a kill fee for articles or a cancellation fee (usually the number of hours worked to that point times hourly rate) for contract work.

Project Requirements

Finally, before agreeing to any contract work, it is essential that you perform a thorough analysis of the amount of time you estimate the project will require. Writing a tri-fold sales brochure for a company that has compiled all the materials for you on its products and even has solicited customer testimonials is a much different project than one for which you must do the legwork and research to generate those materials. Besides obvious factors like word length and

WRITER'S TOOLBOX
ONLINE RESOURCES FOR PAY RATES

- Periodical Writers Association of Canada:
  www.writers.ca/whattopay.htm
  Here you'll find a set of "Professional Fee Guidelines."

- Editorial Freelancers Association: *www.the-efa.org/Code2.html*
  Guidelines on setting fees and rates.

- National Writer's Union: *www.nwu.org/hotline/hotsurv.htm*
  The results of a survey carried out in 1999 by the National Writer's
  Union on freelance and contract writer rates.

- Donald Denier: *www.writing-world.com/business/worth.html*
  Some valuable thoughts about personal "worth" and helpful links about
  this topic.

research, there is also travel required—if you're traveling for a
client, you are most likely not working for another. Travel time is
usually billable. Ask any lawyer.

NEGOTIATE THIS! GETTING EVERYTHING YOU WANT IN A FREELANCE CONTRACT

Who writes the contracts that publishers send to you? Uh huh.
And whose interests are those corporate lawyers looking out for?
Hint: Not yours. Keep those two points in mind whenever you sit
down to read a publisher's contract. You have every right to discuss
the terms of it. Whether you want to negotiate or not is your option and should be exercised wisely, but you certainly have the
right to negotiate.

As an editor who had to acquire freelancer signatures on contracts (and who supervised other editors doing the same), it didn't bother us that a writer questioned certain clauses and wanted further information. Matter of fact, we had more respect for those who did and especially for those who knew how to ask for certain changes in the boilerplate contract. Knowing how to ask and what to ask spell the difference between an amateur and a pro when it comes to contract negotiations.

Another secret: An editor will almost never offer you what he or she can actually afford to pay you. It's called low-balling and editors play such games as well as rug salesmen. After all, this is business: The editor's/publisher's goal is to get the best writing and most rights at the lowest cost possible. Your goal is to sell the fewest rights at the highest cost. Meeting somewhere in the middle is called negotiation. Some tips on doing it:

Tip #1: You Got to Believe

You've got to believe that you are worth what you'll be asking. That belief should be based on an up-to-date knowledge of the marketplace and what other freelancers of your experience and reputation are receiving for similar work. Do your research. Find out what the going rates are. Establish your own rates. Ask for them, without shame or timidity.

Tip #2: You Got to Talk the Talk

Editors and publishers deal with contracts everyday. Their companies probably provide seminars on contracts and negotiations. What about you? You've got to understand the terms and clauses in a contract at least as well as the person you're dealing with. This means getting the information you need. The National Writer's Union publishes an excellent book on the subject: the *NWU Guide to Book Contracts*. Much of the information is also applicable to journalism contracts. See the resources listed in the article "How

Much Should You Charge?" earlier in this chapter. The writer associations listed there provide most of the information that you need.

Tip #3: You Got to Know When to Hold 'Em, When to Fold 'Em

One of your most important tasks is to determine the lowest fee you will accept, the point beyond which you will not go. That point is going to change during your career. When you first start out, you'll be willing to take less and give more in order to get the byline. That's understandable and acceptable. Along the way, your goal is to continually assess what that bottom line is. Above that line is your comfort zone where everything is negotiable in a collegial way. Once you hit the bottom line, you're looking at a decision either to walk or to work for less than is normally acceptable to you.

Tip #4: You Got to Get Ready

While it's probably not essential to actually write out a script to follow before negotiating with an editor or publisher, at least jot down on the contract the points you wish to make and the order in which you wish to make them. Negotiations require as much care in word choice and tone as any situation does when delicate subjects are on the table.

Examples:

No: "That's not enough money for my work."
Yes: "At first glance, I have to tell you, that seems just a bit on the low side to me."

And what if Editor says, "Sorry, that's the best I can do."

No: "To make it worth my time, I must have..."
Yes: "I understand totally. You've got a budget to work with and I appreciate that. But what I had in mind was..."

The point is not just that you get more flies with honey than with vinegar, although you certainly do. Such verbal gymnastics signal that you are reasonable and flexible, that you are unemotional about this issue, that you understand the importance of money and the delicate nature of talking about it.

Such language also invites further conversation about the subject instead of putting the other person on the defensive. One of the first things you learn in marriage counseling, oops, I mean in basic psychology class, is that if someone perceives they are being attacked, the natural and nearly unavoidable reaction for them is to become defensive and to fight back. Use language that allows you to avoid confrontation, not instigate it.

And what if after such politeness, the editor once again refuses to budge? Now load up the detail and put it on your side:

Editor: "Sorry. That's all we're offering for this type of article."

No: "I don't understand why you expect to pay so little for so much."

Yes: "Right, and I remember reading that exact figure in your writer's guidelines. That's perfectly understandable. But remember, I had to do some special digging at the mayor's office for that data you wanted on the homeless numbers in Allentown, which added a lot to the article and was a good call on your part. And there was the quote you wanted me to get from the shelter volunteer. So, I just think, considering the extra time and research put into this, that we should agree on something like 10 percent more. What do you think? That's doable, isn't it?"

Good luck. Never let 'em see you sweat.

SHOULD I WRITE ON SPEC? SHOULD I WRITE FOR FREE?

Sooner or later during your career, you'll be asked to do both. Have your answers ready to go.

On Spec: Once and Done

Here's the pickle: You've already written one article for this editor on spec. She liked it. You got paid. Great, you think, a productive new market for me. So you submit another query. Ouch! She wants to see it, but "on spec" again. Should you or shouldn't you? No, you shouldn't.

Do not write a second article for this editor on spec. If the first article was turned in on time, at the right word count, required minimal rewriting and editing, you should not be expected to write on spec again. There is only one purpose in giving an "on spec" assignment: one for which an editor does not provide a contract or any promise to compensate you, not even a kill fee. That purpose is to test the waters with a writer for the first time, especially when that writer lacks substantial clips. Once you've proven yourself, you should be given contracts with kill fees—the promise to pay a percentage of the article's agreed upon price if the offer is withdrawn or the article doesn't make it to publication.

As someone trying to make a living, you cannot be expected to provide your services on speculation. Can you imagine a plumber or auto mechanic doing so? "I'll fix your pipes and, if you like the job I do, you can pay me." Writing for a specific magazine can often mean producing a piece that has little marketability elsewhere. If the on-spec assignment doesn't work out, you've not only wasted your time, you've actually lost money that you could have earned by writing something else or fixing someone else's pipes.

My advice: Give such an editor one more chance. Simply say, "I'd really love to do this article for you. I thought the last one worked out great. But, I'm sorry, I can't write a second assignment on spec." Then pause. Wait. Put the onus on the editor to respond, whether you're talking on the phone or corresponding by email. If you get a contract, great. Put this behind you and chalk it up to business: Many editors (and I was one of them) will always try to negotiate the most favorable terms for them. No big deal. Part of the game. But if this is the kind of editor who can't make contractual commitments to qualified freelancers, run like hell. To the editors who can.

Why Free Rarely Is

Throughout your career you will occasionally be asked to write something for free. And there may indeed be situations when doing so makes sense.

Writing no-pay articles for web sites can help get your name in front of editors, readers and other experts in your area. An important book marketing technique is for an author to offer free content to web sites what will allow a byline that includes a promotion for the book. When breaking into a new genre, it may make sense to write for free just to establish your presence and some credentials there. Finally, you may write for free because it's a good cause. Whether it's your college alumni magazine, a newsletter for battered husbands, or your local neighborhood watch group.

In each of those situations, you could argue that there is a fair exchange (albeit non-monetary) taking place. What is definitely to be avoided is any situation which tries to take unfair advantage of your time and your talents. As a freelancer, those are what you offer the marketplace. And as my grandfather from Arkansas used to say, "Why buy the cow if the milk's for free?" Grandpa was talking about premarital sex—I think. But his wise words also apply to writers: To be considered a professional, you have to conduct business as one, and that means putting a clear and reasonable value on your products and services; otherwise, I hear Wal-Mart is hiring greeters.

Bottom line: Unless you are receiving an important non-monetary value, a fee, not free, puts dinner on the table.

THE CHECK ISN'T IN THE MAIL: WHAT TO DO WHEN YOU DON'T GET PAID

And you thought writing was the hard part! Sometimes getting paid is harder than pinching mercury, and not nearly as much fun. When I became the person who had to ensure freelancers got paid, I made a promise to myself: they would be paid on acceptance (not publication) and within 15 days of that acceptance. It wasn't about money. It was about respect. If you worked hard for me and the company I represented, you deserved our respect. I endeavored to honor freelancers by bestowing upon them one of the most respected things in our society—money.

Unfortunately, corporations don't always see it that way. The current trend in many large publishing companies is to hold off paying invoices for as long as possible. In the last company I worked for, new managers had instituted a *de facto* accounting procedure that stipulated freelancer invoices should be sat on until the freelancer screamed, longer if possible. I became the first editor with a phone block put on him by the accounts payable department.

As a freelancer, you will also get to experience the frustration, the living Hell, of corporate accounting offices. Here's what to do:

1. Make sure you have a contract.

   Please say this aloud with me: "Never work without a written contract." Sorry. You weren't loud enough. One more time: "Never work without a written contract." If an editor refuses to give you a written contract, you should do two things: (a) submit one yourself; (b) don't work until it's signed. Samples of contracts can be downloaded at the National Writer's Union site and the Science Fiction Writers Association. I've also included my own in Appendix 4. Help yourself.

2. Include an invoice with the completed manuscript.

   Do not wait on anyone to invoice you. Your invoice should include all information necessary for payment, a clear statement of the work performed, the terms for payment (usually 30 days net, meaning all of it within 30 days of receipt of the invoice). Microsoft Office has an invoice template that you see a lot of these days. Included in Appendix 2 of this book is a copy of the one I use. Feel free to steal it. You can even leave my address on it if you wish. I promise to forward your checks. Really.

3. Send it again.

   Make multiple copies of your invoices and fully expect to send in an invoice more than once, both to editors and to the accounts payable department. A common delaying tactic by accounting departments is to claim your invoice was "misplaced." And the dog ate their homework.

4. Keep all documents.

   Emails, love notes between you and the fact-checking department, contracts, invoices—everything that pertains to the assignment. Make and keep notes of phone conversations, especially when they include discussion of pay and rights issues. You'll need them at some point to resolve differences of, uh, memory.

5. Expect to be paid.

   Translation: Approach this aspect of freelancing in a professional and, if necessary, persistent way. Don't get huffy and rude. Calmly and pleasantly inquire about what is owed you, be helpful in resupplying needed information, get the check, then decide whether it's worth partnering with that outfit again.

6. Report abuse.

When all else fails, send professional letters of complaint to higher up officials at the publication, and if that doesn't work, your next step is the National Writer's Union and similar advocacy groups.

WHO PAYS FOR REQUESTED SUBMISSIONS?

"An editor asked me to make sure the featured craftsperson in my article sends images of six of the dollhouses she makes. Who pays for the postage? Can you tell me if the editor does, or do I? I asked the subject and she agreed to send them, so how do I do this? Hope you can help."

Since the editor specifically asked to see the images, the editor should pick up the postage. But the cost would usually be handled as part of your freelance invoice as agreed to by the contract you signed. When you send in the finished article, you normally include an expense invoice and receipts to document each item. Questions for you: (1) Is the editor paying your expenses? (2) If so, what is the limit? (3) Will the cost of sending in images of these six houses put you over your limit? Avoid phoning again over a simple business matter like this. If the editor is paying your freelance expenses, then a simple email should suffice:

Dear Editor Big Bucks,

I checked with my subject about the cost of sending in images of the six houses you requested. The postage will be $XX for UPS (or FedEx, Airborne, etc.) delivery. If this is fine with you, I'll simply add the postage to my expense report.

HOW LONG SHOULD I WAIT AFTER SUBMITTING BEFORE CONTACTING THE EDITOR?

"An editor called me—three days after I mailed my query—and said she was interested in my idea but needed more information. We spoke for a few minutes then she said she'd get back to me. How long a time is reasonable for me to wait to hear from her before I pitch other magazines?"

That was a very quick, and therefore encouraging, response from an editor. I'd say that time is less a consideration right now than making sure the line of communication stays open so that you know what her final decision is: to give you an assignment or not. I suggest immediately writing a follow-up email or making a follow-up phone call, both of which are acceptable since the editor has called you. Simply say that you enjoyed talking and ask if she has had a chance to make a decision yet on your proposal. Say that you are excited about possibly working for her and that you are looking forward to her response.

Since an editor has taken the time to call you, she was more than likely interested and has the obligation to follow up on her phone call to you. If you have no response in three to five business days of trying to make contact, consider it a negative response and move on. And never take rejections personally and try not to shut the door on this editor or any others in the future. You do not know what may be happening in that person's office or at her magazine that prevented her from following up in the manner she would've liked. Business is business. Always be open to it. Put your personal emotions aside.

SHOULD I GET A BYLINE OR A TAGLINE?

"When I agreed to write a filler for a national magazine, the editor and I discussed a byline. Although the page

my work will appear on usually doesn't have bylines given, he assured me (because I asked) that I would get one. The article is finally getting to see print after nearly a year. Should I mention the byline or not?"

I wouldn't. It might come off as vain and amateurish—pros usually think in terms of pay and prestige of the publication, and have long gotten past the thrill of seeing their name in print. At least that's what you're supposed to pretend. Also, you don't really need it. It is your published work, whether or not it has a byline/tagline. If you use the published filler as a clip, you will send it in along with other materials clearly identified as yours. Besides, having a byline/tagline on it does not change the piece's length, its purpose (filler) or its quality. In my opinion, you should drop it. When you get paid, thank the editor for taking good care of you, then hit him with a hot idea for a feature.

Last point: Unless it's a long sidebar, usually you get a tagline for fillers, sidebars and the like. A tagline, if it appears, is usually at the end of the sidebar, flush with right margin, and set off by an em dash and in italics:

> This is the text of your filler for a national magazine. It will be inside a box usually set off with a rule, which is a thin line.
>
> *—WordFreak*

WHAT ARE MY OBLIGATIONS DURING THE FACT-CHECKING PROCESS?

"I've sold an article! Now the fact-checkers are calling me right and left. Every couple of hours, it seems like. They demand things ASAP. What are my obligations? How much time do I have to spend doing this?"

Congratulations on your sale! Now, cement the next sale to this editor by cooperating fully, quickly, and meticulously in the fact-checking process. As a freelancer, you're the brick layer. Your words are your bricks. Your job is to follow the master blueprint and put the exact number of bricks where you're told to. The quickest way never to get another assignment from that editor is to get into a debate over requested revisions or fail to supply requested fact-checking materials. In fact, many major magazines require fact-checking materials to be delivered to them by the article's deadline—sometimes via FedEx. While you can and should ask for clarification and even offer your own point of view on editing and fact-checking issues, never argue. In the end, it's the editor's budget and magazine, not yours. Same is true for the amount of rewriting done to your manuscript by the editors. It's their money and their magazine. If you don't like the way they work, move on to a place where you are more comfortable. Simple as that.

MY ARTICLE WAS KILLED. NOW WHAT?

"Last September I got a call from a national magazine wanting my story. They assigned me 200 words. I submitted the article and they paid me $250. In the contract it said that I could not publish the piece again until it appeared in their publication first. Trouble is, there was a problem when they tried to confirm information. The piece has still not appeared. So, do I still have to wait for them to publish the piece?"

First, make sure their check cleared; the money is yours. Next, determine if the editors have killed the piece (decided they no longer plan to use it) or if they still have plans to run it with revisions to resolve the problem. If they've killed it, you are free to do what you want with it. But please find out what the problem was with the inability to "confirm information." Was a fact wrong? Did a source disappear? Whose fault was it that the info could not be fact checked?

If they are still exercising their option to run it (holding it for future publication), you have to wait until they do so, as stipulated in the contract you signed. Some contracts put a time limit by which a piece must have appeared. If it hasn't appeared by that date, your contract with them is terminated and you are free to market it elsewhere as a first rights story.

*"Publishers use boilerplate contracts
to get as much as they can,
like car salesmen."*

CHAPTER SIX

SERIOUS STUFF: ETHICAL & LEGAL ISSUES

- Top 10 Questions about Copyright Permissions
- Do I Need Permission to Use Screen Shots?
- What Every Freelancer Should Know about Fair Use
- Contracts and Copyrights—Yours
- What Is Libel? How Do I Avoid Trouble?
- Do I Need Model Releases?
- Are Fam Trips Unethical?

When I first attended a Rodale Press workshop on legal issues for editors, I was stunned by how much I didn't know, and by the fact that there weren't more editors and writers serving time in our nation's fine penitentiaries. Then I realized that if, as a freelancer, I hadn't known this stuff, then gosh, maybe the freelancers wanting to write for me didn't know it either. And if they made a mistake that caused trouble, I was responsible.

The blade of distrust stabs quick and red.

The bedrock of a freelancer's relationship with an editor is trust. Anything that softens that trust is bad. Anything that builds trust, like, say, your expert knowledge of the "fair use" provision of copyright law, will make an editor smile—with confidence in you.

TOP 10 QUESTIONS ABOUT COPYRIGHT PERMISSIONS

Want a good reason to be well versed in copyright permission codes? As a freelancer, it's your job to get permissions. And the editor's rear end if you don't. Editors do not like getting calls from lawyers. Makes their stomach drop and skin prickle. Lawyers never call with good news—only when there's trouble, the kind that gets you noticed by people with "Senior Vice President" and other such scary titles after their name. If you, the freelancer, are the cause of that trouble, you will be made to pay, one way or another. So, do not let an editor hear you ask any of the following questions:

1. **Does giving full credit in the text substitute for permission?**
   Not at all: The law says that copyright infringement is the "unauthorized use." To be authorized, you must have permission before using it, not thanks afterward.

2. **I plan to write an adaptation of a copyrighted work, do I need permission?**
   Definitely: Adding a layer of copyrighted material (yours) to an original work does not negate that original work's copyright protection. This is especially important for screenwriters. An option on a previously published book or life story is essential before adapting it for the screen; otherwise, you could waste a lot of time. Agents and producers usually will not consider or commission a screen adaptation without a signed option agreement.

3. **Do works in the public domain require permission?**
   Sometimes: A work may still have legal protection once its

copyright expires. The character of Sherlock Holmes is trademarked; ideas may be protected under contract law; information may constitute a trade secret; and human beings have the right to control how their likeness and name are used. Make sure the public domain work is not protected in any of those ways.

4. **Should I wait to get permission until after the manuscript is done and I'm sure that the work is being used?**
Definitely not: A copyright owner is never obligated to give you permission, or may charge whatever he or she wishes. Your work could become hostage to copyright permission. You could miss a deadline. You could get chewed.

5. **Do I need permission even if my work is for nonprofit, educational purposes?**
Yes: In deciding copyright infringement, courts focus on what harm has been done to the value of the copyrighted work, not your motives. Harm can be done by a not-for-profit publication as well as a for-profit one. Unless you are certain that your use falls under the "fair use" provision of copyright law, you should acquire permission. Be conservative: it's better to know than not know that an author disapproves of your use.

6. **Do I need to get permission since the work I'm using is now out of print?**
Yes. Out-of-print does not mean out-of-copyright. Out-of-print could be a temporary condition.

7. **Since I'm using only a small portion, am I covered under the "fair use" provision?**
Not necessarily: The courts have no mathematical formula for

determining what is and isn't fair use. However, the courts have ruled, "you cannot escape liability by showing how much of [the] work you did not take." The prevailing issue is harm caused by your use, not the amount. Did your use cause commercial harm to the copyright holder? That's the bottom line.

8. **The work I'm using is a U.S. government publication. Do I still need to get permission?**
No. U.S. government publications are not copyrightable. However, you must provide a full and accurate citation using your publication's preferred style guide.

9. **If the work doesn't contain a copyright notice, do I still need permission to use material from it?**
More than likely: For works created after 1978, statutory copyright automatically exists when the author first expresses his creation in "tangible form." Before 1978, works published without a copyright notice did indeed risk losing their protection. But not today.

10. **Do anonymous works posted on the Internet require permission for use?**
Not likely but make sure: Copyright law specifically protects anonymous and pseudonymous works, but posting anonymously in hopes that others will share it is common on the Internet.

In sum: The need for copyright permission can be summarized thusly—When in doubt, don't do without.

DO I NEED PERMISSION TO USE SCREEN SHOTS FROM THE WEB?

"I have a publisher whose lawyers have asked me to get

WRITER'S TOOLBOX
COPYRIGHT GUIDES FOR FREELANCERS

- *The Copyright Permission and Libel Handbook.* Lloyd J. Jassin, Steve C. Schecter.

- *Every Writer's Guide to Copyright and Publishing Law.* Ellen M. Kozak.

permission to take screen shots from web sites to accompany site reviews. I recoil at this request, but am not sure whether I am on solid legal ground. Do you know what the state of the law is on whether a screen shot is the legal equivalent of a photograph? And if you know of no precedent, can you tell me whether you would seek permission before publishing a screen shot? If you don't have a policy, then this is my question: Would you seek permission from, say, a restaurant you were reviewing before publishing either the review or a photo of the front of the restaurant? I am certain that in asking permission, I will be asked by the people I'm reviewing to send them the text of my review. If they consider it unfavorable, I am betting that permission will be denied. Arrrggghhh...my tummy hurts!"

Do what the publisher's lawyers want you to do. From a legal perspective, it's the company's buttocks on the line, not yours. Regarding screen shots, it's my layman's opinion that, yes, you do need permission to use screen shots even if your usage is for criticism, comment, news reporting, teaching, scholarship or research (the allowed uses according to American copyright law's "fair use" doctrine). Screen shots, which contain the text and graphical elements of a web page, may include copyrighted work of a number of contributors, and therefore screen shots shouldn't be compared to printed texts. Remember that "fair use" is a defense in the event you are sued for copyright violation. Believe me, your goal as a writer should always be to avoid that situation by attaining permissions before publication, not legal exoneration afterward.

Second, although the subject being reviewed can ask to see prepublication copy, you are under no obligation to provide a subject prepublication copy for review or for any other reason. If the subject wants to give you permission, fine. And I suppose there is a safety and a goodwill element in asking in the first place. But there is no connection between giving copyright permission and having the right to see prepublication copy, which is a dangerous habit for writers to get into.

CAN I QUOTE FROM ANOTHER AUTHOR'S MAGAZINE ARTICLE IN MINE?

"I found a great quote in a woman's magazine. Should I give credit to the mag and the person they quoted too?"

There are three possible answers to your question:
1. If you're writing professionally for publication, the answer is no. You should get your own quotes. Quotes from secondary sources are not good journalism, except in a few special instances.

2. If you're writing for college, the answer is probably yes. This is the sort of thing that often passes for "research" in college writing courses, although some professors do not allow consumer magazines to be used as sources.

3. Whenever you use a quotation, it should always be sourced

not only to the speaker, but also to the speaker's identity and qualifications to speak on the subject:

Example: "According to John C. Fine, author of *The Hunger Road* and a former U.S. State Department official, 'Over 1 million children starve to death each year, and 6 million live in what the UN describes as absolute poverty.'"

WHO ACQUIRES PERMISSIONS: THE AUTHOR OR PUBLISHER?

"I'm planning on using some copyrighted material in a book manuscript I'm preparing. Should I go ahead and be getting permissions to use that material or is that something the publisher takes care of?"

Definitely begin getting the permissions before the manuscript is finished. Acquiring them is your job, as is paying any fees required by the copyright owner. Usually the publisher supplies the author with guidelines for obtaining permission and blank permission request forms to do so. Please see the sample permission form (which you have permission to use) in Appendix 3.

When permission is necessary, you should contact the copyright owner or the owner's authorized agent. The copyright owner is named in the formal copyright notice that accompanies the original work. Because official notice is no longer required to obtain copyright protection, sometimes non-book publications lack the notice or include the name of someone who is not the actual or current copyright owner. Reference librarians can be helpful for finding actual names and addresses of copyright holders.

The Copyright Clearance Center (*www.copyright.com*) can also simplify the process by acting as an agent on behalf of thousands of publishers and authors to grant permission, but there is usually a cost. Remember that copyright owners have wide discretion when responding to your request for permission. Your request may be granted or denied. If granted, it may be contingent on paying a fee. The fee may be modest or exorbitant. Copyright owners also have no obligation to respond at all. For nonprofit educational and research uses, you will usually find copyright owners to be cooperative. But there are no guarantees.

Before sending the permissions request form, a simple phone call can be helpful to establish exactly who should receive the form. If permission is granted to you verbally over the phone, the permission is valid. But in everyone's best interest, obtain the duly signed permission form for your files.

WHAT EVERY FREELANCER SHOULD KNOW ABOUT FAIR USE

Will you get in trouble for using someone else's work in your own? Depends upon your ability to apply the four-point "fair use test." In a nutshell: Fair use is an exception to the exclusive protection of copyright under American law. The fair use provision permits certain uses of copyrighted material without your having to obtain permission from the author or owner, if your use meets certain criteria. Before we review those criteria—the infamous four-point fair use test—here is the actual statute from the Copyright Law of the United States of America, Chapter 1, section 107. As a freelancer, you should keep a copy of it handy:

§ 107. Limitations on Exclusive Rights: Fair Use

Notwithstanding the provisions of sections 106 and 106A, the fair use of a copyrighted work, including such use by reproduction in copies or phonorecords or by any other means specified by that section, for purposes such as criticism, comment, news reporting, teaching (including multiple copies for classroom use), scholarship, or research, is not an infringement of copyright. In determining whether the use made of a work in any particular case is a fair use the factors to be considered shall include—

(1) the purpose and character of the use, including whether such use is of a commercial nature or is for nonprofit educational purposes;

(2) the nature of the copyrighted work;

(3) the amount and substantiality of the portion used in relation to the copyrighted work as a whole; and

(4) the effect of the use upon the potential market for or value of the copyrighted work.

The fact that a work is unpublished shall not itself bar a finding of fair use if such finding is made upon consideration of all the above factors.

—*Contained in Title 17 of the United States Code.*
Text revised to July 2001

The four numbered points are the infamous "fair use test"—infamous because its ambiguity allows very different conclusions about the same use.

Working with the Fair Use Test

Each of the test's four factors has its own ambiguities. Convincing yourself that you pass the four factors does not insure that others, especially those whose work you may be using, will feel the same. However, the test is comprehensive and is generally a good indication of what you can and cannot do when it comes to using copyrighted works. Courts must consider all four criteria together to determine which way the scales of justice tip. No one factor by itself can condemn you—or save you.

Factor 1: Purpose and Character of Use

The courts consider three elements when weighing purpose and character of use:

1. if your use was of a commercial or a nonprofit nature;

2. if your use involved any of the purposes stated in the statute's preamble: criticism, comment, news reporting, teaching, scholarship or research; and

3. the degree to which you transformed the original work in your use of it.

Predictably, preference in judgments has been given to nonprofit uses, but a commercial use does not automatically make you guilty, especially if your use involved one or more of the preamble's stated purposes: criticism, comment, news reporting, teaching, scholarship or research. Courts have been clear about protecting your ability to use parts of a copyrighted work to carry out the preamble's functions. The third element, transformation, looks at whether your new work supplants the original (not a particularly fair use) or whether it adds something new: a further purpose, new expression, new meaning or new message that contributes to public discourse. If it does, that tips the scale in your favor.

Factor 2: Nature of the Copyrighted Work

This factor considers a work's worthiness to be protected under the copyright law. Courts look at the original work in question and try to determine where that work falls along the continuum of worthiness.

This factor acknowledges the reality that some works are simply more deserving of copyright protection than others. Court opinion over the years has established a "least deserving" end of the continuum comprised mostly of published works based on facts (the longer they've been published, the better). On the "very deserving" end of the continuum are unpublished works of the imagination that receive the most protection.

Factor 3: Relative Amount

This third factor looks at the amount and substantiality of the portion of the work you used. Some commentators have tried to say that using less than 3 percent is okay, but 30 percent or more and you're in trouble. The fact is, amount usually isn't the core issue.

The critical determination is the value of the materials you used, especially in comparison to your reason for using them. Courts recognize that using a whole work may be fair use in some circumstances (a teacher who copies an entire article for students), whereas using a tiny fraction of a work in a commercial publication may not qualify as fair if you can't justify its use as criticism, comment, review, teaching or research.

So, judgments aren't based merely on "small amount" and "more than a small amount," as some analysts have said. Quality and importance of the copied material must be considered. Some justices have looked to see that "no more was taken than was necessary" to achieve the purpose for which the materials were used.

Factor 4: Effect upon Potential Market

The last factor considers the extent of harm caused by your use to the market or potential market for the original work. This factor takes into account harm to the original, as well as harm to potential derivative works.

This is the most important factor when determining fair use. If you injure the market for the copyrighted work, the entire scale tilts toward unfair use. The most egregious examples occur if you rob sales from the original, or if you are trying to avoid paying for permission to use the work in an established permissions market. On the other hand, tipping the scale in your favor are such factors as the original being out of print, or the copyright owner being unidentifiable.

The Beauty of Ambiguity

The fair use statute's ambiguity is both a curse and a blessing. As one U.S. Supreme Court Justice put it:

> *"The primary objective of copyright is not to reward the labor of authors, but 'to promote the Progress of Science and useful Arts.' To this end, copyright assures authors the right to their original expression, but encourages others to build freely upon the ideas and information conveyed by a work. This result is neither unfair nor unfortunate. It is the means by which copyright advances the progress of science and art."*
> —*Justice Sandra Day O'Connor*
> *(Feist Publications, Inc. vs. Rural Telephone Service Co., 499 US 340, 349[1991])*

The genius of United States copyright law is that it balances the interests of copyright owners with society's need for the free exchange of ideas. Central to this exchange is the concept and practice of fair use. Use it well.

CONTRACTS & COPYRIGHTS—YOURS

It's more important than ever these days for freelancers to become

WRITER'S TOOLBOX
ONLINE FAIR USE RESOURCES

- Lloyd Jassin: *www.copylaw.com*
  Web site of copyright lawyer Lloyd Jassin, co-author of *The Copyright Permission and Libel Handbook.*

- U.S. Copyright Office—Copyright Search: *www.loc.gov/copyright/search*
  Allows a search for copyright holders of books, music, serials and other documents.

- Why and How to Register Your Articles:
  www.asja.org/pubtips/copyrite.php
  A primer on copyright prepared by the American Society of Journalists and Authors Contracts Committee.

- Copyright and Electronic Rights—Laws and Agencies:
  www.canauthors.org/links/copywrite.html
  Prepared by the Canadian Authors Association, a descriptive document of web resources for U.S. and Canadian writers.

- Copyright and Fair Use: *www.fairuse.stanford.edu*
  Resource page from the Stanford University Libraries.

- The Fair Use Test: *www.benedict.com/info/fairUse.asp*
  Informal, plain English explanations from Benedict O'Mahoney's award-winning copyright web site.

their own experts in understanding and negotiating the copyright portions of contracts, especially e-rights. Here's why.

First, you've got your electronic revolution: Since the explosion of the world wide web in 1995, the periodical publishing industry has been engaged in a massive land-grab of electronic rights as they try to launch new e-ventures and drive them to profitability.

Unfortunately, many of those publishers want freelancers to bear a substantial portion of the financial risk of these new ventures by demanding a writer's e-rights for free along with print rights. Others have simply stolen e-rights.

Imagine musicians getting paid only when someone buys their CD, not when the same songs are played on the radio. Or, as another writer put it, imagine building an apartment complex and charging renters only one month's rent for the rest of their life.

Next is the repurposing of content: Today's publishers have found a profitable model for taking previously published content and creating new products to sell, thereby cranking up profit margins on things like special issues, anthologies, foreign editions, CD-ROMs, fax-on-demand, not to mention electronic databases.

And then there's consolidation: Periodical publishing, whether newspapers or magazines, is being done by fewer and fewer, larger and larger corporations. They've got legal muscle and publishing contracts longer than the article attached, with the standard impenetrable legalese to match.

The result: Blithely selling all rights today will make you a publisher's sweetheart and a mortgage company's nightmare. Time to get back to basics: *If profits are being made from a work that you created and own, why shouldn't you be getting some?* Rhetorical question, of course, but it's amazing how many freelancers don't ask it. Wish I had a nickel for every time I sent a freelancer the boilerplate contract given to me by the corporate legal eagles and got it back signed with a flourish and no changes, giving the company ownership of the writer's work in "all media whether now known or hereafter imagined or created."

Yes, editors and publishers will try to take as much as you give them, just like used car salesmen. So, you'd better know how to read a contract, identify what's valuable, and negotiate to the limit of your self-interest, not the publisher's.

Never Work without a Contract

Speaking of basics: There are few absolute statements that don't leak worse than a Congressional Sub-Committee, but this one comes close—*never work without a contract*. Having a contract in place is standard business practice, even among friends. Don't learn the hard way that contracts are like medical insurance: they're there just in case. No one plans on getting cancer. No freelancer expects to get into a dispute. But when it comes to money, disputes are—sooner or later—inevitable. Thus a contract's first benefit: protection for you in the case of a dispute. A contract gives you a way to resolve that dispute without mediators, lawyers and judges.

Contracts also help you avoid the honest misunderstandings that are the basis of most disputes, whether it was a deadline date or the amount of an expense check. Because contracts spell out expectations on a number of issues, they force you and others to focus attention on all aspects of your business relationship.

Finally, a contract allows the stipulation of "material terms" (those related to subject matter, payments, quality of work and duration of the contract). Indefiniteness or absence of these material terms could be used to show that a valid contract never existed.

Top 5 Myths about Contracts
Myth 1: A Valid Contract Must Be written

Some types of contracts must be in writing: The Copyright Act requires all transfers of copyright ownership to be in writing. But as a freelancer writing for periodicals, you aren't transferring ownership; you are licensing your rights. As a result, your publishing contract can be oral, written or electronic, formal or informal. It's certainly best that a contract be detailed and written, but don't believe a publisher's claim that a prior verbal agreement isn't valid because no written document exists.

Myth 2: If a Publisher Sends Me a Check and I Cash It, I Have Agreed to the Publisher's Terms

Not true. Payment does not constitute a contract. A contract must be agreed upon by both parties in order to be valid.

Myth 3: An Altered but Signed Contract is Valid

Not unless the change is initialed. For any stipulation in a contract to be valid, both parties must agree to it. By crossing it out, you have indicated it is unacceptable to you, but the change must be initialed and agreed to by the publisher or publisher's representative in order to be valid. And vice versa.

Myth 4: When I Sign a Contract, the Publisher is Buying My Work

Unless it is a work-for-hire contract, as an independent contractor (freelancer) you own what you write. You do not sell your work; you sell the right to make copies of it: "copyrights." Indeed, a legal term for a publishing contract is an "Assignment of Rights" contract. Only work-for-hire employees sell their copyright.

Myth 5: Freelancers Who Try to Negotiate Contracts Are Freelancers Soon to Be Unemployed

Just the opposite: Continually giving away rights to your work without adequate payment is a much surer way to rejoin the ranks of corporate drones.

What Should a Contract Contain?

As a general rule, more rather than less. To be specific:
1. Names and addresses. Official contact info so nobody can claim that they didn't get something because you didn't send it to the right place. And vice versa.

2. Dates. For which the contract is effective; necessary for the contract to be legally valid and enforceable.

3. Your status. It should be clear that you are a freelancer or independent contractor, not a work-for-hire employee, if that is not the case.

4. Title of the work. Can be a working title.

5. Due date(s). Can include a schedule of deadlines.

6. Grant of right clause. Rights being purchased and the media to which they apply.

7. Compensation. Get what you want now or forever hold your peace.

8. Payment terms. When your compensation is due—standard is "net 30 days" (full payment within one month). This section can also include a schedule to allow for an advance, etc.

9. Late payment penalties. Standard business practice. Also consider giving a reward for early payment: If the agreed-on fee is $1,000, lower it by 2 percent to $980 if paid in 15 days. You can make up the $20 by paying your own bills on time.

10. Writer's obligations, liabilities and warrants. Publishing companies have a right to protect themselves, just as you do, from the unscrupulous. These clauses normally deal with the quality of your work and its legality, especially plagiarism.

11. Termination conditions. Stipulation of payment of kill fees

or cancellation fees if the contract is terminated before completion.

12. Expense reimbursement. Expenses should be payable within 15 days of submitting your expense invoice and receipts.

13. Byline or tagline. How you wish your name to read as well as any associated credit line, e.g., "Head Writer" instead of "Writer."

14. Contributor copies. Should be provided to you free.

Getting It Right, Getting It Good

The heart of this financial exchange called a contract is item #6 above: the "grant of right" clause that describes what rights you are licensing (not giving) to the publisher and for how long you are licensing them. The first thing to tell yourself is that, as copyright owner, you have a bundle of rights that you may assign in any manner you choose. Before beginning negotiations, it's helpful to make a priority list of rights from that bundle that you "must keep," "would like to keep," and "don't expect to keep." The "must keep" list usually consists of dramatic, broadcast and merchandising rights. "Don't expect to keep" usually includes second serial rights and book club rights. The rest is probably negotiable to some extent.

The second thing to tell yourself is that, as a freelancer, you go into a contract negotiation owning all the rights and the licensing of them. You are in control. You have something that somebody else wants. You have some leverage. The law of supply and demand is at work. You are the supplier. Here's what you have to sell:

All Rights

This license leaves you with very few: no reprint or anthology rights, no digital or other media rights. In fact, unless your contract states that rights revert to you at some point, an all-rights contract can mean that you may not use your work again for a long time. All-rights contracts are common for many smaller departments and fillers, where your chances of reselling are slim anyhow. Beginning freelancers are often forced to accept all-rights contracts in order to nail those crucial first bylines. Later in your career, especially with longer pieces, there is usually little reason for a freelancer to give up all rights to his or her creations. Nonetheless, ask if a phrase can be put into the contract reverting the rights to you after a period of time.

E-Rights

The electronic rights to your work (its digital form that can be published via the Internet on web pages, in email newsletters, CD-ROMs, e-databases and so forth) are now fully protected thanks to several court cases. The courts, including the U.S. Supreme Court, have made it clear that an author's e-rights are distinct from any other copyrights and not automatically granted to a publication unless an author expressly licenses those rights. That said, e-rights are currently being sold for very little, usually 5 percent to 25 percent of the amount paid for first publication rights. At many publications, licensing of e-rights is expected without further compensation.

First North American Serial Rights

This is the most common copyright licensed to periodicals. Remind yourself, when reviewing a contract, that FNSR does not include anthology rights, reprint rights, e-rights, subsidiary rights or foreign rights. FNSR means only:

- "First"—you are warranting that the publication you are selling to is the first to publish it and the work has never appeared in any other copyrighted publication.

- "North American"—the agreement includes publications in Canada, the U.S. and Mexico, but not elsewhere.

- "Serial"—publications that appear periodically, as opposed to books.

- "Rights"—the permission to publish your work.

One-Time Rights

Also known as "simultaneous rights," this clause gives the publisher the nonexclusive right to use your work one time, but you don't guarantee the same work won't appear in other publications. One-time rights are appropriate when selling the same work to non-competing markets (see "Hidden Freelance Market: Newspaper Weeklies and Dailies" in Chapter 4).

Reprint Rights

Also called "second serial rights." Reprint rights give the publisher the right to print something that has already appeared in another publication. Reprint rights are by definition nonexclusive.

Subsidiary Rights ("Sub Rights")

Subsidiary rights are those that may be used secondary to print publication: electronic rights, performance rights, audio book rights, book club rights, foreign and translation rights, movie and television rights, anthology rights, merchandizing rights, etc. The licensing or sale of sub rights is usually to a third party and proceeds of the sale go to the publisher and author. If the publisher wants some or all of your sub rights, it is important that you ascertain if the publisher has the means to exploit them. Otherwise, those rights will be tied up unnecessarily and unprofitably.

WRITER'S TOOLBOX
LEGAL REMEDIES

The purpose of business contracts is to avoid getting to this point. Nonetheless, smelly stuff happens. If you've exhausted your personal supply of patience and diplomacy, it may be time to take advantage of the legal and quasi-legal services of one of the national-level writer organizations:

- American Society of Journalists and Authors: *www.asja.org/cw/cw.php*
  ASJA's "Contracts Watch" is a free service from its Contracts Committee. "Contracts Watch" collects and publishes contract information for freelance writers, keeping you informed about the latest terms and negotiations in the world of periodicals, print and electronic publishing.

- Canadian Authors Association:
  www.canauthors.org/links/writing.html#national
  Maintains a list of all Canadian writer organizations.

- Editorial Freelance Association: *http://the-efa.org/Code4.html*
  Publishes a "Code of Fair Practice" and maintains a Fair Practice Committee to provide guidance and assistance in these matters to members.

- National Writers Union: *www.nwu.org*
  Besides the helpful page on contracts, copyrights and negotiations, NWU members in good standing can obtain grievance assistance or contract advice by sending email to: advice@nwu.org.

- Periodical Writers Association of Canada:
  www.pwac.ca/who/committees.htm
  Provides a mediation service to help resolve disputes between members and their clients. Also open to publishers who use the PWAC Standard Freelance Publication Agreement in dealing with PWAC members, against whom the publisher may have a complaint.

WRITER'S TOOLBOX
SAMPLE CONTRACTS

These can be downloaded and altered for your own use; however, the groups and individuals who wrote the templates assume no liability regarding your use of them. Included in Appendix 4 of this book is a copy of two contracts I use. You're welcome to adapt them for your use with the stipulation that I am not liable for any consequences of such use.

- Standard Freelance Editorial Agreement:
  www.editors.ca/pubs/contract.htm

- Standard Journalism Contracts: *www.nwu.org/journ/jsjc.htm*

- Internet Writing (Writer's Guild-East):
  www.wgaeast.org/mba/internet/internet_agreement.html

- Freelance Assignment Agreement:
  www.austinidealist.com/samplecontract.html

- Freelance Publication Agreement:
  http://shopmystate.com/Agent/Writer-AGREEMENT2.pdf

- Sample Copyright Development and Transfer Agreement:
  www.lawforinternet.com/pdf/WorkforHire-Contractor_Extra.pdf

WHAT IS LIBEL? HOW DO I AVOID TROUBLE?

"What are the nonfiction writer's restrictions in using real names of people in a disparaging way? How far can you go legally? Can you change the names and be safe? Public figures seem to be fair game but how about government agencies and their employees?"

You have just touched upon one of the most complex issues that a journalist must face today. It's also an area where you can't afford to make mistakes. You are exactly right that public figures are treated differently, so are public officials. But the differences can be fine. Luckily there is a guidebook for us: the "Briefing on Media Law" portion of *The Associated Press Stylebook*. And if you want to know what it says, you've got to go to the library or pay for it. You can order it online at the AP's web site. Accept no substitutes: *www.ap.org/pages/order.html*.

Here is a brief guide to libel and slander as I've come to understand them through cases I've been involved with:

Libel, Slander and Defamation

Libel can be personal libel or trade libel, which is also known as "product disparagement" and can include a product, service or company. Libelous statements are published statements that are false and damaging. Slander is the same as libel in most states, but in spoken rather than written form. The terms "libel" and "slander" are often subsumed under the term "defamation." It is a tort (a wrongful act) to harm another's reputation by defaming them. How do you know if you might defame someone or something in what you are considering publishing? There are three tests which the defamatory statement must meet in order for a plaintiff to prevail in a suit against you:

1. Untrue. In order to be defamatory, the statement must be untrue. If the statement is true or substantially true, then it is not defamatory, and the case is over.

2. Damaging. In order for the plaintiff to prevail, the statement must have caused real and substantial harm to the person or business. The plaintiff must present evidence of substantial harm done.

3. Knowingly false. The plaintiff must also show that the defendant knew the statement was untrue, but published or broadcast the statement despite that knowledge.

From this brief explanation, you can deduce that the best way to avoid a libel charge, or to defeat it, is to: (1) Write only that which is true and can be shown to be true through your meticulous research and note taking; (2) Keep all research for a period of years, depending on the statute of limitations that applies where you are. In sum, you can say or publish just about whatever you wish in our open society—so long as it is true.

Regarding your comment that public figures "seem to be fair game"—you are correct in that public persons and private persons are treated differently. But I don't agree that they are "fair game." Since a freelancer's writing often concerns public as well as private people, it's important for us to know the boundaries of the playing field.

Public Official vs. Public Figure

The same liberal rule applies to both categories: To prevail in a libel case against you, in addition to showing that the statement is untrue and caused significant harm, a public official or a public figure must also prove "malice"—that you acted in reckless disregard to the facts known to you and with intent to harm. Obviously, because of this stipulation, you enjoy considerable protection when it comes to public personages, since proving malice (intent to harm) places a heavy burden on the prosecution.

Who are these public people? The status of "public official" is relatively easy to determine from public records. The trick comes in determining who falls into the category of "public figure."

The courts have determined that there are two types: A "general purpose public figure" is someone who enjoys social prominence. Entertainers are in this category. But there is also a "limited purpose public figure"—someone who has intentionally placed themselves into prominence, such as a vocal activist on a given issue. The reasoning is that the press has a First Amendment duty to report on such newsworthy people, and therefore published statements warrant such protection.

Who is a private person? None of the above. Now you see why lawyers get the big bucks.

CAN I BE SUED FOR LIBEL WHEN WRITING FICTION?

"I want to write a book on a person who lived over a hundred years ago. He was somewhat of a character and from what I've been able to come up with on him, the information would make a great story and maybe even a better movie. My problem is this: Even though he was written about several times and was in the public eye for several years, there is very little information about his personal life. After six months of part-time research I am feeling like there may not be enough on his personal life to fill in a good book or movie. I have been unable to even come up with any present day relatives.

"The answer to my problem would be to fill in areas of his personal life with fiction. Can this be done? Are there any disclaimers that would have to be mentioned about the accuracy of the life events? Would any long lost relatives be able to cause a problem on any of the fictional events? I'm sure many books and movies drift back and forth between truth and fiction, but I'm a little unsure how to proceed without knowing the legal implications for libel. Thanks for your help."

Yes, you can fill in the gaps with fiction. And, yes, there are possible legal implications, which vary according to the publication format you choose: movie, historical fiction, historical biography.

Movies and Life Rights

Before a producer would touch a property about a real-life figure, there must be some sort of "life rights" agreement in place. Producers pay subjects for the right to tell about their lives. In return, a life-rights agreement usually gives the producer the right to change elements of fact in order to make the movie. This is why you see the phrase "based on a true story" under a movie's title. The work has some basis in fact, but the viewer is also being warned that not everything they're about to see really happened. Before you write a screenplay, you should either acquire the life rights or have a very clear notion that life rights aren't required, which is likely in the case of someone who lived over 100 years ago. Same for any book you wish to adapt for the screen: get the option on the book first, before you start writing.

Historical Fiction

So long as you have at the beginning of the book the usual disclaimer—"This is a work of fiction. Any similarity to real people, events or places is purely coincidental"—you should be fine from a legal point of view if filling in the gaps with plausible fictions. All the names must be changed. In this case, you would be using the real person's life and times as the basis of the fictional work. You are correct: this is done quite often.

Historical Biography

Here you must be as accurate and truthful as possible, to the extent that you (and your publisher) could defend your work in a court of law. The key is truth—so long as what you write is true, any libel suit against you will always fail in an American court. It doesn't sound as if there is enough info for you to do a biography.

DO I NEED MODEL RELEASES TO PROTECT MYSELF FROM LAWSUITS?

"Some of the photography I'm sending in with my article contains pictures of people that I took myself. Should I have gotten model releases?"

Whenever you use a photograph of a person without a written release form, you risk being sued for invasion of privacy. A conservative guideline: If the identity of the individual can be discerned in the image, then you should secure a model release from that subject to protect yourself. If the subject is unrecognizable in the image, then you're probably okay.

A model release is a consent form signed by a photograph's subject that gives you permission to publish the photograph without invading that person's privacy or copyrighted image. Professional models often have strict limitations on how their image can be used.

Generally, the photographer's right of free expression is not

WRITER'S TOOLBOX
MODEL RELEASES AND PRIVACY

- See Appendix 5 for a copy of a model release used in the "Kids Wanna Know" TV production.

- Sample online model releases:
  www.pdnonline.com/businessresources/modelrelease.html
  www.istep.com/photostop/Legal/adult_release.html
  www.istep.com/photostop/Legal/minor_release.html
  www.apogeephoto.com/mag4-6/adultlon.htm

- Online legal discussions of model releases:
  www.apogeephoto.com/mag4-6/mag4-6model_releases.shtml
  www.danheller.com/model-release.html

questioned if the subject of a photograph is newsworthy. This is what allows paparazzi to harass celebrities anytime they're in public. However, the privacy rights of a non-newsworthy person can prevail when the image is used for a commercial purpose, especially in trade or advertising. In some states, "trade or advertising" includes only promotional materials, not editorial. In other states, any money-making use, including editorial use, could require permission. As you can see, there are no hard and fast rules in this area, only ambiguity and contradiction. "Hooray!" shout the lawyers.

It's best to get a model release from anyone who is recognizable, and especially permission from the parents or guardian of any minor. Caption the photo correctly and make sure it wasn't taken while you were trespassing on someone's property.

WHAT'S THE DIFFERENCE BETWEEN A FAM TRIP AND A PRESS TOUR?

"I'd like to know the difference between a fam trip and a press tour. I've been published several times, but have just taken my first expense-paid press tour. A friend said I took a fam trip. What's the difference?"

"Fam trip" is the term heard most often from PR agencies trying to promote their travel-service clients; it's short for "familiarization." "Press tour" is the more traditional term. For example, the Army may arrange a press tour of its frontline positions in Afghanistan, or a press tour of a new battleship or the newly remodeled White House wing. The phrase "press tour" is usually heard outside the travel industry and the promotions game. But sometimes PR flaks try to give their fam trips more prestige by calling them press tours.

Regardless of what it is called, be careful of any agreements you sign before going on a free fam trip. Some PR agencies want you to guarantee their client positive editorial at a certain minimum number of words, within a certain time frame. To do so would compromise your ability to write objectively. If you're going to write a work-for-hire advertorial, have fun!

ARE FAM TRIPS UNETHICAL?

> *"A while back you helped me understand the difference between a press tour and a fam trip. I submitted a story idea to a newspaper. The editor wants the story—but, he says he cannot pay if it was a fam trip. I'd like to write it for free. What do you think?"*

First, I've never heard of a similar policy (not paying a freelancer because he or she was on a fam trip). I suspect it is peculiar to this editor, if it's true. I don't know the editor, and my policy is always to assume the best about someone until proven otherwise. So, for now you can assume that the editor truly has an ethical concern here. On the other hand, it could be about his wanting to save money and take advantage of a first-time freelancer. That would be the cynical view, and I'd hold off on that, giving the editor the benefit of the doubt for the time being.

Next step: Ask the editor for some further explanation as to why having participated in a fam trip (which did not involve his newspaper) disqualifies you for pay. There's a contradiction at work: On the one hand, he considers your work worthy of publication, including research done on a fam trip. Yet that same work isn't ethical enough for you to be paid for it? I don't get it. The only other explanation I can think of: the editor may be running your story as a puff piece or "advertorial"—in which case you wouldn't be paid by the editorial department, you'd be paid by the advertising department.

On the whole, I think writing for free is a bad precedent to set for yourself and the freelance community as a whole. This is a business. A serious business. You want to be taken seriously as a writer, one whose craft is legitimate, whose skills are manifest, and who has every right to be paid for application of those skills and the time you take to craft something for publication. Frankly, if a free-lancer ever sends me a query and offers to write for free, I automatically reject it without reading anything else. It's a clear signal he/she isn't a pro yet. On the other hand, you have to start somewhere. And a clip IS a clip. No one else has to know (or should want to know or even has a right to know) how much you were paid. But ask yourself this: if you give this piece to him for free, what can you expect to be paid for the next one?

"On the web, say it in few words or be skipped. In plain words, or be flamed."

CHAPTER SEVEN

WEB MATTERS: HOW TO WRITE AND SELL YOUR PIXELS

- Print vs. Web: Understanding the Differences, Implementing the Fixes
- Jakob Nielsen: Putting It All Together
- E-Rights: Control and Controversy
- How to Prepare for a Career in Web Writing
- Opportunities for Travel Writing on the Web

Bold prediction: In 500 years the name Tim Berners-Lee will be as familiar as Johannes Gutenberg's is today, and the date 1990 as memorable as 1440. Berners-Lee is credited with developing the information sharing system that led to the development of the world wide web. Like Gutenberg and his converted wine press, Berners-Lee built upon the ideas and technical advances of those before him and of his contemporaries. Nonetheless, it's the web that enabled the Internet to embrace the world, and it's Berners-Lee's name that has become attached to the phrase he coined: the "world wide web."

More telling is the perfect fit to the web of this description of the importance of the printing press: "It paved the way to the world of knowledge and communication in which we live today."

Guess we better learn how to write for both.

PRINT VS. WEB: UNDERSTANDING THE DIFFERENCES, IMPLEMENTING THE FIXES

Fortunately, in this brave new world of the Internet, most of the old writing rules still apply. But what about the ones you never dreamed of? The Law of Unintended Consequences applies to the Internet just as it did to that other revolution in information distribution: the printing press. No one predicted that Johannes Gutenberg's little experiment in subsidy publishing would form the foundation for the Renaissance and the Protestant Reformation. Oops.

One of the ironies of the Internet is that, true to the Law of Unintended Consequences, the medium that was supposed to make books obsolete has fueled a publishing bonanza and an offline reading explosion. Glory be! The Internet is just as dependent on the written word (and the scribes who get paid to produce those words) as books, magazines, newspapers and TV. But there the similarities end.

Writing for the Web: An Overview

Some of the differences between print reading habits and web reading habits are apparent, but others have only recently emerged through empirical research. In both cases, it's essential for web writers to be aware of the differences between the world of linear text flowing like a river, and the fragmented world of hypertext on a computer screen. The most successful web writers have identified the key differences. They are:

Web vs. Print Difference 1: Scanning/Skimming

Web-user studies at Sun Microsystems' Science Office uncovered several of the key differences between the two media. One of the most stunning is that 79 percent of users scan and skim a web page instead of reading word-for-word. Scanning means letting the eyes rove over the entire page until they see something that causes them to stop. Then web users skim: passing swiftly over the words. Wait, it gets worse.

Studies at User Interface Engineering labs have found that web readers do not read a computer screen in the typical left-to-right manner. Instead, a web reader's eyes are most likely to focus first in the center of the page, then track to the left—exactly opposite of what happens with print documents.

Finally, one of the most dramatic findings comes from a large-scale eye-tracking study carried out by Stanford University and The Poynter Institute. The study found that new visitors to a web site largely ignore graphics. Moreover, the text that they focus on is highly limited. Seventy-eight percent of a web reader's attention is on headlines, summaries and captions.

Taken together, these findings clearly support two of the most important recommendations for writing web copy:

Make Text Scannable

Effective web writers frequently use bullets, numbers, boxes, colored type, background shading and other devices to break up the screen into discernible and digestible chunks that facilitate scanning.

Write in Chunks

Breaking a long article into a variety of related components allows readers to scan and read only the parts interesting and relevant to them. As a result, chunking provides a type of customization driven by the demand for personalization on the web, and it signals an important advance in helping web-page viewers to process information in a hypertext environment on a computer screen.

Generally, chunking is achieved by a combination of three methods:

1. Visual separation.

   This most often means the use of white space to frame chunks: spaces between paragraphs, the space around centered texts, and other visual arrangements.

2. Visual progression.

   This refers to giving sequence to chunks via bullets, numbers, flags and other devices in horizontal and vertical arrangements.

3. Visual differentiation.

   Visual differentiation relies on typography, the use of various type styles, sizes and colors, as well as background shading to make each chunk graphically distinct.

Web vs. Print Difference 2: Reading Speed

Studies at Sun's Science Office also found considerable differences in reading rates. Reading from a computer screen is 25 percent slower than reading from paper.

The increased difficulty of reading from a screen, as evidenced by a 25 percent slower reading rate, also discourages word-for-word reading and encourages scanning. Why is reading from a computer screen slower and more difficult? Researchers have identified a number of factors: (1) poor character resolution and background contrast in comparison to print; (2) the inability to hold the entire document at once; (3) the need to scroll one page at a time in order to read a web document; (4) the need to use hyperlinks. Given these factors, it comes as no surprise that web readers resist scrolling and often leave a document after viewing only a single screen.

The web seems to have produced readers who are impatient, highly specific in what they are hunting for, want it at the top of their screen, and are intolerant of any elements that hinder their hunt. These strong reader preferences have combined to make the lowly paragraph the basic unit of text on the web. In print works, we usually think in basic units of chapters, articles and stories. But on the computer screen, it's the paragraph that has been atomized as this medium's basic unit.

This constellation of web reading habits suggests three more important guidelines for writing web copy:

Invert the Pyramid

Journalism's inverted pyramid—where the story's summary comes first and information flows from most important to least—has found a new and welcome home on the web among readers who demand information at the top of a page in summary fashion. The most-to-least-important arrangement allows readers to stay a short period of time (to get main points only) or stay longer to increase the level of detail they receive.

Limit Paragraphs to One Idea

Non-scrolling, impatient, skimming web users typically read only the top part of the article and paragraph, just as the typical newspaper reader does. As a result, a strong trend in web writing is to reduce paragraphs to only a few sentences, perhaps only one, which is also similar to newspaper journalism.

Reduce Word Count by 50 Percent

Conciseness is demanded by the impatient reader who wants to find his targeted info fast. As a result, the onus is on the writer to make information searches easier by writing clearly and succinctly. On the web, the writer's goal is to convey reliable information in as few words as possible, preferably in a summary at the top of the page, with a list, or as a caption.

Implementing these rules without producing a series of seemingly disjointed chunks on a screen is one of the challenges of writing good web copy. One solution is to treat each screen like a painting that is framed by the computer's monitor. On this electronic canvas are elements that you, the artist, weave together, linearly and nonlinearly, to form a visually coherent whole that can be accessed with little or no exploratory reading. Your tools are the techniques and devices already discussed, plus one more important one: hyperlinks.

Web vs. Print Difference 3: Hyperlink Access

On the web, pages of a document can no longer be seen only in linear sequence. Because of embedded hyperlinks, a user can enter a document at multiple points, coming from very different contexts. A web page that begins with "The next element to be considered" is a potential problem for a surfer who clicked directly there from a remote server on the web. A page's text and vocabulary must stand by themselves in discrete chunks.

Because of hyperlink access, surfers also depend upon clear headings, subheads and other chunking devices to find what they're looking for. Now web writing incurs an additional burden of helping the surfer navigate individual pages and, ultimately, the web itself.

Make the Navigation Clear

Writing in the world of hypertext places a premium on good organization of content and on devices that signal the content's organization to the web user. On the page level, this means:

- headings and subheadings that provide clear summaries, not clever writing;

- use of topic sentences and transitional words;

- concepts framed as lists;

- graphical elements that aid navigation, not distract from it; and

- paragraphs limited to 100-word chunks or less.

On the macro level, clarity means consistent navigational elements and buttons that communicate fully: "Next" could mean either the "Next page" or "Next search result" or "Next chapter." Although these issues usually fall to the web programmer, don't forget that programmers simply make your text a technical reality. You, the writer, are still very much in the driver's seat.

Provide Hyperlinks

Hyperlinks are necessary in web copy for three reasons: users expect links that help them drill for information; links to definitions, explanations and sources allow a web page to be independent; links provide credibility. So use 'em, but don't abuse 'em.

Credibility is substantially more difficult to establish on the web than it is in print. The proliferation of the web (three billion pages and counting), the ease of publication, the protection of anonymity and the remoteness of servers make it essential that the writer pay attention to elements that help establish that credibility. According to Canadian web writing consultant Doug Lavendar, outbound links to authoritative sites and sources are currently seen as the primary way of establishing credibility. Here are some guidelines.

- Avoid too many links, which can be confusing.

- Limit their purpose to link to data, explanations and sources not on the page.

- Hyperlink words that serve as a title for the link. Examples:

  No: "For information on how to conduct searches, *click here*."
  Yes: "Information on *how to conduct searches* is available."

  No: To read an article by Marcia Bliss, *choose this link*.
  Yes: Articles by *Marcia Bliss* are available for free.

- Avoid teaser links. Links should tell readers what they will find, summarizing what the link points to. Examples:

  No: Officials came to a *surprise conclusion* as to why the company's stock rose dramatically.
  Yes: Officials surprised the public with *their conclusion* that the company's stock rose dramatically due to a false beta rather than net earnings.

Web vs. Print Difference 4: Rigorously Democratic

The user is very much in control of this interactive experience. Print and television provide one-way communication to a passive recipient. The web has turned this communication model—and the notion of who is and isn't an expert—on its head. Pretentiousness of any sort, especially in language and attitude, is a frequent target for flames. What has emerged is a democratic medium with a distinctive voice:

Be Informal and Objective

The best-received language is characterized by a lack of marketese and slogans, jargon, subjective claims, hyperbole, emotion and lit-

WRITER'S TOOLBOX
CHECKLIST: WRITING FOR THE WEB vs. WRITING FOR PRINT

- **Make text scannable.** Few web users read word-for-word. Even fewer want to.

- **Write in chunks.** Set apart concepts visually with devices that allow users to quickly select information they want.

- **Invert the pyramid.** Put conclusions or main points at the top of their paragraph or chunk, as in journalism's inverted pyramid.

- **Limit paragraphs to one idea.** When paragraphs are necessary, limit them to a single idea expressed in 2–3 sentences.

- **Reduce word count by 50 percent.** A highly visual medium, the web requires tight integration of graphics and words in equal proportions.

- **Make navigation clear.** Since users may enter a web site on any of its pages, each page must provide clear, stand-alone heads, subheads and other navigational tools.

- **Provide hyperlinks.** Users expect hyperlinks in order to drill for information and for the credibility they provide.

- **Be informal and objective.** Preferred style is succinct, plain language that communicates clearly and directly.

erary affectations. Instead, this is language boiled down and simplified for a utilitarian use.

Jakob Nielsen: Putting It All Together

One of the best demonstrations of the differences between print

MEASURING THE EFFECT OF IMPROVED WEB WRITING		
Site Version	Sample Paragraph	Usability Improvement*
Promotional Style (control condition using the "marketese" found on many commercial sites)	Nebraska is filled with internationally recognized attractions that draw large crowds every year, without fail. In 1996, some of the most popular places were Fort Robinson State Park (355,000 visitors), Scotts Bluff National Monument (132,166), Arbor Lodge State Historical Park & Museum (100,000), Carhenge (86,598), Stuhr Museum of the Prairie Pioneer, (60,002) and Buffalo Bill State Ranch Historical Park (28,446).	0% (by definition)
Concise Style (word count reduced 50%)	In 1996, six of the best-attended attractions in Nebraska were Fort Robinson State Park, Scotts Bluff National Monument, Arbor Lodge State Historical Park & Museum, Carhenge, Stuhr Museum of the Prairie Pioneer, and Buffalo Bill Ranch State Historical Park.	58%
Scannable Layout (same text as control condition in a layout that facilitates scanning)	Nebraska is filled with internationally recognized attractions that draw large crowds of people every year, without fail. In 1996, some of the most popular places were: • Fort Robinson State Park (355,000 visitors) • Scotts Bluff National Monument (132,166) • Arbor Lodge State Historical Park & Museum (100,000) • Carhenge (86,598) • Stuhr Museum of the Prairie Pioneer (60,002) • Buffalo Bill Historical Park (28,446)	47%
*Relative to control condition Reprinted by permission from "Jakob Nielsen's Web Site," *www.useit.com/alertbox/9710a.html*		

text and the brave new world of concise, scannable and objective web texts is provided by the guru of web usability, Jakob Nielsen, and his famous Alertboxes on www.useit.com.

MEASURING THE EFFECT OF IMPROVED WEB WRITING		
Site Version	**Sample Paragraph**	**Usability Improvement***
Objective Language (using neutral rather than subjective, boastful, or exaggerated language)	Nebraska has several attractions. In 1996, some of the most-visited places were Fort Robinson State Park (355,000 visitors), Scotts Bluff National Monument (132,166), Arbor Lodge State Historical Park & Museum (100,000), Carhenge (86,598), Stuhr Museum of the Prairie Pioneer (60,002), and Buffalo Bill Ranch State Historical Park (28,446).	27%
Combined Version (using all three improvements together: concise, scannable, objective)	In 1996, six of the most-visited places in Nebraska were: • Fort Robinson State Park • Scotts Bluff National Monument • Arbor Lodge State Historical Park & Museum • Carhenge • Stuhr Museum of the Prairie Pioneer • Buffalo Bill Ranch State Historical Park	124%
*Relative to control condition Reprinted by permission from "Jakob Nielsen's Web Site," *www.useit.com/alertbox/9710a.html*		

If you can appreciate the differences in the samples in this table, then you're ready to write for the web:

E-RIGHTS: CONTROL AND CONTROVERSY

Don't let the little "e" fool you: e-rights have become a very big deal. Because they're part of a bundle of rights that freelance writers automatically own, e-rights should first be seen in the overall context of copyright. As a writer, you have no guarantee of success. You invest your time and talent in the same way a wildcatter sinks an oil shaft: you hope and pray to strike oil, and you're willing to take a risk for the opportunity to do so. Copyright is your deed to the oil well; copyright helps guarantee that you will recover your investment if and when the well comes in.

This "copyright deed" is a serious issue for writers, musicians, artists and anyone who produces creative works for sale. You should take all of your rights seriously and respect them. Copyrights are very much like your money in that regard: if you don't respect it, you're likely to lose it.

The recording industry has historically done a better job than the publishing industry of protecting the copyrights of its artists with automatic licensing through agencies like BMI and ASCAP. But even that industry is undergoing a serious struggle as it comes to terms with the technologies that enabled Napster to become one of the most popular sites on the web during its day.

New technologies have also created new opportunities and challenges for publishers and writers, but so far one of those two has benefited significantly more than the other. This inequity, along with strong-arm tactics by publishers and outright piracy at times, made it inevitable that the issue of e-rights would end up in the courts.

Jonathan Tasini, now the president of the National Writer's Union, and five other freelancers filed suit in December 1993 against the *New York Times* and several online database companies, to whom the *Times* had sold the freelancers' work for archiving and retrieval without any further compensation to the freelancers. The publishers claimed they had the right to do so under section 201(c) of the U.S. Copyright Act, which gives publishers the right to distribute collective works such as newspapers and magazines and any future revision of the collective works. The publishers claimed that the databased articles represented an allowed revision of the original works in which the freelancers' work appeared.

Nearly eight years after the original Tasini filing—including lower-court reversals, appeals, and failed settlement attempts—the

U.S. Supreme Court heard the *Tasini* vs. *NY Times* case and ruled in favor of the freelancers in June, 2001. The court held that, because the freelancers' articles appeared as isolated works in the databases, the articles were no longer part of a collective work and the publisher's 201(c) revision privilege did not apply.

Freelancers won back their e-rights. Now, what are you going to do with them? This is not a spurious question. Few publishers are making enough money with their electronic ventures to be able to offer you print-like fees, yet these publishers need your work online in order to remain competitive. Are you willing to walk away from an otherwise acceptable contract over a few measly dollars for e-rights?

Another result of the Tasini case is that contracts these days include stipulations regarding e-rights, with the publisher or editor wanting more for less. Some points to keep in mind:

1. The world wide web is just that. By licensing your e-rights, you are agreeing to make your work available to the world, not just North America.

2. If different media yield different financial results for a publisher, this is an argument for adjusting the amount you receive for your e-rights, not for giving them away.

3. Unlike print magazines on a newsstand, an article on a web site has the potential for being read for decades.

4. If online database services are paying publishers for your work, can you sell your work directly to such services and realize more benefit? This is just what the National Writers Union is organizing with its Publication Rights Clearinghouse initiative (see "Hidden Freelance Market: Publication Rights Clearinghouse" in Chapter 4).

Bottom line: Your e-rights have value. Otherwise publishers would not be fighting you for them or expending resources to take that fight to the U.S. Supreme Court. But the fight isn't over. During contract negotiations, you'll likely hear a variety of arguments designed to acquire your e-rights for probably less than they're worth. Here's how to be ready for them.

Publisher Tactics and How to Counter Them

These responses aren't meant to make you combative, but simply to ensure that you understand what may be said to you and what options are available to you for response.

- Tactic 1: The phrase "First North American Serial Rights" does not distinguish acquiring serial rights from e-rights; therefore, I automatically acquire rights to the electronic version of the story.

  Response: The U.S. Supreme Court has ruled that electronic use of articles originally appearing in print are not part of serial rights. E-uses are considered additional and are not permitted without a signed contract stipulating them.

- Tactic 2: Allowing your work to be archived is for the public good.

  Response: We're all for the public good. But the selling of my work for e-use is a business transaction, of which I must be a part. *Keep snide response to yourself.* I'll allow my work to be archived for free if you'll offer your publication for free.

- Tactic 3: Your work must be archived in order to be found. Over 80 percent of users find content via online databases and search engines.

  Response: Most search engines are free to users. If an

electronic database company or anyone else pays you to use/view my work, it's only fair that I be paid, too.

- Tactic 4: Your work was bought under a work-for-hire agreement. I can use it as I wish.

    Response: Let's look at the contract. It must stipulate that I licensed "all rights" or created a "work-for-hire"; otherwise, a writer maintains any right not specifically licensed away.

- Tactic 5: Online databases are just another way of distributing the work. I don't pay you extra if I increase the number of print subscribers or newsstands that carry the magazine.

    Response: Newsstands distribute collective works, for which you have paid me. Databases distribute individual works. If a database paid you to acquire my individual work, it's only fair that I participate in that transaction.

- Tactic 6: We're simply archiving that issue of the magazine on the web, like we used to do with microfilm, like we do with our print magazines on office shelves and in warehouses.

    Response: Microfilm contained the entire issue and everything in it, just as it once appeared in print. On the web, users can call up my individual article divorced from the original print publication. You aren't archiving print issues on the web; you're archiving individual articles for individual use.

- Tactic 7: Our web site is not making money right now. I can't pay you.

    Response: When you started the print magazine, were you profitable from day one? Yet you still paid freelancers who contributed to a non-profitable print magazine. Why is the web any different?

- Tactic 8: Unlike a print magazine which subscribers pay for, we don't charge download fees and therefore can't pay you for web use.

    Response: Do you still accept paid advertising on your web site? Advertisers are paying to reach the users who are coming to your site to read articles, not to look at ads.

- Tactic 9: We don't have the technology to determine if your article is being accessed or how often.

    Response: I understand. In that case, pay me a flat fee based on the number of months you wish to use my work on your web site, or the number of unique visitors to your web site.

- Tactic 10: The cost of writing small checks is greater than the small fees I owe you.

    Response: To help you reduce costs in this area, I can make arrangements with a service like the Author's Registry, which will keep small accounts for writers.

- Tactic 11: The web provides great exposure for you, getting your name and work in front of millions you otherwise could not reach.

    Response: I appreciate that. But so does your print magazine, yet you pay me for it.

- Tactic 12. Other authors are signing the same contract with no problems.

    Response: Thank you for that information. Naturally, you

WRITER'S TOOLBOX
E-RIGHTS RESOURCES

- Standard Online Contract—National Writer's Union:
  www.nwu.org/journ/jsjcweb.txt

- Copyrights and Beyond in the Digital Age:
  www.piercelaw.edu/tfield/digital.htm

- Recommended Electronic Rights Policy—National Writer's Union:
  www.nwu.org/journ/j15pct.htm

- Electronic Rights Negotiation Strategies—National Writer's Union:
  www.nwu.org/journ/jstrat.htm

- Electronic Publishing: Fiction and Fact—American Society of Journalists and Authors:
  www.asja.org/pubtips/ewrongs.php

- The Digital Millennium Copyright Act of 1998:
  www.loc.gov/copyright/legislation/dmca.pdf

and I can't discuss the details of your financial arrangements with other writers. I can only speak to the contract in front of me and its clause concerning my e-rights. *Keep snide response to yourself:* When you were a kid and tried that one on your parents, I bet they didn't care either.

E-Strategies That Work for Both

Instead of arguing, it's best to find a win-win formula that protects and benefits both. Some ideas:

- License the right to use the e-version of your work when print rights are bought, but for a finite period that coincides with the on-sale date of the publication. If the publisher wishes to archive the work online longer, the period should be specified and paid for up front.

- License the automatic, non-exclusive rights to additional usages in the future (i.e., the publisher sells bundled works to an online database), but in return the author receives a flat fee up front for agreeing to this clause.

- Define e-rights as specifically as possible. Maybe it's just for the web, or a certain database. Knowing for sure can help you determine the value of what you're licensing.

HOW DO I PREPARE FOR A CAREER IN WEB WRITING?

"I am just out of my second semester of grad school in counseling, and have decided to pursue a writing career instead. I am particularly interested in content editing/New Media and other jobs that involve writing, editing, researching and the Internet. Though I have a BA in journalism, I have few clips or references left from the days when I was actively freelancing.

"Can you give me some direction on how I can best prepare and market myself for these positions? It's frustrating knowing that I have the talent and experience needed to do these jobs well, but lack the resume credits to convince employers to give me a chance. Any thoughts?"

This is a fascinating question about the role of the freelancer in the new age of web journalism. There are indeed important differences right now between freelancing for the print world and for the web. Here are the ones that strike me as most important:

Web Freelancing Doesn't Mean Just Text Articles

Thinking back on the successful web freelancers I've employed, they offered programming, not just a one-shot article. For example: Bill Toomey licensed his daily "Sherman's Lagoon" cartoon to us; we used a Dive Safety Tip of the Day, Photographer of the Week, and a week's worth of live coverage of a new free-dive record in Cabo San Lucas. Yes, there are some web sites that still use a print model. But mostly what I'm seeing is "web producers" who are capable of providing programming, not one-shots of content.

Do Their Own Programming

The best web freelancers do their own programming: html, Java, digital images, and the rest. They offer a multi-media package, not just ASCII text. They know how to include video and audio effectively, as well as hyperlinks.

Web Freelancers Are Highly Specialized

The Internet has broken down all the walls—political, national, social, economic. As a result, people are coalescing into Internet "tribes": small groups closely knit by their special interests and beliefs. Some tribes you belong to are short term (car buyers) and some are long term (enthusiasts). But I think it will be difficult to find enough work as a web freelancer without having one or more specialties.

Specific advice to you:
- Work on turning your professional expertise (graduate work will qualify you as a credentialed professional) into your freelance specialty.

- Learn the basic web programming tools. Build your own home page to send editors to when applying for online writing assignments.

- Spend time finding web sites that fit what you have to offer.

- Become an expert in your field and let people know that you are. Market yourself on the web.

- Remember that the most powerful nonfiction is often expert driven. But on the web you must learn to sound objective and informal.

You have a remarkable opportunity to combine two of your loves and strengths: communication and psychology.

CURRENT ONLINE MARKETS

Like the web itself, the online market for freelancers is very much in the developmental stage, making it difficult to know what the next three to five years will bring. So far, much of the content on the web has come from print sources. This is true of corporate sites and well as magazine sites. But I see this as a start-up phenomenon that has run its course. Today's emerging model is exclusive web programming, not repurposed print content.

Another factor is that many web sites are being designed and written by web development companies. Much of the original writing on the web is being created inside these web development companies, a situation that suggests a possible new approach for freelancers: In many cases, it's more appropriate to contact the web company that developed a site you're interested in contributing to, not the owners of the site. The owners may be outsourcing design and content creation.

WRITER'S TOOLBOX
ONLINE MARKET RESOURCES

- Online Market Directory:
  www.bacons.com/directories/internetmedia.asp
  Bacon's Internet Media Directory. Over 6,000 web site listings organized by media type and subject matter. Subscription is $300, but available at many libraries in print or online versions.

- Job pages for journalists and freelancers
  www.freep.com/jobspage
  www.newslink.org/joblink.html
  www.elance.com ("It's a madhouse!"—Charleton Heston, *Planet of the Apes*)

- Freelancer Online Communities:
  www.thewell.com
  www.contentious.com

- Print Resources:
  Online Markets for Writers. Anthony Tedesco (Owl Books).
  Writer's Online Marketplace. Debbie Ridpath Ohi (Writer's Digest Books).

The four areas where the most opportunities seem to be right now for original writing are:

- entertainment sites;

- online game sites;

- children's programming; and

- news and information sites.

That's not to say that new areas won't develop or that these will remain hot. After all, this is the web, where development seems to take place at the speed of thought, as some guy named Gates said.

WHAT OPPORTUNITIES ARE THERE FOR TRAVEL WRITING ON THE WEB?

"I am planning to work and backpack my way around the world and was wondering if it is possible to get a magazine or newspaper to provide some sort of sponsorship in return for a type of diary I could send each day via email or something. A sort of daily column you could say.

"Is your ability to write really important? Or could I just write a journal and have one of the writers working for the particular newspaper or magazine adjust my entry?

"Any advice on how to approach companies on this and to make my writing successful would be much appreciated."

Interesting question. Today, we're seeing a re-emergence of field reporting on the web, where the correspondents send daily updates using wireless modems, satellites, digital cameras and the like. So there is one part of your answer: your best shot at landing this kind of assignment is from a web property.

A second part of the answer: which web property? What you're doing is adventurous, so I'd start with the web sites focused on offbeat, adventure travel for a twenty-something audience. You'll need to do some research to find web sites that fit that profile. The next step would be for you to study the writing found on the target web sites and make sure that what you do fits their content slant and especially their voice and attitude.

How to make your writing successful? Read the greats. In

your case, I'd highly recommend Tim Cahill for his powers of observation, his humor and distinctive voice when it comes to adventure travel. Paul Theroux brings an unparalleled wisdom to his travel writing. The writing of Gretel Ehrlich and Bill Bryson approaches poetry at times. David Quammen may not be the world's greatest prose stylist, but he is always interesting. You should of course buy and devour *The Best American Travel Writing*, published annually.

Is your ability to write really important? Of course. Does dribbling count in basketball? However, there is an inverse correlation between the interest-level of the content and the quality of writing required for the content to be marketable. Even if I were only semi-literate (and some think I am) I could sell the story of my secret torrid affair with the First Lady in the Lincoln bedroom—with the Secret Service watching—and no publisher would care a fig about my grammar. Hey, it worked for Monica.

Short of those kinds of topics, yes, you must be a good writer. By the way, Shakespeare spelled his name 9 different ways during his lifetime and John Keats was dyslexic. So don't get hung up on the trivial parts of writing. The important aspects of style are:

  • authenticity;

  • honesty;

  • specificity; and

  • directness.

Finally, although grammar is a part of writing, it's not the most important part or the part that requires the most knowledge, power or skill, nor the one that gets the most applause, nor the one that

wins the game. Don't confuse good grammar with good writing, although the two are always found in the same place.

CAN I PUBLISH THE SAME STORY ON MY WEB SITE AND IN A PRINT MAGAZINE?

> *"I will be* au pairing *in Germany for one year while I save money for a backpacking excursion. I plan to write a biweekly column while there about my experiences as an American girl in Germany and as an* au pair. *My intention is to publish the column on my own web site and at the same time publish it in various magazines and newspapers. Can I do that?"*

It depends on whether or not you keep control of your e-rights in any contract that you sign. If you license exclusive e-rights along with print rights to your material, publishing in both places would be a violation of your contract.

However, I'm not sure you should be looking only at print magazines and newspapers as paying outlets. Lots of web sites need lots of copy these days. Take a look at the *Writer's Online Marketplace* book from the Writer's Digest. There is also the *Internet*

Media Directory from Bacon's, a comprehensive source particularly rich in news-related sites. Although a yearly subscription is $300, it is available at many libraries.

It's possible that an even more fruitful area would be the teen market: As an *au pair*, you are probably a teen or in your early 20s. Teen 'zines publish a lot of PEs or personal experience, first-person stories. You have a unique slant: How is a teen's life in Germany different than in America? How does American culture influence German teens? How are German teens' attitudes toward sex, parents, education, dating, etc. different than their American counterparts'? What elements of the German teen scene would American teens be fascinated to hear about?

So, my advice: Take a digital video and still camera with you and a laptop. Have the ability to upload jpegs and mpegs (lots of 'em) along with your stories to the web and then get in touch with web sites that are travel- and teen-related—preferably both. Since you will have the ability to upload daily and weekly, this sort of project should find a home on a teen-related web site. Also, make it as interactive as possible: allow teens to ask you questions, suggest places for you to go and things to write about and photograph, conduct interactive interviews, set up chat groups, etc.

Remember, newspapers superceded magazines because newspapers were daily. Radio superceded newspapers because of the human voice. TV superceded radio because of the moving image. And the Internet is superceding TV because of interactivity. Explore and exploit that facility.

"For today's information entrepreneur, publishing a book is part of the package, like business cards."

CHAPTER EIGHT

BOOK WRITING: THE ROAD TO CREDIBILITY

- How to Write a Book Proposal and Query
- Hidden Freelance Market: Book Packagers
- Agents: How to Find, Use and Feed Them
- When Do You Need an Agent?
- Should You Use a Literary Submission Service?
- What You Should Know about Copyediting
- I've Got a Book Idea. Now What?
- Is Self-Publishing the New Industry Model?

Credibility? Sure. Has Barnes and Noble opened any new "periodical superstores" in your area lately? When's the last time you got something off the "magazine shelf" in your home? Do you own stock in a company named "Magazines-a-Million"?

This chapter is last because the logical outcome of your ability to research, write and publish as a freelancer will be the application of those skills to a longer format, one that has the potential to pay you more, to open more doors and, I bet, to give you a powerful and unique satisfaction about your craft and yourself.

Given the proliferation of information about self-publishing and self-marketing, the ease of gathering research on the Internet, and the public's unslaked thirst for information about every aspect of their complex lives, it's only a matter of time before you, the successful freelancer, are talking about perfect binding and paper stock with someone who has the look of ink in their eyes.

HOW TO WRITE A SUCCESSFUL NONFICTION BOOK PROPOSAL AND QUERY

Congrats: you've done the research, planning and written some chapters. Now, is anyone interested in publishing your masterpiece-in-waiting? There's only one way to find out: a book proposal, an essential marketing tool. It should be given the spit and polish that will enable it to make a quiet but definitive announcement: "Herein lies the work of a professional." That's your first goal in writing a book proposal: to look like a professional so that you avoid the slush pile—that stack of unwanted book proposals and manuscripts which is large and growing larger. It is currently estimated that writers send in approximately 10 million submissions each year. That was not a typo: 10 million.

However, both large and small publishers combined print about 120,000 books per year. That wasn't a typo either. Some quick math suggests that your literary effort has a .012 chance of being accepted and published. And you thought getting a date in high school was tough.

How do you increase those pathetically miniscule odds? Simple: Find out what they want, then give it to them—good. The first step in doing so is to request a copy of submission guidelines from the agent, agency or publisher that you are targeting. The discussion of queries and book proposals that follows should be considered only general guidelines, because each publisher or agency may have its own set of specific requirements outlined in their submission guidelines, from the font they want you to use in your letter, to the order of materials in a submission packet. Know before you blow it.

Next, make absolutely sure that the agent or publisher wishes to see books in your genre or topic area. Surprisingly, publishers and agents continue to bemoan the number of manuscripts and proposals they receive for perfectly fine books in categories they do not handle. Lastly, determine if the agent or publisher wishes to see a query first, then the submission packet. Some prefer to skip the query and want your entire proposal.

Query Letter

Your query letter will probably be about 3–4 pages long. The most accepted format for the query letter is paper. Email is sometimes acceptable but a fax is almost always unacceptable.

Your query letter should include these components:

- Brief statement of purpose. In other words, why you are contacting this person.

- Synopsis. Also called a summary. It is a 300- to 500-word condensation of the entire work written in the objective third-person (do not try to hype your work). Remember Cliff's Notes that you cribbed from in school? Like that. If you've never written a synopsis before, get help, practice, and show yours around before sending it in. Writing a good synopsis requires special skill and practice. But sure to get them both.

- Genre. Never say yours is a unique genre that can't be classified. Agents and publishers must know how to market and sell your work within established categories of the book industry.

- Brief writing biography. In no more than a paragraph, establish your writing background and expertise for authoring this book.

- Marketing info. Here you must demonstrate that you have done your homework. How many books similar to yours are currently in print? How are those books selling? How will your book be like those others? How will yours be unique? Emphasis on this last one: Your work must offer some new value that will make readers cough up the cash.

- Graphics, illustrations, photographs. These not only increase the value of your book, they also make it more complicated and expensive to produce. Indicate any of these elements that are a part of your book, their number and size, and in what format you will provide them: line art, transparencies, electronic images, etc.

- Copyediting. Indicate if your book has already been professionally copyedited and, if not, your plans for doing so. Agents do not provide this service.

- SASE. If you don't want your materials back and aren't including a SASE for that reason, be sure to say that your materials are disposable.

If your query is successful, or if you have targeted someone who accepts unsolicited submissions, you are now ready to compile what is usually considered the traditional book proposal.

Nonfiction Book Proposal

- Cover page. A block containing your personal information (name, address, contact info) goes in the upper left. In the page's center goes your book's title in all caps, with any subtitle double-spaced below it in caps and lower case. Your by-line is double-spaced beneath the title and "by" is in lower case. Ten lines below your byline comes the word length: "Approximate length: ____ words" rounded off to the nearest thousand. Nothing else should appear on this page.

- Writing biography. Approximately one single-spaced page providing more background than in your query letter. Highlight your strongest points: previous publications, especially books; professional experience related to your book's subject; relevant professional affiliations.

- Table of contents and chapter outlines. How you format the chapter outlines (as descriptive paragraphs, bulleted points, numbered outline) is far less important than the meat. Use 100 to 200 words to give a clear picture of the compelling content in each chapter.

- Sample chapters. Most want to see at least two chapters, and some prefer sequential chapters, not random ones.

- Graphics, illustrations, photographs. In addition to what was submitted in the query, include specific location in the sample chapters of any artwork.

- Marketing. This section should represent considerable research and thought on your part. There is no faking it here. Either you've got a good concept or you don't. The only question is whether or not you write this section well enough to convince someone else that this book can be marketed successfully. Its parts:
  1. Logline. Distill the concept into a *TV Guide*-type of sentence. Example: "*Band of Angels* tells the inspiring, sometimes horrifying story of American WWII nurs-

es in the Philippines captured by the Japanese—the only group of women ever held as prisoners of war."

2. Rationale. Why this book is important and to whom it is important.

3. Market position. Why this book is different from and better than all other books in print on this subject. Avoid saying "there are no books that compare to this one." First, it's likely to be untrue, therefore indicating poor market research. If such a statement is true and there are no other books written on the topic, maybe there's a good reason—lack of consumer interest.

4. Competition. A list and brief annotation of competing titles (author, publication date, a descriptive sentence).

• Ancillary materials. Although not required, these can be helpful: They include a meaningful introduction, preface or foreword written by you or by someone with significant credentials. Having the right person write front matter not only will give your work more credibility, it will also show your willingness to help market your work. And don't forget pre-publication reviews and endorsements.

Put It All Together

Assemble your materials just as you would the pages in your book, with cover page on top and ending with your sample chapters. Binding methods vary according to agency and company; check their guidelines. Most prefer large butterfly clips or loose pages in a box. Place all materials either in a pocket folder (no fasteners or rings) or in an appropriate-sized manuscript box or paper box, according to how many pages you have. Affix a plain white label on the folder or box that contains (centered) your book's title and your byline.

Play the Waiting Game

Send it, forget it. The tendency will be to have a letdown after a large project is finally in the mail. So you probably won't get any heavy-duty creative work done for a few days. Be prepared to fill your time with other essential duties: organizing, researching, writing follow-up letters on other projects. Keep your writing business moving forward and, above all, don't be a pest. Forget about your submission for four to eight weeks before you think about bugging someone about it.

How to Bullet-Proof Your Book Proposal

In case you haven't had your daily dose of reality yet, take a swig of this: *Editors and agents will look for reasons to reject your submission.* Sounds cruel but it's natural: You've got 25 manuscripts sitting on your desk and one hour to sort through them. Such initial sorting must done by applying two threshold criteria: those proposals that followed submission guidelines and those that didn't; those that look professional and those that don't. According to agents and editors I've worked with, the following are the lowest-common denominators for getting past those hurdles. Clear them and at least your work has a chance of being read.

- It looks like a proposal. Agents and editors have read thousands of them. As a result, they have a clear set of expectations about what a professionally-done proposal looks like on the outside, regardless of what is on the inside.

- It's addressed to the right place. In other words, the writer has bothered to consult a copy of the pertinent guidelines or has

WRITER'S TOOLBOX
RESOURCES FOR YOUR BOOK PROPOSAL

Web

- Write a Nonfiction Book Proposal:
  http://co.essortment.com/bookproposal_rjwi.htm

- *How to Write a Non Fiction Book Proposal That Sells* by Anne Wayman, PDF (e-book):
  www.booklocker.com/books/24.html

- The Book Proposal Series:
  http://store.yahoo.com/youcanwrite/thebookpropgroup.html

- Preparing a Book Proposal:
  http://uk.cambridge.org/information/authors/proposal.htm

- How to Write a Great Nonfiction Book Proposal:
  www.shepardagency.com/writing_proposals.html

- *The Nonfiction Book Proposal: Put Your Best Foot Forward* by Patricia L. Fry:
  www.writing-world.com/publish/proposal.html

Print

- *The Fast Track on How to Write a Nonfiction Book Proposal.* Stephen Blake Mettee.

- *How to Write a Book Proposal.* Michael Larson.

- *Nonfiction Book Proposals Anyone Can Write.* 2nd edition. Elizabeth Lyon.

- *Write the Perfect Book Proposal: 10 That Sold and Why.* Jeff Herman, Deborah M. Adams used an up-to-date directory to determine the correct person to contact, the categories being accepted, and the procedure for submissions. Failure to follow their rules can doom your chances of even being read. After all, if you can't comply with these simple instructions, what's it going to be like to work with you over an extended period of time on a book project?

- It doesn't contain red flags. Such as misspellings, bad grammar, incorrect word use. If the writer didn't bother to get it right here, he or she probably can't be trusted in book-length form to be accurate, fair and honest.

HIDDEN FREELANCE MARKET: BOOK PACKAGERS

Want to get your first book credit without lots of rejections? Many book writers got their first byline in the clandestine world of book packagers, one of the least-known markets for freelancers. Two of publishing's dirty little secrets are that not all big-name authors write the books with their names on them, and not all big-name publishers design, create and edit the books with their imprint on them.

Ask R.L. Stine when was the last time he wrote one of his best-selling scary books for kids. Likewise, a book packager is an individual or company that publishers turn to when they want to outsource the design, writing and editing of a book or series of books. Book packagers are "ghost publishers" and function like "ghost writers" except with different responsibilities.

Book packagers most often focus on research-intensive, graphic-intensive or highly-technical works that require special expertise, for example: *Wild and Beautiful Glacier* (photo book); *Word 2000: A Professional Approach* (for the popular Microsoft program); *New England Furniture* (written for a museum). A book packager's projects may also include book series, since big publishers are set up mainly to work with single authors. Example: *Concise*

Dictionary of Scientific Biography, 2nd Edition. Don't knock it. Maybe George Kuran Reference Books (a book packager) is hiring for the 3rd Edition right now.

Why Do They Need Freelancers?

For the same reason that publishers need writers and editors: to get the job done. A publisher usually outsources work to a book packager because the publisher lacks the available in-house talent to do the planning, research, writing and editing. The book packager either has these resources in place or hires freelancers to do it. The packager usually pays freelancers a flat fee based upon the kind of work (writing, research, editing, proofing, indexing) and the amount of it that you perform. Your contract terms are typically negotiated up front.

Getting in Touch with Book Packagers

As usual, you should first research the book packager to determine protocol and preferences. Whether you send a postal letter or an email, it will most likely include:

- a description of yourself as a writer and your availability. Are you currently writing full-time for a living? If not, how many hours per week are you available?

- a list of your writing credits. Tell a little (one or two sentences) about each.

- a sample of your relevant clips. Not every clip from your portfolio, but only those that pertain to the subject matter that the packager specializes in. If the packager works in several genres, use a variety of clips to show your versatility.

- all of your relevant contact info: ground, electronic, cellular.

There are two ways to find book packagers. In the current *Writer's Market* from Writer's Digest Books and by typing "book producer" or "book packager" as a search phrase into an Internet search engine.

LITERARY AGENTS: HOW TO FIND, USE AND FEED THEM

These secrets about agents will help you land one who can make your writing life a whole lot easier and more rewarding. Agents are a good and necessary thing if you plan to make your living writing books, screenplays, teleplays or other major formats. They enable you to write while they go about trying to sell your work to the right people at the highest price and the most favorable terms.

Besides that primary role, agents can also be an invaluable source of business and professional advice, caretakers of the sensitive soul, and even the warden who can enforce the rules and provide, ahem, motivation to do what you should be doing. The agent is also your business partner, reviewing royalty statements and monitoring licensees' marketing of your work. That is, if they are a good agent. Here are some recommendations on separating those who are from the lazy, unethical, uninterested—and generally to be avoided.

Finding the Right Literary Agent for You

First, virtually all literary agents are book agents or agents for manuscripts such as screenplays or television scripts. Very few represent short stories, articles, poetry, greeting cards or essays. So start your agent search (see this chapter's "Writer's Toolbox: Agent Resources") only after you've either completed your manuscript or you're at a point where you can write a winning proposal that includes sample sections. Never submit anything less than your best work to an agent. Most surveys indicate that literary agents reject 98 percent of everything they receive.

Although they are hard to get, a literary agent is becoming increasingly necessary for those wishing to sell to large publishing firms and production companies, who often will not consider unagented manuscripts. So your first job will be to identify a large group of agents who specialize in your subject matter.

Pre-Screening

Your next step is a commonsense one: contact fellow writers, editors or publishers who produce the kind of works you'll be writing and ask for recommendations of agents. If you belong to any relevant professional organizations, its members may have recommendations. Same for creative writing teachers. You will have narrowed your search to agents who are having success in your field and who have managed to establish good enough professional relationships that others feel comfortable recommending them to potential clients like you. Lists of agents such as those in *Literary Market Place* can help you follow up this initial list with more detailed information.

Large or Small?

What about the block-buster, big-name agent who just landed an umpteen-million dollar contract for a client? Probably will not be a fruitful first contact for the unpublished book writer. Even if you make it past the mega-agent's receptionist, do you really want to be the newest pony in a such a luminous stable of fellow scribes? How much attention would you get? You'll likely end up with mega-agent's new assistant fresh out of grad school. You may be better off with a smaller agent, eager and hungry, who will go the extra mile for you because you represent an important part of his or her business.

Personal Chemistry

When negotiations start and there's money on the table, you need to be in a relationship of mutual trust and respect. If you're looking for a first agent, your tendency may be to be grateful to anyone who will take you on. That could backfire if the chemistry isn't right to begin with. Try to find people you really like. When things get tense—and they will—you'll need a reserve of goodwill.

What do you do when the agent you desire wants nothing to do with you? Don't despair. Keep sending your work to publishers. Play the rejection game. Then, when you do get an offer from a publisher, return to the agent of your choice and put the offer on the table. It'll be one he or she can't refuse: a commission for taking you on.

How to Approach an Agent

Once you've narrowed your list of agent prospects, it's time to follow the etiquette of contacting him or her for the first time.

Use the Mail

That's right: put down that phone and walk away from the fax machine. Get your letter or email ready (not your manuscript) by describing your project and yourself much as you might to an editor to whom you're trying to sell your work. Don't go over two pages. Write or email the agent by name.

You can contact as many agents on your list as are appropriate, just don't overdo it. And make sure that each of the agents on the list is equally desirable to you. This isn't like applying to college where you have a few "reach" schools and a few "sure things." If you say yes to an agent, then get a call from a more desirable one, you may not sleep well that night.

What about Exclusivity?

There are generally two situations in which exclusivity comes into play. First, if you've met an agent, hit it off well and discussed your work, it would be of your benefit to follow up on this wonderful situation by offering an exclusive read of your work. Second, if you've been recommended to an agent by another of the agent's clients, by an editor the agent works with, or by another agent, this is again one of those special situations where exclusivity would benefit both parties.

Of course, if you already have a contract that promises an agent an exclusive look at your next work, you must abide by that, in the same way that if you promise an agent an exclusive read, professional ethics demand you keep that promise.

What about Emails?

Used to be *verboten*, but now they're as common as ego trips at a writers' conference. A majority of today's agents and agencies have welcomed the efficiency of email queries and opened up their inboxes. A few tips:

1. Avoid attachments. Usually not opened for security reasons. Save those until invited.

2. If you send multiple email queries, treat each as a separate letter with only one name in the "To" line.

3. Include a non-spam subject line with the words "query," "book proposal," "looking for representation" or something similar.

4. Don't confuse instant messaging with email.

5. Don't refer an agent to your web site to "find out more."

Compose Your Letter

Your letter of introduction should contain three parts:

- Part 1: Introduce yourself as a writer, giving a brief history of your published work, focusing on your books. No credits? Don't try to fake it. Focus on your professional experience that gives you the needed credibility to write this book.

- Part 2: Describe your book or script in detail. Use six to eight paragraphs: introduce its topic, unique approach, and its overall content. Writers of dramatic works call these summaries, treatments or "pages." Book writers call them synopses or summaries.

- Part 3: Sign off. Simply ask if they would like to take a look at it. If so, then they can contact you at....

It's fine to include the summary, treatment, synopsis or whatever you call Part 2 as a separate document and combine Parts 1 and 3 as a cover letter. It's also usually OK to discuss two projects in one contact, but never more.

Then wait six to eight weeks. Don't make any contact before that. Hopefully you remembered to cover all your bases by including a SASE for those agents who prefer to write, an email address for the Internet-enabled, and a phone number for the chatty.

Beware

Since you conducted a pre-screening though other writers, editors and publishers, you won't likely encounter any of the below. If you do, cross these agents off your list, immediately:

- A fee to read your work

- A fee to take your submission

- A requirement for you to sign a written release

WRITER'S TOOLBOX
AGENT RESOURCES

There are excellent online and offline sources for literary agents. After all, they're experts in marketing, right?

Online

- Association of Authors' Representatives, Inc. *www.aar-online.org*.
The premiere online resource for literary agents. The AAR was formed in 1991 through the merger of the Society of Authors' Representatives and the Independent Literary Agents Association. Members are screened, must meet eligibility requirements and pledge to abide by the Association's code of ethics.

- Literary Market Place.
www.literarymarketplace.com/lmp/us/index_us.asp.
The online version of the standard reference book.

- WritersNet. *www.writers.net/agents.html*.
A searchable database of 357 American agents and agencies. These agents are not screened and some may charge a reading fee.

Print

- *Literary Market Place.* The industry bible.

- *2003 Guide to Literary Agents.* Annual edition; be sure you purchase the latest.

- *Writer's Digest Guide to Literary Agents.* From Writer's Digest Books.

- *Writer's Guide to Book Editors, Publishers, and Literary Agents, 2003–2004: Who They Are! What They Want! and How to Win Them Over.* Annual edition; be sure you purchase the latest.

More Tips on Getting Your First Agent

OK, you're alone on your mountaintop writing away. No agents know who you are. Worse, no agents want to know who you are. What to do? First, stay on the mountaintop and keep writing. You'll see why in Tip 1 below. Next, pick up the mountaintop's phone and boot up the email; it's time to network and sell—yourself. If you got problems with that, stop reading here and, please, enjoy the rest of your life.

Tip 1: Keep Writing!

Agents want to see a fountain of prose, a cornucopia of words, a blizzard of pages. The reason is obvious: the more you write, the more they have to sell. Prodigious output also indicates prodigious seriousness. It marks you as a writer with legs. The real thing. A steady income for you both.

Tip 2: Find Friends

Get to know the people who know agents. Get plugged into the network. Nurture your relationships with producers, editors, actors, publishers and anyone else in your industry who works with agents.

Tip 3: Win a Literary Prize

Any prize will do, but the more notable and competitive, the better. Take that award and use it self-promotionally as a reason to contact your dream agent.

Tip 4: Keep Dreaming

Keep reading the trades in your industry and keep track of the agents who are doing the kind of deals with the kind of literary properties you are producing. Don't get stuck on one agent or agency. Keep your list active and keep submitting your query to the new names that pop up on it.

WHEN DO I NEED AN AGENT?

"I have enough material for a book. Is writing the first few chapters then looking for an agent the best way to go, or should I write the whole book? Also, how much does an agent get? Where can I find one?"

Since this is nonfiction, I think you should do both: (1) Write the first two or three chapters, then send them along with a professionally done book proposal to an agent or a publisher. (2) Continue writing the rest of the book as you continue to look for an agent or publisher. If a publisher offers you a deal on your book, at that point you won't have any problem getting an agent, I assure you. (Submitting fiction to an agent almost always means the entire manuscript.)

How much does an agent get? Usually around 15 percent on books, 10 percent on scripts. But the most important thing for you right now is to write a great book that people will want to read. Where can you find agents? Tons of lists online and off (see "Writer's Toolbox: Agent Resources"). Read the descriptions in these listings closely to find one near you, someone willing to work with a writer at your level, and someone with experience representing books and scripts in your area (medical, diet, self-help, biographies, etc.).

A question you didn't ask but implied: Do you really need an agent? The answer is no, not right now. What you need first is a great idea, then execute it well on a topic that fulfills a clearly defined reader need. One of the crucial elements of any book proposal is the "Market Analysis" portion. In it, you detail what other works are extant in this field and how yours will be different. Without demonstrable knowledge of the major works in your field and without a different slant for yours, the proposal is dead in the water, regardless of whether you send it to an agent or directly to the publisher.

WRITER'S TOOLBOX
MANUSCRIPT SUBMISSION SERVICES

- AuthorLink. *www.authorlink.com/asublist.html*
  The site's description reads: "The award-winning rights marketplace where editors and agents buy and sell unpublished and published manuscripts and screenplays. Providing the serious writer with access and exposure to the broadest range of legitimate publishing professionals." In business six years. The above link is to the FAQ page.

- Publishers and Agents. *www.publishersandagents.net*
  Provides submission services for book authors and screenplay writers to agents, publishers, producers; also provides submission help to columnists looking for syndication.

- Writer's Relief, Inc. *www.wrelief.com*
  In addition to submissions, also provides proofreading, copyediting and electronic keying of texts.

So, you don't have to have an agent. But is one recommended? Yes. They have contacts with publishers and want to help you make your book as saleable as possible. A reputable agent will be honest with you about your book's merits and shortcomings. Listen closely. Like a personal lawyer in a divorce case, they fight for your best interests in contract negotiations.

SHOULD I USE A MANUSCRIPT SUBMISSION SERVICE?

"I've seen a web site where, for a fee, they will submit your work to appropriate agents, even write your cover letter or query letter for you. What do you think? Worth it?"

Quite possibly a submission service is right for you. I know of three such services, the oldest and best regarded being *www.authorlink.com*, a division of Ingram, the world's largest book wholesaler and a major player in the book publishing industry. Hey, if you can't trust Ingram....

Submission services normally evaluate your manuscript first and decide if they can represent it as is or, for an additional fee, perhaps assign you to a book doctor to upgrade your offering into something they can represent. Once the manuscript is tuned up, the service taps into its databases to select appropriate agents, producers, publishers or whatever your work requires. The service then packages your work with your cover letter/query letter (or will write it for you for another fee), and sends it out to the targets.

Unless the service maintains good relationships by sending out useable material and behaving in a professional manner, it won't be in business long; so there is a definite incentive for them to offer legitimate services to you and quality work to its buying outlets. Fees generally range from $50 to $150, depending upon the package of services that you purchase.

WHAT ARE THE DIFFERENT TYPES OF BOOK EDITING?

"I'm confused and hope you can help me. I'm preparing my first book for submission and have been reading about all the different phases of getting it ready. But I'm not exactly clear on the differences between proofreading, copyediting and content editing? Which comes first?"

Wise question, especially the last part about which comes first. You are exactly right in that there is a sequence that must be followed to prepare your book manuscript (or any other manuscript) for successful submission:

1. Content editing. This comes first and refers to major content revisions (additions and deletions) or "substantive editing." Either you or another professional steps back from the com-

pleted work and analyzes it from the point of marketability, focus and completeness. You will be examining the largest elements of your writing: (a) Is the content and tone on target for your intended audience? (b) Does the work as a whole contain a logical, effective developmental structure? (c) Are there important content elements either missing or lacking sufficient development? You may also be challenged to take a closer look at larger stylistic elements such as transitional elements between sections, chapters and paragraphs. Does the text need to be divided up differently or into smaller chunks? It's often said that "good writing is rewriting," and the content-editing process proves it.

2. Copyediting. Now that the author's major tasks of research, structuring, drafting and revising are done, a professional copyeditor takes over to tune up the manuscript: grammar, spelling, consistent adherence to a style sheet or manual, consistency in headings and subheads, sharpening up sentence clarity, reducing wordiness, and other aspects to bring your manuscript to the professional level. Fact checking may be a part of this phase or the next one.

3. Proofreading. Absolutely last and also usually not the author's responsibility. Proofreading is the last chance to catch errors of any sort before the proof goes to the printer, when corrections become truly costly. A work that has been properly proofread contains no typos, misspellings; no inconsistencies in folio, headlines or subheads; no widows or orphans; and so on. In essence, proofreading ensures that the printed page is free of any distraction so that the great content comes shining through with no clouds of credibility-reducing errors.

SHOULD I HIRE A COPY EDITOR?

"I received a book manuscript back from an agent who told me to hire a good copy editor. What does that mean?"

It's probably a personalized rejection slip that means the agent found lots of stylistic and proofreading errors. It also means that other authors who try to do their own copyediting and proofing are likely in for the same sort of letter someday.

Copyediting is a highly specialized subdiscipline in the publication industry. And I assure you that being a decent writer doesn't mean you're worth a flip as a copy editor. To paraphrase Flannery O'Connor: "A good copy editor is hard to find." When you do find one, pay them well and remember their birthday. They can make your manuscript look and read professionally. They can even save your reputation and protect your livelihood. As a result, the good ones are worth their weight in Sharpies.

Unfortunately, many freelancers must sometimes serve as their own copy editor. That means getting a copyediting manual and paying your dues as you learn this very special skill. Turning in a poorly copyedited manuscript usually means automatic rejection. If the mechanics aren't right, how much faith can an editor have in your writing?

Making a Pass

Perhaps the most significant difference between how an untrained person reads and how a proofreader reads is creating a system of "passes." A "pass" is a read-through of the entire work, during which the reader examines a single element, and only that element. For example, when proofreading bluelines (a proof that has been made from final film and from which the actual printing plates will be made), a proofreader might make seven separate passes, examining each of these elements in turn:

- Margins

- Type alignment on facing pages

- Crossovers of type

- Rule lines

- Color placement

- Trim size

- Page blemishes

Professional copy editors and proofreaders have a separate list of passes for each stage of the editing process. In the case of sending a manuscript to an editor for consideration, you may wish to make separate passes for each element you should check: from spelling to punctuation, margins to header consistency, page numbers to page breaks.

More Tips for Self-Copyediting

When you absolutely, positively have to do it yourself:

1. Wait until the very end. Once you begin this stage of copy-editing, try not to do any further revisions, only corrections. Revisions (more writing) inevitably introduce more errors and require another round of proofing.

2. Get someone to help. A friend, spouse or other non-payable help. A second or third pair of eyes can be helpful, even if they are untrained. Tell them to read only for spelling, typos,

punctuation, spacing and other mechanics. At least buy them dinner.

3. Get verbal, get slow. To have any chance of doing it yourself, you have to radically alter the way that you normally read your own work. Now that you're familiar with it, you will automatically correct and insert missing words in your head as your eyes glide over the prose in a rhythm made familiar by having read it numerous times. At this stage, read the work out loud, word-for-word, and slowly.

4. Read out of sequence. Instead of reading pages in their normal sequence, choose pages at random to prevent you from getting into the flow of your writing.

5. Let it get cold. This is hard to make time for and may not always be possible. But keep in mind that the colder the manuscript becomes, the more likely you will be to spot problems.

A WRITER'S GUIDE TO BOOK ROYALTIES

Are you getting paid what you're worth? Can you read a royalty statement? Do you need this handy guide? Answers should be yes, yes, and yes. If you answered no to any of the above, here's what you need to know.

In its simplest terms, a "royalty" is a payment based on the sale of your book, the rights to which you have licensed to a publisher. A "royalty rate" is a figure (usually a percentage) that is multiplied by another number, usually the income received by the publisher from selling your book. The basic formula for calculating your royalty payments is:

Book's selling price x your royalty percentage x number of books sold = your royalty payment

Unfortunately it's a bit more complicated than it appears. Unless you sell directly to the consumer via your own web site or direct mail, the retail price of a sold book is rarely the amount you receive. Instead, you receive:

- Invoice price.
  This is the book price that your royalty is based on when a freight allowance, usually 50 to 75 cents, has been deducted from the cover price. The allowance allows booksellers to recoup the cost of shipping books.

- Wholesale price.
  This is the book price that your royalty is based on when a buyer is given a discount off the cover price. Most sales will be through a discount given to wholesalers and others who purchase your books in quantities. When your book has been sold at a discount, which can be as much as 55–70 percent off the retail or cover price, your royalty will usually be based on that wholesale price.

- Net receipts.
  The figure that your royalty is based on once returns have been accounted for. Publishing is one of the few industries that take back unsold merchandise after it's been distributed. Your royalty calculation may include a "less returns" clause.

- Royalty Escalation.
  Finally, a good thing. Your royalties may begin at 10 percent of the selling price of a hardcover book (less for paperbacks) for

STANDARD ROYALTY RATES†	
Book Type	**Royalty Rate***
Hardcover trade	10% of selling price, escalating to 12.5%, then 15% after 10,000 copies
Trade paperback	6 to 8% of selling price, escalating after 50,000 copies
Mass-market paperback	8% of cover price
Textbook	6 to 15% of net receipts
Professional/Reference book	10 to 15% of net receipts

†Current rates will vary according to your market, level of experience and publisher.
*Note: Rates are for the adult book market. Authors of books for children and young adults typically receive less.

the first 5,000 copies, then escalate to 12.5 percent for the next 5,000 and then jump to 15 percent for copies over 10,000.

- Advance.
An advance is money paid to the writer before the work's publication. Authors are usually advised to get as much advance as possible because of the long delays that can occur between a manuscript's acceptance and its actual publication.

- Recoupable advance.
Ah, the rub. Advances are paid against future royalties. So, if you get a $5,000 advance, you won't see any more money until your book has earned you $5,001 in royalties.

I'VE GOT A GREAT IDEA FOR A BOOK. NOW WHAT?

"I am looking for advice. I have been to over 1,100 places in the Washington, D.C. metro area by public transporta-

WRITER'S TOOLBOX
IVAN HOFFMAN'S WEBSITE

Be sure to check out the web site of Ivan Hoffman, an attorney who specializes in publishing and intellectual property law. It's chock-full of legal advice for writers and publishers. Including:

• A Guide to Royalty Calculations in Book Contracts:
http://www.ivanhoffman.com/royalties.html

• 10 Key Negotiating Points in an Author-Publisher Agreement:
http://www.ivanhoffman.com/points.html
Taken together the 10 points provide another excellent reason to have a book agent by your side.

tion and I am thinking about trying to publish my information and make it into a book. I would like to know what is the best way to go about this task. My dream would be to publish a book which would list the 1,100 things which I have done in the Washington area by public transportation. I would like it to be something simple and something people would like to read. My only problem is I don't know where to go from here. What can you suggest to me?"

First, I think you may have an excellent idea for a book about one of the world's most touristed cities. Second, there's no way of knowing if it is a saleable idea until you complete the most important phase of writing a book proposal: market research. In other words, is there a need for this book?

To answer the essential question, you must ferret out all similar books in print. If there are but a few like yours, you're in great shape. If there are a number of similar ones (and there probably will be), you need to study them to determine how yours will be different—therefore adding a value to yours that the others don't have. Your public transportation angle sounds unique.

Next, write a formal book proposal. There are several acceptable formats. See the guidelines and resources earlier in this chapter. After you've written your proposal, you need to shop it around. There are three options here:

1. Get an agent and let him/her work their publishing contacts to shop it around.

2. Send it yourself to the acquisitions editor at publishing houses that do this kind of book.

3. Self-publish it. With today's e-book publishing, print-on-demand technology and the power of the Internet that allows writers to successfully market their own work, there is no need for you to wait—if you are willing to invest your own money and to outsource all the things royalty publishers do for writers: professional editing, design, printing and distribution. Get your work out there. Get reactions to it. Learn what your readers want and don't want (see the section on self-publishing at the end of this chapter: "Catch the Wave").

DO I NEED A CO-AUTHOR?

"I am trying to write a book about my early childhood. I suffered as a child unspeakable acts of abuse. I want to write it more to open the eyes of our government and its officials about how little punishment is given to persons who abuse others, physically, mentally and sexually. A person gets more time for shoplifting than scarring a child for life. Do I need a co-writer or someone to

help me articulate the abuse and the damage it has caused?"

Sounds like you may be proposing an "as told to" book. In this scenario, a professional writer with credits in this format and subject matter fashions the words and experiences of a nonwriter into a book that has the nonwriter's byline and an "as told to" byline. This is different from a co-authorship, where two professional writers collaborate, each bringing a set of writing, editing and research skills to the joint project. You also may be proposing two books and need to choose which one to write first:

- Book 1: A personal memoir in the vein of Maya Angelou's *I Know Why the Caged Bird Sings*, which brings home the unspeakable horror of such abuse by taking readers on a hellish ride through it themselves. Books in this vein raise the consciousness of readers, help them understand the great damage that can occur, and generate a sense of outrage. The reader can then use the experience of the book to vote, voice opinions, and personally interact with other victims in a more effective, enlightened way.

- Book 2: A nonfiction exposé of the status of child abuse in our culture, the rate at which it happens vs. the reporting of it and, more importantly, a documentation of what happens to the victimizer and the victim in the judicial system.

Both books are substantial undertakings, but are doable if you commit to do the research and writing work necessary. There are also other outlets for the concern, anger and even rage that you expressed: activism in your local community about the legal issues and even volunteer work with the victims of abuse. Working in these areas would also provide a wealth of perspective and experience on which to draw when writing about this topic on a local and national level.

SHOULD I SIGN AN "ALL RIGHTS" BOOK CONTRACT?

"As a first-time book author, should I agree to sign an 'all rights' contract just to be on the safe side and help my work get in print?"

Absolutely not. "All rights" means exactly that, leaving you next to nothing: no reprint or anthology rights, no digital or other media rights. If you do sign it, you'll definitely be on the publisher's safe side, not your own. In fact, unless your contract states that rights revert back to you at some point, an "all rights" contract means that you can never use your work again for many years. Beginning freelancer magazine writers are often forced to accept all-rights magazine contracts in order to nail those crucial first bylines. But I don't think a book author should do so. Your words have value. Some publisher thinks so. You own your words. You should strive—politely, professionally and in good faith—to retain as many of your rights as you can. Yes, first-timers often have to give up more, because the publisher is taking more of a risk on you. But you don't have to give away the farm.

Get an agent, ASAP.

HOW DO I PROTECT MY ARTWORK WHEN SENDING IT IN?

"I want to send in artwork to accompany my book, but I'm hesitant to do so. What if some of it is lost or damaged? What do the pros do?"

Two words: *delivery memo.* A delivery memo is a document that accompanies photographic work that has been commissioned and requested, not over-the-transom materials. The memo specifies the value of each image and places liability for loss or damage on the recipient. However, do not send in artwork unless it has been requested.

If you are submitting original photography, for example, you should include a delivery memo. It lists each image being delivered and contains a notation (number and short description) that corresponds to the same notation on the actual image, the use being made of the images, and any other previous agreements. The delivery memo also asks for a signature from the employee who receives the photography or artwork to ensure all is present and not damaged. A copy of the signed delivery memo is returned to you. All work—photographic and text—is best delivered by a service that tracks and ensures your creations: FedEx, Airborne Express, UPS, etc.

WHAT ARE "GALLEY PROOFS"?

"What's the difference between 'proofs' and 'galley proofs' and such? I hope to get some of them of my books some day. Should I insist on seeing proofs? What are they exactly?"

It's inevitable. If you work hard enough and long enough, it will happen. And getting a set of proofs in your hands is a glorious day. Your book is finally a reality like it's never been before.

Before your book is typeset, you're likely to receive a *design proof*: samples of your pages indicating how major design elements are being used: fonts, leading, styles of titles and headings, and other aspects of an interior design. After your text is typeset, it is returned as *first proofs* or *galley proofs* (named after the long sheets of paper that books used to be printed on). Galley proofs from magazines usually omit artwork, captions and other graphical elements. However, galley proofs from book publishers today closely resemble the finished product. As they are completed, galley proofs are usually provided by publishers in batches to authors and editors so that proofreading can commence. *Second proofs* are a follow-up set of pages that contain the requested revisions as well as all art elements. These proofs are what the published page will look like. After these page proofs are completed by the author and editors, *printer's proofs* are sent by the typesetter to the printer. In turn, the printer makes a last set of proofs—*film proofs* or *bluelines* (because they are usually printed in blue ink). Film proofs are sent by the printer back to the publisher for one last look. If an error or problem (page smudge, incorrect page number) isn't caught here, it will appear in the published form. Bluelines are not meant for editing; only for you to check the printer's interpretation of your margins and other page specs.

CATCH THE WAVE: IS SELF–PUBLISHING THE NEW MODEL FOR THE BOOK INDUSTRY?

It is certainly "a" new model, and it also seems to be part of the revolution currently underway in book publishing. To wit:

- R.R. Bowker, the official registry for ISBNs and unofficial registry for publishers, is currently averaging about 7,000 new publishers a year with a current total of around 50,000 publishers.

- In 1994, Barnes and Noble, America's largest bookstore chain, reported that the top 10 publishers accounted for 75 percent of its total book sales. Five years later, those same top 10 publishers accounted for only 46 percent of BN's sales.

- Today, the majority of books are being sold by independent publishers, self-publishers and small presses.

- Indeed, 53 percent of America's books are not sold in bookstores.

These facts suggest a seismic shift during the last decade in the publishing world, of which self-publishing is a part. Consider, for instance, recent self-published successes like *Erroneous Zones*, *The Celestine Prophecy*, *Who Moved My Cheese?* and *The One-Minute Manager*, all of which trace their tradition back to the 1970s self-published phenom, *What Color Is Your Parachute?*

Ardent self-publishers are quick to point to a literary heritage rich with kindred successes, from Mark Twain's *Huckleberry Finn*, which critics sometimes call The Great American Novel, to Walt Whitman's *Leaves of Grass*, Edgar Rice Burroughs' *Tarzan of the Apes*, James Joyce's *Ulysses* (considered one of the greatest novels in English) even *Robert's Rules of Order* and a Cornell University English professor's small tome, *The Elements of Style*. The list trundles on.

Also important: Our society has evolved into a group of readers perpetually hungry for information, especially specialized information packaged in books, tapes, e-books, e-zines, CDs, pdf special reports, and other formats that large publishers and their large economic models have had difficulty responding to.

Nature abhors a vacuum, especially an information vacuum. The giant sucking sound you hear is that of small presses, independent publishers, self-publishers and university presses rushing in to fill the void.

Should You Catch the Wave?

It's hard to ignore the advantages of self-publishing. One of the movement's champions, Dan Poynter, touts them loud and often in his various publications and appearances:

- Money.

Royalty publishers typically offer 6 percent to 15 percent in royalties. Being your own publisher will get you 35 to 40 percent after discounting, even 100 percent if you sell directly from your own web site. Don't have your own web site? Then you must not Yahoo! The cost for having your own basic web site ranges from $0 to $25 a month these days, including hosting. Build-it-yourself web tools have become as common as pop-up ads on AOL.

- Speed.
Why bite your nails during a one- to two-year production cycle when an industrious self-publisher can have a new work out in three to four months?

- Control.
From your book's title to how it is marketed. One of the big myths about big royalty publishers is that they promote the books they buy. Fact is, they do little promotion for the vast majority of books on their list, and the 80–20 rule is very much at play: 80 percent of the marketing resources are spent on 20 percent of the books. The rest are left to find their own audience. If you do rise from the midlist by virtue of luck or your own promotional bootstraps, then you might get some marketing attention. Without your own marketing or the publishing company's, your book is likely to become a statistic: only 1 in 10 books ever make back their advance. Believe it: "Promote or perish."

- Acceptance.
With 10 million manuscripts being submitted to publishers each year, even getting a reading is difficult. Calculating the odds of acceptance requires a Pentagon supercomputer.

- Personal growth.

  As a successful self-publisher, you must go beyond your writing skills to learn virtually every aspect of the book industry, from marketing to prepress, printing to distribution networks. With that knowledge comes greater control over your book's destiny and your own.

Self-Publishing Self-Assessment

While the rewards of self-publishing are tempting, the personal commitment and sacrifice to realize those rewards deserve your careful cogitation:

1. Are you prepared to be an independent businessperson?

   Here's where the "publisher" part of the phrase kicks in. A publisher makes a significant financial commitment to something that may or may not pay off. Got an extra $10,000 to play with? How's your 401(k) doing? You must be capable of casting a cold eye on what the reading public wants and compare that in an impartial way to your own manuscript.

   Being a publisher also means doing work you've probably never done before: soliciting and choosing bids for cover and interior designs, printer quotes, wholesaler and distributor contracts, maybe even a publicist, if you've got the bucks, and certainly becoming your own tireless promoter. Each of those professions represents a world of knowledge—and jargon—that is likely uncharted territory for you. Are you ready to doff the writer's mantle and put on your business suit?

2. Have you targeted a sufficient niche or vertical market?

   One important economic reality is that, unless you are Oprah or Budweiser, you probably don't have the resources to conduct an effective mass-market promotion and marketing campaign. You will be stretched enough to reach your

WRITER'S TOOLBOX
SELF-PUBLISHER LIBRARY

Still not sober? Well, then, you just might be self-publisher material. Since you are reading a self-published book right now, let me share with you the online and print materials that have helped guide me through this long, wonderful, stressful, scary, enlightening, joyful, frustrating, life-altering, mind-bending, soul-shaking and genuinely fun experience that has resulted in getting *The Freelance Success Book* into your hands:

Online

- Brian Jud:
  www.bookmarketingworks.com/toc.htm
  Warm up your printer and put in a fresh cartridge: You'll want to print out every one of the 40+ articles on how to market your self-published book.

- Moira Allen:
  www.writing-world.com/selfpub/FAQ.html
  www.writing-world.com/selfpub/basics.html
  Moira's site contains one of the largest collections of authoritative articles for writers on the web. In addition to featuring Brian Jud as a regular columnist, she also has authored an extensive section of how-to articles for the self-publisher. Great free newsletter.

- Pneuma Books:
  www.pneumabooks.com
  Brian Taylor has succeeded in creating a complete online resource for self-publishers. This is the only place I've found on the web where the self-publisher can learn the inside scoop on design, layout and printing issues. Pneuma also offers a free manuscript critique and a free 15-minute consultation on whether or not you should self-publish your book. Don't miss their free e-book, "Smart Start Kit":
  www.pneumabooks.com/smart.pdf

continued...

...continued

- Wise Owl Books:
www.wiseowlbooks.com/publish/articles_on_book_publishin.html
Mark Ortman is another leader of the self-publishing movement, and this web site contains not only excellent articles but also a long list of valuable links.

- Para Publishing:
www.parapub.com
Lots of free goodies on Dan Poynter's site and invaluable links to reports, lists and books. Great free newsletter.

Print

- *1001 Ways to Market Your Books.* John Kremer, 5th edition, 1998. Open Horizons. Considered the bible for self-publishers learning how to promote and market their works.

- *The Complete Guide to Self-Publishing: Everything You Need to Know to Write, Publish, Promote and Sell Your Own Book.* Tom and Marilyn Ross, 4th edition, 2002. Writer's Digest Books. If the Rosses don't get you motivated, check your pulse.

- *Jump Start Your Book Sales.* Marilyn and Tom Ross, 1999. Communication Creativity. The dynamic duo seems to know every trick. You'll learn something helpful on each page.

- *The Self-Publishing Manual: How to Write, Print and Sell Your Own Book.* Dan Poynter, 13th edition, 2002. Para Publishing. One of the tribal elders and a pioneer of contemporary self-publishing.

- *A Simple Guide to Self-Publishing.* Mark Ortman, 3rd edition. Wise Owl Books. Don't miss his *Simple Guide to Marketing Your Book*, too.

smaller, targeted market. You must know that there are channels to your market and that your potential sales are large enough to support your book and your family.

3. Are you willing to stop writing for a substantial portion of the day and to start marketing?

   That's right: Once you've typed "The End" or ###, the fun has just begun. Unless you're willing to learn how to market and promote your book, then spend 50 to 75 percent of your day doing so, you may want to go back to being a wage slave.

4. Can you sell at least 1,000 books?

   Seriously. You'll run out of family and friends anywhere from 50 to 100 copies. And now your credit card—which you used to pay your copy editor, indexer, designer and printer—is racking up interest about 19.6 percent faster than you could ever make new friends or family. Most self-publishers do an initial print run of 1,000 to 3,000, which equals a total production cost of $5,000 to $10,000. If you net $5.00 per book you sell, you've got to push 1,000 units to breakeven on a $5,000 investment; twice that for the more common $10,000 investment.

5. Can you sell direct?

   Because that's where the profit margin is. Wholesalers, distributors, bookstores, Amazon, UPS—all take a cut, often leaving you with a single-digit profit percentage. If you have your own web site and do your own picking and packing, now you can cut out the hungry hands in the middle and, maybe, make back your investment.

*"The two most engaging powers
of an author are, to make new things
familiar, and familiar things new."*
—Dr. Samuel Johnson

A WRITER'S GLOSSARY

ABC. The Audit Bureau of Circulations. This is a quasi-independent organization that verifies the circulation claims of its member publications. But since the members are the source of its revenue, ABC is usually reluctant to be too harsh on errant members. Still, it is the most reliable audit service in America for determining the circulation numbers of most consumer periodicals. The bigger the circ, the bigger your paycheck should be.

Advance. This is one you hope to hear a lot: a sum of money given to an author (usually books) by the publisher prior to publication. Authors are advised to get as much of an advance as possible due to the long delay between acceptance and actual publication.

Advertorial. Also called a "puff piece." This is an advertising feature that promotes a person, group or business. According to ASME guidelines (American Society of Magazine Editors), advertorials and special ad sections should be made distinct from the editorial of a magazine or newspaper by virtue of: (1) being labeled as "Advertising" at the bottom and/or top of each page; (2) printed in a different type face than editorial text; (3) be graphically distinct from editorial design. Provided these guidelines are followed, there's nothing wrong with writing advertorials and getting paid for them so long as no one attempts to fool the reader as to what they really are.

Agent. The person who serves as liaison between the writer and everyone else: publishers, producers, even editors. The agent is responsible primarily for selling the literary work, for which he/she receives a 10 to 15 percent commission from the advance and royalty.

All rights. A contract that leaves the author very little of them: no reprint or anthology rights, no digital or other media rights. In fact, unless your contract states that rights revert back to you at some point, an "all rights" contract means that you can't use your work again for a long, long time. "All rights" contracts are common for many smaller departments and fillers, where your chances of reselling are slim anyhow. Beginning freelancers are often forced to accept all-rights contracts in order to nail those crucial first bylines. Later in your career, especially with longer pieces, there is usually little reason for a freelancer to give up all rights to his or her creations.

Anthology. A collection of works by different authors. Mentioned here because anthology rights, like other subsidiary rights, are important rights to keep in order to realize continued revenue on your works.

Assignment. When someone commissions you to write something. You receive them most often once you've been writing regularly for a specific magazine, editor, or in a specific genre. You and your work become a known commodity, so editors feel comfortable in seeking you out and assigning you ("commissioning") a story. Although some expenses may be paid up front, usually there is no advance in magazine or newspaper freelancing.

Auction. A nice situation for a writer to be in: when companies (publishers, producers, etc.) bid for the acquisition of rights to a work perceived to have high commercial potential. The competitive event usually drives the sale of the property to extremely attractive levels. Usually conducted by the agent.

Avant-garde. Work that is highly innovative and cutting-edge in form or subject matter.

Backgrounder. A story that is not assigned a deadline or publication schedule, but is for internal informational purposes. Also, a published story that details the background or profile of a subject.

Backlist. A list of books that were not published during the current season. Not out of print, but getting close.

Banner. A headline that extends across the page or screen.

Beat. The area or subject matter that an editor or reporter regularly covers. Also: a word used to signify a pause during a character's speech in a screenplay.

Belles lettres. Literary writing, which these days usually means stories focused on the internal lives of its characters. What is, and isn't, belles lettres changes from generation to generation.

B/W or B&W. Abbreviations for black and white images.

Bio. In a query letter, the bio section comes usually at the end of the letter and establishes your credentials and ability to write the kind of work you propose. Bios at the end of articles and on a contributor's page are usually written by the editors.

Boilerplate. The standard contract of a publisher. You can pretty much count on it being strongly in the publisher's favor. Unless you're a beginning writer hungry for bylines, editors and art directors usually consider the standard contract as a beginning point for negotiations. Caution: Do not earn a reputation of being difficult about contracts. Editors are busy people and there are lots of freelancers out there. Instead of hassling with you every time, they are quite likely to get someone else. Be nice and realize when no means no.

Boil down. Reduce a story's length by making it more concise.

Book packager. Also known as a book producer or book developer. This person or company is hired by publishers to put together all elements of a book, from concept to cover design to marketing. Book packagers often specialize in highly technical or art-intensive books that are beyond the usual publisher's capability.

Bump. To move a story ahead or behind its original publication date. Sometimes it can apply to pay rate, as in "I'm bumping up your per-word rate."

Byline. The author's name, usually preceded with the word "by." Don't expect bylines for sidebars and fillers, but you can ask for a tagline: your name at the end of the piece.

Captions. Sometimes called cut lines or cutlines. If you submit photography or illustrations with your text, you should also provide ample caption information, especially the names of any persons in the photographs.

Casebound. Printer talk for a hardbound book.

Category fiction. Also called genre fiction: horror, fantasy, mystery, western, romance, thriller, etc.

Chapbook. A small book of poems, drawings, oral stories or other short forms.

Chunks. Also chunking or chunked. A term from the field of human engineering, it refers to dividing information into digestible blocks or "chunks" and is based on the cognitive precept that human short-term memory (also called "working memory") has a maximum capacity of 7 simultaneous units, $+/-2$.

In magazine and newspaper writing, the concept often goes by the name of "multiple-entry journalism," or providing readers many entry points on a single page instead of one large unit of print.

Thus, many articles today are divided into sidebars, lists, charts, nutgraphs, and illustrations with captions that are tied together (if at all) by a shortened main story.

Today, most successful consumer magazines divide text on the average of every 100 words. Some, like today's top-selling magazine, *Maxim*, divide text every 40 words.

Chunking allows readers to scan an article (its chunks) and read only the parts most interesting and relevant to them. It is a type of customization that is being driven by the demand for personalization on the web and Internet, and it signals an important advance in helping readers and web-page viewers to process complex information.

Generally, chunking is achieved by a combination of three

methods: visual separation, visual progression and visual differentiation. Visual separation most often means the use of white space to frame chunks. Visual progression refers to giving sequence to chunks via letters, numbers, colors, horizontal and vertical arrangements. Visual differentiation relies on the use of various type styles, sizes and color shading to make each chunk graphically distinct.

Today's freelance writers are well advised to study their target publication to discern how the editors are using chunks, then divide up their story accordingly.

Circulation. Although it refers to the number of readers of a periodical, circulation comes in many varieties. There is "rate base"—the number of readers that are guaranteed to advertisers. There is "readership"—the total number of readers including "pass alongs" or people who were given the magazine by a subscriber. There is paid circulation and nonpaid circulation, controlled nonpaid and so forth (see also *ABC*).

Clean copy. This is what every editor hopes for from a freelancer. The better you can produce it, the more gainfully you will be employed. Clean copy is characterized by writing that fits the assignment and audience, strong sentences and structure that don't have to be deciphered and revised, no spelling or grammar errors, useable heads, subheads and decks, and most of all, 100 percent accuracy in its reporting.

Clips. When you're starting out, get them by any legal or ethical means possible. Clips are a collection of your published works with your byline or tagline on them. When submitting clips, submit copies on regular 8 1/2 x 11 paper, not actual clips that have been cut out.

CMYK. Cyan, magenta, yellow and black—the colors used to produce all others in today's four-color separation and printing process. The best publications are the ones that use four-color separation to produce graphics that are sharp and clean.

Codex. Any book made of bound pages.

Column inch. The number of words that appear in one vertical inch of typographic space. It is essential for freelancers to count the average number of words given to the features and departments in the magazines and newspapers they are writing for. This is usually done by counting the number of words in a column inch, measuring the number of column inches given to the story's text, then multiplying them.

Commercial. A work that is commercial appeals to a mass audience. Can be novels, screenplays or other works with a broad appeal.

Commissioned work. See *Assignment.*

Concept. A statement that summarizes the feature article, novel, screenplay or teleplay before it is actually written.

Confessional. A work—article, novel, poem, screenplay—in which the author reveals highly personal elements about themselves and others. When identities are only vaguely disguised, the work is called a "roman à clef."

Consumer magazines. A group of magazines that appeal to general and special interests of the public. These are usually the magazines that you see on newsstands. Trade magazines, on the other hand, focus on the membership of professions, trades, athletes and other specialty areas and are distributed mainly via memberships lists.

Contact sheet. A sheet of photographic paper containing all images from a roll of film to allow a preliminary review. Contact sheets are being replaced by CD-ROMs of images and by web sites where low-res versions of images are stored for review and selection. If you will be submitting photography, many editors now prefer dealing with electronic formats.

Contributor's copies. Free issues sent to authors who have work in it. At the beginning, this may be your only form of payment. But it's OK to start somewhere.

Co-publishing. In this form of subsidy publishing, the publisher bears some of the costs of production, fulfillment and marketing.

Copy. A story's text.

Copyediting. Also copyreading. The art of editing a manuscript for publication. A freelancer must often be his or her own copy editor. That means getting a book to learn this very special skill. Turning in a poorly copyedited manuscript usually means automatic rejection. If the mechanics aren't right, how much faith can an editor have in your reporting?

Copyright. The legal protection from unauthorized use of your work. Copyright is different from your rights to the work you create. You own the rights to your work as soon as you create it, sometimes called "common law copyright." Publishers then license from you the right to publish it, yet you can and should maintain your copyright—you've merely sold some ancillary part of it. First publication rights, digital rights, foreign publication rights, reprint rights, anthology rights—all are various types of rights that publishers have to license from you unless you sign a "work for hire" agreement, in which case you give up your copyright. Writers working full time for magazines and newspapers usually do not own the rights to their works; the company does.

Copywriting. Usually refers to copy written for advertising or marketing purposes.

Cover. To research and put together a story, as well as the frontmost portion of a publication.

Cover letter. A brief letter accompanying the submission of a manuscript, usually in response to an assignment or query. If you don't have anything necessary to say in a cover letter, don't waste an editor's time. Necessary things include: "Enclosed is a diskette with an electronic copy in Quark formatted for a Mac," or "My contact information has changed; please send my check to...," etc. If all you have to say is, "Here's my story," save a tree and some time.

Creative nonfiction. A style of writing that blends a reporter's objectivity and accuracy with a fiction writer's emotive impact and techniques of plot, narrative, character development, conflict, resolution, literary tropes and more.

Credit. To acknowledge the source for a given fact, or an acknowledgment of a person's contribution to your work.

Crop. Also cropping. Deleting unwanted parts of a photograph before publication. Although you can suggest certain cropping to an editor you're submitting your photography to, don't do any cropping yourself. Also, the smart freelancer will notice how photos are being cropped in a target magazine—how large the central image is, how much empty space is left, how many verticals vs. horizontals are being used—and provide photography that fits the photo editor's needs.

Deck. Also called a teaser or bank. The deck is usually a single sentence or phrase printed below the article's title and before the text begins. It serves to summarize and suggest the article's slant and reader payoff. If your target publication uses decks, study them: Are they humorous or serious, short or long, based on a pun or straightforward? But don't provide your own decks if you can't write them well enough not to embarrass yourself. Example: Title—"Minimize Your Risk of Cancer." Deck—"How to reduce it to the level of lightening strike and alien abduction."

Delivery memo. If you have been asked to submit photography or other artwork, you should include a delivery memo, which lists each image being delivered with a notation that corresponds to the same notation for the actual image, the use being made of the images, and any other previous agreements. The delivery memo asks for a signature from the employee who receives the photography or artwork to ensure all images are present and not damaged. A copy of the signed delivery memo is returned to you. All work—photographic and text—is best delivered by a service that tracks and insures your creations: FedEx, Airborne Express, UPS, etc. A delivery memo only accompanies photographic work that has been commissioned and requested, not over-the-transom materials. The memo specifies the value of each image and places liability for loss or damage on the recipient.

Derivative work. A new work based upon an old one in some form, as a translation, abridgement, adaptation, condensation and so forth.

Desktop publishing. Today's desktop and laptop computers, software and printers allow the knowledgeable individual to produce quality publications and distribute them with the use of a traditional pre-press and printer for typesetting and duplication. Desktop publishing has also produced a flood of substandard books by those who fail to bring professional-level management to all aspects of publishing, from copyediting, to cover and interior design, to printing.

Docudrama. A film or TV show based, often loosely, upon a real event of recent occurrence.

Dummy. A pre-publication mock up. For magazines, a dummy is usually a large piece of paper or electronic equivalent that contains thumbnails of all pages, which are then used to position editorial and advertising elements together, providing a schematic of the magazine. A book dummy usually consists of the covers with cover art and blank pages inside.

Dupes. Short for duplicate slides. When submitting transparencies to an editor, do not submit originals unless requested to do so. Instead, find a reliable photographic lab that produces high-quality duplicates of your original slides. Indicate to editors that you are submitting dupes, and that the originals are available on request.

Eclectic. A publication or publisher that produces a variety of writing styles and types, rather than being limited to one subject category or literary genre.

Electronic submission. A story or other work submitted via the Internet or on media such as a CD-ROM or computer disk.

E-Rights. The electronic rights to your work (its digital form that can be published via the Internet on web pages, in email newsletters, CD-ROMs, e-databases and so forth) are now fully protected thanks to several recent court cases. The courts, including the U.S. Supreme Court, have made it clear that an author's e-rights are distinct from any other copyrights and not automatically granted to a publication unless an author expressly gives up those rights. That said, e-rights are currently being sold for very little, usually 5 percent to 25 percent of the amount paid for first publication rights. With many publications, e-rights are expected without further compensation.

Erotica. All-encompassing term that refers to sexually oriented material of any kind.

Fact checking. The process of verifying the accuracy of all statements and claims of fact, spellings, quotations, dates and more. In many small publications, you are responsible for your own fact checking. Any inaccuracies that are pointed out after publication decrease your credibility and usefulness accordingly.

Most larger publications maintain their own fact checkers who work with you and the materials you provide to carry out this important process. For some publications, you may have to cite the sources of your facts in your manuscript when you submit it, as well as all research materials you used.

Fact checking is not only an important part of the publication's ability to maintain credibility; it also serves a legal purpose in libel cases, resulting in fact-checking materials being stored at least until the statute of limitations for libel have been exceeded.

Fair use. This provision in copyright law allows the quotation of short passages from a copyrighted work without violating the author's copyright. The actual number of words used is less important than if the use is an allowed one (for criticism, comment, news reporting, teaching, scholarship and research) and the commercial impact on the work from which the words were taken.

Feature. In newspapers, a feature is a story that contains elements of human interest rather than merely news. In magazines, it usually refers to the longest and most important stories in that issue.

Filler. A short item usually contained in a sidebar or box that is used to fill a hole in a page where another story appears. Editors often collect fillers of various sorts to have on hand for last-minute use. A common practice is for fillers in a specific magazine to be organized around recurring themes. Some writers specialize in writing fillers for selected magazines.

First North American Serial Rights. The most common portion of your copyright sold to magazines and newspapers and the most desirable since you give up the least. You are not giving up anthology rights, reprint rights, e-rights, subsidiary rights or foreign rights. Here's what the phrase means:
- "First"—you are warranting that the publication you are selling to is the first to publish it and the work has never appeared in any other copyrighted publication.

- "North American"—the agreement includes publications in Canada, the U.S. and Mexico.

- "Serial"—publications that appear periodically, as opposed to books.

- "Rights"—the permission to publish your work one time.

Flak. A low-position spokesperson for a company, sometimes used disparagingly for those in public relations and marketing.

Folio. The total number of pages in a newspaper or magazine, not counting covers. Also used to refer to the page numbers and any associated text in a page's header or footer.

Follow-up. A piece that details developments about the subject of a previously published story.

Formula story. A mainly derogatory term that refers to work that is predictable and familiar by its use of a well-recognized theme and plot structure.

Front matter. In a book, all the opening text with folios that would be printed as lower case Roman numerals if they were present. The length of the front matter is adjusted only after the main body of the text is done, since the total number of pages in a book must be divisible by 16. Back matter is also sometimes used to make this adjustment.

Front matter can include (in this order): blanks or advertisements, half-title page, list of other works by the author, title page, copyright page, list of contributors, blank, dedication, table of contents, table of illustrations, foreword, preface, acknowledgments or credits, explanatory notes, half-title.

Full bleed. When a photograph or other art element runs from edge to edge of the page it appears on.

Galleys. Sometimes called "galley proofs." This is the edited, typeset version of your story or book before it is published. Most magazine editors don't appreciate writers who insist on seeing galley proofs, and only the most highly paid writers get away with doing so. Editors will sometimes offer to show galleys to the author for a final check, but you should insist on seeing galleys only at your own peril.

Ghosting. Also called "ghost writing." A work-for-hire agreement in which you agree to let someone else put their name on your work.

Glossy. A photograph with a shiny surface as opposed to one with a matte finish.

Graf. Short for paragraph.

Gutter. The area where the left and right pages of an open publication meet in the middle and are bound.

Hammer. A term used to describe the third element of a three-part cover line. For example, in "Special Report: The Truth About Ginseng—It'll Make You Cry," the last element is the hammer.

Hard copy. The form of your manuscript supplied by a computer's printer.

Headline. The main title of your story. Sometimes called the "head" or "hed."

Head shot. A photograph of someone that includes the head and shoulders only. See also *Mug shot.*

Honorarium. This is usually where most freelancers begin: a token payment in cash, a byline or sample copies.

Hook. A technique used at the beginning of a work to nab a reader's interest (see also "lead"). Editors expect a hook because of the tremendous competition for a reader's attention today. Something must signal the work's freshness and unique appeal.

How-to. The most popular form of nonfiction writing today. Sometimes called "reader service journalism," it is writing which attempts to improve the reader's life by providing information and inspiration on virtually every topic that touches our lives. Reader service journalism has replaced fiction and literary essays as the dominant genre in American publishing.

Hyperlink. Also called "hypertext." It is a word or group of words linked by html coding to another page on the worldwide web. When writing for the web, your text should contain a variety of hyperlinks that make use of the instant interconnectedness of the web.

Illustrations. A catch-all term for any artwork included with your manuscript: photographs, jpegs, drawings, charts and tables, etc.

Imprint. The name of a publisher's line of books, for example, "The Idiot's Guide" series is an imprint of Alpha Books.

Interactive. A piece of software or computer application that allows user input and responds according to that input. It is the basis for a type of writing that is growing in popularity—interactive fiction and nonfiction—as well as for that revolution in communication called the Internet, the first many-to-many communication device.

Invasion of privacy. A legal term that describes photographing or writing about someone without their permission.

Kicker. The first sentence or first few words of a story's lead, sometimes set in a font size larger than the body text. Also applies to cover lines. Example: "Stay Alive: How to Drive During the Holidays"—the first two words are the kicker.

Kill fee. If a story you have delivered via a contract assignment is "killed" (canceled) and if a kill fee was part of your contract, you are entitled to a portion of the original sale price. Can be as little as 5 percent or as much as 100 percent, with 25 percent being common.

Lead. The opening section of a work (see *Hook*).

Lead time. The time between when something was assigned and when it is due, or between when it was received by the editor and when it was published.

Libel. There are two types of libel that writers are most often vulnerable to: personal libel and trade libel (also known as product disparagement). Both involve accusations or published statements that must meet three legal criteria to be considered libelous: The statement must: (1) be false; (2) have caused demonstrable harm; (3) have been made knowingly.

The truth of the statement is always considered first. If the statement is shown to be true, then the other two criteria do not come into play and the case is over. Only unprivileged communications can be libelous; privileged communications include statements protected by client-lawyer confidentiality, reports of legal proceedings, etc.

Writers can best protect themselves from libel by following the normal processes of fact-checking and keeping all research, notes and drafts used in the preparation of a manuscript. Reputable publishers carry writers' liability insurance and will defend their writers and themselves against a libel charge.

Magalog. A direct mail solicitation or catalog that contains teaser bits of editorial designed to generate interest in what is being sold. Some of the highest paid writers in America specialize in writing effective direct mail pieces and other types of advertising and promotional materials.

Masthead. The list of a publication's staff in hierarchical order, usually found in the front. The hierarchical order is important because the same job title may denote widely different duties and status at companies. Smart freelancers use a masthead to find the most appropriate editorial person to contact regarding a story idea, which could be directed toward a specific department editor, the features editor, etc.

Memoir. A fictional or true account of the narrator's or writer's personal history.

Model release. A form signed by a photograph's subject that gives you permission to publish the photograph without invading that person's privacy or copyrighted image. Professional models often have strict limitations on how and how often their image can be used.

Mug shot. A photograph of someone's head and shoulders.

Multimedia. The integration of various forms of media, including video, text, still photos, illustrations, animation, and sound.

Multiple submissions. Sending an editor more than one manuscript at a time. It is considered good etiquette to ask if the always-harried editor would like to see multiple submissions before sending them. Not to be confused with *Simultaneous submissions.*

Net sales. The number of books sold minus those returned by distributors.

Newsbreak. An important, late-breaking story added at the last minute to a newspaper's front page or to a section in a magazine.

News peg. Any current news item that gives immediacy and relevance to your story.

Nostalgia. A form of nonfiction writing that focuses on the fond recall of past events, products, people. More or less sentimental, depending on the publication.

Novella. A work of fiction in the 7,000 to 15,000 word range, also called a long short story or novelette.

Novelization. Creating a novel from a screenplay or teleplay, also called a "tie-in" and often published concurrently with the creation it novelizes.

Nutgraph. A paragraph in a story containing the key details of the entire story. Also, a list of information in paragraph form using some graphical device (bullets, flags, etc.) to separate their elements. See also *Chunking.*

One-time rights. Also known as "simultaneous rights," this agreement says the publisher has the nonexclusive right to use your work one time but you don't guarantee the same work won't appear in other publications. One-time rights are appropriate when selling the same work to non-competing markets.

On spec. Short for "on speculation," it's what you might hear after you've pitched a story to an editor and he/she is interested in seeing it, but doesn't know you well enough to commit to a contract. An on spec assignment does not obligate the editor to purchase the story once it is completed. After a successful on spec assignment with an editor, you should receive contracts with kill fees for any future assignments.

Opener. In magazine layouts, editors and art directors try to design compelling opening pages that clearly designate the story as a feature or a type of department, convey its emotional tenor, and draw the reader in. As the opening paragraph of your manuscript, the opener is considered the story's most important 100 to 200 words. It must have some sort of sizzle that marks it as fresh, strong writing and also adequately sets up all to follow.

Outline. Outlines of articles, books, screenplays and teleplays each have their own format. An article summary contains its subheads with one or two sentences each; same for a book summary, which uses chapter headings. A summary of a screenplay or teleplay, however, contains a scene-by-scene description and is called a "treatment."

Over the transom. A quaint phrase from the days when doors had transoms. It refers to unsolicited manuscripts that often go into the "slush pile" on the floors of agents and editors. A good freelancer doesn't do a lot of unsolicited submissions, but rather focuses on getting assignments first in order not to waste time chasing a story that no one is interested in.

Package deal. Selling your text and your photography to a publication at a discount.

Pad. To make a story longer.

Page rate. Instead of per-word payments, some magazines pay authors per printed page. "Page rate" is still commonly used by photographers.

Parallel submission. Also known as "multiple sales." The smart freelancer gets the most from his/her research by mining it for multiple articles, coming at it with different slants, and selling the stories to as many outlets as possible.

Paste-up. Also, a page proof. A page's textual elements assembled along with its graphical elements.

Payment on acceptance. Payment that occurs when your manuscript is deemed acceptable for publication. Obviously preferable to the next form.

Payment on publication. One of the many reasons why freelancing can be a tough life. What if your story keeps getting bumped from issue to issue? You could starve.

Perfect bound. A magazine or book whose pages are glued to a central spine, as opposed to being stapled (saddle-stitched), stitched, coil bound or other method.

Permissions. The right to use copyrighted material. This job is usually the author's, including any copyright fees that must be paid. Usually the publisher supplies the author with guidelines for obtaining permission and blank permission request forms.

Pitch. An idea for a story, book, movie or other project. Also a verb.

Plagiarism. Whether intentional or unintentional, it is illegal and unethical to pass off as your own work something that has been created by someone else. There is word-for-word plagiarism, mosaic plagiarism (using the same sentence structure but substituting synonyms periodically), and structural plagiarism (appropriating someone's approach to a topic).

Pork. Material held for later use.

Prepress. The process of creating color proofs and film that will be used by a printer to set the publication to paper and bind the pages together. This is when original artwork is scanned digitally and the four-color process is applied. Also includes "ad stripping," or preparing the ad materials on the page along with editorial copy.

Press junket. Usually a "free" trip offered to writers by travel-related businesses and their marketing agents. Great way to get free travel, but they're also like going to the Poconos for a "free" weekend and spending the day listening to a time-share sale pitch. Be aware that you will be a captive audience and that the provider will expect positive coverage in some publication in return for their largesse. The provider may also require an "assignment letter" on an editor's letterhead. Obvious caution lights. Don't promise something you can't deliver. Determine how you will deal with the expectation that you provide positive coverage upon your return, even if the service was dreadful. The most common way of dealing with this is to work out a very clear understanding between you and the provider about what you will and will not write, or can and cannot deliver. You may also be asked for pre-publication copy.

Proofreading. The careful reading of a manuscript to detect errors in spelling, punctuation and other typographical elements. Effective proofreading is a discipline that requires a different way of reading than how we normally go about it when editing or revising.

Proofs. Text sent to a typesetter is returned to the publisher as "first proofs" or "galley proofs" (named after the long sheets of paper they used to be printed on). Galley proofs from magazines usually omit artwork and captions or other graphical elements. However, galley proofs from book publishers today closely resemble the finished product. Proofs are provided to the author in batches as they are completed so that proofreading can commence.

- "Second proofs" or "page proofs" is a second set of pages that contain the requested revisions as well as all art elements. These proofs are what the published page will look like.

- "Printer's proofs" are proofs sent by the typesetter or pre-press house to the printer.

- "Film proofs" or "bluelines," or simply "blues" (because they are usually printed in blue ink) are sent by the printer to the publisher for one last look. If an error or problem (page smudge, incorrect order) isn't caught here, it will appear in the published form.

Proposal. An idea for a book, movie or TV show is submitted as a proposal. The formats for book proposals are often specified by a publisher or agent. If it isn't specified, standard formats can be used and usually include a cover letter, prospectus (single-page overview), analysis of the proposed market, analysis of competitive books, author biography, chapter outlines, sample chapters, and related research. Same for movie and TV show proposals: each requires a different format.

Prospectus. Or abstract. A brief description of a written work.

Public domain. Material that is not copyrighted or whose copyright has expired.

Puff piece. Also, simply "puff." A work that contains editorialized, complimentary statements about a person, place or business.

Pull quote. A quotation from an article, sometimes edited for brevity, and displayed in larger type as a sort of illustration to the article to generate reader interest.

Query letter. Or just "query." A query is a question. In this case, you are asking an editor if he or she is interested in seeing the manuscript of the story you're describing. Whether on paper or in an email, keep your query brief (one page) and focused on describing your story in such a way that it clearly fits the editor's publication, audience and current needs.

Reprint rights. Also called "second serial rights." Reprint rights give the publisher the right to print something that has already appeared in another publication.

Response time. The amount of time an editor or producer takes to respond to your query or submitted manuscript. Many state their response time in their submission guidelines. If you are working without guidelines, allow 4 to 6 weeks for a response. At that point, send a reminder note or email asking politely for an update on your submission. If there is still no response, politely ask for your materials back and move on to greener pastures.

Saddle-stitched. A magazine or book with pages stapled together.

SASE. Self-addressed, stamped envelope. Any correspondence you send that you would like a written response to should include a SASE. An editor or producer is under no obligation to return unsolicited materials without a SASE.

Self-publishing. The original form of publishing. These days more and more authors are paying for the production of their own work and finding ways to market it directly to readers, realizing more of its profits. The Internet is a strong force in the self-publishing movement.

Sell through. Percentage of net sales for a book or magazine. If 10,000 copies were printed and 5,000 sold, a book had a 50 percent sell through.

Sidebar. An element of the main story called out for separate treatment. Sidebars are essential elements of today's multiple-entry journalism prominent in magazines and on the web. See *Chunking*.

Signature. Also called "sig," it refers to your name and contact information at the end of an email. It can also refer to a group of pages printed together in four, eight, 16-page increments or higher. In the latter, 16 pages would be printed on the front of a large piece of paper, and 16 pages on the back. Then the large piece of paper is folded and cut to produce the individual pages that are bound together. In this latter use of the word, "signature" dates from the time that workers signed their name on the pages they compiled.

Simultaneous subs. "Subs" refers to submissions. The practice of submitting the same article to more than one publication at the same time. At the very least, your cover letter should indicate that you are also submitting the story to another publication. Some editors are open to simultaneous submissions; many are not due to the competitive nature of publishing.

Skyline. The area at the top of a magazine cover, above the logo. The skyline usually contains one or more cover lines and secondary images. Because of newsstand placement, often only a magazine's skyline is visible.

Slant. There are various levels of slant. On one level, slant is the approach you take to your material in order to make it fit a specific publication's audience. For example, it is not enough to write an article for women. You must slant your material for the particular take on women that each magazine has. The same material would be slanted highly differently for *Cosmopolitan* than it would be for *Oprah*. Slant can also refer to the theme and tone that you give to the material, and usually answers the question: "What will readers take away from reading my story?"

Slides. Slide film is processed differently than print film and produces a transparency that is close to the true colors and details of the original subject. Print film, on the other hand, contains colors adjusted by a technician at a color lab and printed on paper that may dull or distort original colors. High-quality slide film or high-resolution digital images are almost always preferred over prints.

Both of these forms of emulsion technology are being rapidly replaced by digital photography.

Slugline. A slug is a department title or other feature of the story that is repeated on subsequent pages so that the reader can better find its parts.

Slush pile. The place where unsolicited manuscripts are often placed for later (usually much later) consideration. The larger the publication, the less likely someone important (or anyone at all) will read the submission to determine its worth. Some book publishers and magazines have editors whose job it is to wade through the slush. Some have stopped accepting unsolicited manuscripts. In either case, as a freelancer, you have to ask yourself why you're submitting something no one has asked to see, has expressed no interest in, and will be treated with the lowest regard. Slush piles have very low priority because editors and experienced freelancers know that sending in something unsolicited is usually a waste of everyone's time.

Small press. A publishing business that operates on a considerably smaller financial model than do large publishers. As a result, a small press can specialize and take more risks since it doesn't require the huge mass market success to keep afloat, as do most larger publishers. Small presses publish most of the nonfiction in America.

Source. An individual whose statements are used for material in a story.

Spread. Two facing pages in a magazine devoted entirely to the artwork, graphics and text of a magazine feature.

Stet. Proofreader's mark for "restore to condition before mark up." In other words, disregard the marked change and go back to the original.

Style manuals. There's a flavor for almost every day of the week. Their proliferation speaks to the need to understand your specific market and tailor your writing in every way for it. From *The Associated Press Stylebook* to the *ACS Style Guide*, the list of style manuals suggests the variety of these markets. Keep in mind that many publishing houses generate their own style sheets that serve as in-house style manuals—their own way of doing things—and this can result in many unexpected changes to your copy.

Subsidy publishing. See *Co-publishing*.

Synopsis. A brief summary or précis. If you can't give a clear, effective synopsis of something you've written, chances are readers (and editors) will also miss the point.

Tagline. Your name at the end of a contribution, usually in italics and preceded by a dash.

Target Audience. Few terms are more important to writers than this one and "target market." The intended audience has a direct impact on virtually every aspect of the work: from the topic selected, to the slant toward it, its length, language and most everything else. Here's an example: Imagine telling your best friend about your hot date last night. Now, imagine telling your grandmother about the same experience. How would the details, the language, the theme of what you relate change between the two people? Audience analysis is one of the hidden keys to successful writing. As is the next term.

Target Market. Market can refer to a number of things: the genre (romance market, science fiction market); the type of publication (women's magazine market, mass paperback market); age groups (teen market, adult male market). Most often, it refers to the specific entity you are writing for. That entity can be a television network: CBS garners a very different market than does Fox. For freelancers, it most often means the specific publication. Take the men's market for example. Although all may print stories about "male potency," you can bet that each of the men's mags, from *Men's Health* to *Maxim*, will have a very different take on it.

The successful freelancer studies at least six back issues of a target magazine before crafting a piece for it. The purpose of such study is not only to determine if your story has been recently done. Its more important purpose is to help you to understand how that publication needs a story written for its particular take on the audience it is serving. That "take" affects virtually every element of a story as you craft it.

Tearsheet. The actual page from a publication that contains your work.

Tie in. The part of a story that reiterates past events in order to make recent developments clear. Also, "tie back." A promotional tie-in is a work that helps market another work, e.g., the novelizations of "Star Wars" and "Star Trek" movies.

TK. Proofreader's insertion mark for material or data "to come." Also "TKTK."

TOC. Table of contents.

Trade magazines. Publications aimed at members of occupations, professions and groups. They usually do not appear on the news-stand but are available via subscription to a membership.

Trim. To reduce the length of a story. Also refers to the size of a publication, as in "trim size."

Vanity press. A publishing house that requires the author to pay for all costs of production. Usually the publisher offers little marketing help or marketing help that is ineffective. As the name suggests, vanity presses aren't for the serious writer. Few bookstores and fewer reviewers will consider works from a vanity press.

Well. Sometimes called the "feature well," it is the center or heart of the magazine where the most important stories appear, usually without commercial interruption.

Work for hire. In a work-for-hire contract, you have no rights to your creations, which are owned fully by the publication or company you are writing for. Freelance contractors who are making a living by writing for one publication are often on work-for-hire contracts, but are being paid a sufficient and regular salary.

Writer's guidelines. A list of suggestions that identify the freelancing opportunities at a magazine, publishing house or production organization. The guidelines usually include the kinds of stories and how to approach them, submission guidelines, contact info and payment information. These guidelines should not be used to substitute for the real work of reading and studying a target market before writing for it.

"Of all those arts in which the wise excel,
Nature's chief masterpiece is writing well."
—Duke of Buckingham
Sheffield (1649–1720)

 **APPENDIX II**

SAMPLE
INVOICE

To download printable copies of this form, go to:
www.peakwriting.com/sampleforms
    The author accepts no liability with respect to the proper completion of this form or alterations made to it. The invoice begins on the following page.

INVOICE

David Taylor • 37 Fairmont Ave., Savannah, GA 31406 • (912) 921-1121

Date: mm/dd/yyyy   Invoice: Control#:
Bill to: Client Name   PO#:
             Client's Address 1
             Address 2
             City, State, Zip
             Phone & fax

Date	Description	Amount
	Full description of work and services provided: Title Length Use Projected publication date Expenses (if applicable) Original receipts attached	
Terms	30 Days Net	
	Total	

Pay to the Order of:
Federal Tax ID (if billing as a company):
Social Security Number (if billing as an individual):

Please Mail Payment to: David Taylor
                            Peak Writing, LLC
                            37 W. Fairmont Ave.
                            Savannah, GA 31406

Comments: Thanks for the opportunity to work with you!

Any questions regarding this invoice, please call, fax or email:
Tel: (912) 921–1121 • Fax: (912) 921–1065 • email: david@peakwriting.com

*"I believe more in the scissors
than I do in the pencil."*
—Truman Capote

 **APPENDIX III**

SAMPLE COPYRIGHT PERMISSION REQUEST

To download printable copies of this form, go to: *www.peakwriting.com/sampleforms*

 The author accepts no liability with respect to the proper completion of this form or alterations made to it. The form begins on the following page.

COPYRIGHT PERMISSION REQUEST

October 14, 2003

Dear Permissions Editor or Author:

In preparing a project for publication, I came across the work described below and found it of such value that I would like to include it in my book/article/web site. I am hereby requesting your permission for the nonexclusive right to reproduce an excerpt from the following material:

Description of Work I Wish to Use:
- Author:
- Title:
- Date of Publication:
- Work is found in (book title, web site URL, periodical title):
- Page number(s) or page URL the work is found on:
- Description:

Intended Use of It:
I wish to use the material in this and all subsequent editions of the work described below, in translations, and in other derivative works distributed in all media now or in the future existing.
- Author/Editor:
- Title:
- Media (book, article, web page):
- Projected publication date:

Grant of Permission
Please indicate permission is granted by signing below (digital signature OK) and returning this form to me, David Taylor, via fax, mail or email. If the rights for this material are not entirely controlled by you, please indicate whom I may contact to obtain copyright permission. Thank you for your valuable contribution.

PERMISSION IS GRANTED:

_____

Signature   Date   Please print or type name

Any questions regarding this request, please contact David Taylor:
Tel: (866) 921–1121 • Fax: (912) 921–1065 • email: david@peakwriting.com
37 W. Fairmont, Savannah, GA 31406

"The act of writing is the act of discovering what you believe."
—David Hare

 **APPENDIX IV**

SAMPLE FREELANCE CONTRACTS

To download printable copies of these forms, go to: *www.peakwriting.com/sampleforms*

The author accepts no liability with respect to the proper completion of these forms or alterations made to them. The first form begins on the following page.

PUBLICATION RIGHTS AGREEMENT

This agreement is hereby made and entered into by _____
_____(the "Publisher") and David Taylor (the "Author") of Peak Writing, a Georgia limited-liability company located at 37 West Fairmont Avenue, Building 2, Suite 202, Savannah, Ga., 31406.

Publication _____

Manuscript title _____

Length _____

Due date _____

Compensation _____

Kill fee (%)_____

Expenses _____

Preferred style sheet _____

Projected publication date _____

Credit line in editorial use _____

The Author and the Publisher have agreed as follows regarding the Publisher's acquisition of the Author's written contribution (the "Work").

   1. Author's Warrant

      Author represents and warrants that the Work is the Author's original work; that the Author has the right to sell the Work; that there has been no prior sale, publication or transfer of rights of the Work or any part of it; that publication of the Work will not infringe upon any other party's copyright; that publication of the Work will not violate the rights of privacy of others or their rights relative to defamation; and that Author has obtained all waivers of rights or releases which may be necessary.

Author agrees to cooperate in the defense of any legal action which may be brought against Publisher arising from the publication of the Work, and agrees to retain all notes, drafts and copies relating to the Work for three (3) years from publication.

2. Grant of License

Author hereby grants to Publisher rights as described below for a period of one (1) year from acceptance of the work. All rights are exclusive to Publisher, except as otherwise specified. Beginning one (1) year after acceptance of the Work, all rights are nonexclusive.

A. One-Time First North American Serial Rights
❑ Yes
❑ No
The right to publish the Work prior to any other party in North America in the above-named Publication.

B. One-Time First World Serial Rights
❑ Yes
❑ No
The right to publish the Work prior to any other party throughout the world in the above-named Publication, whether in English or translated into a foreign language.

C. Subsidiary Rights
❑ Yes
❑ No

The right to anthologize the Work at any time in a collection of works from the Publication; to syndicate the
Work in whole or in part for domestic or foreign publication; to publish, distribute and sell reprints of all or
any portion of the Work in any language and in any
country.

D. E-Rights
❏ Yes
❏ No
The right to publish, display and transmit the Work in
electronic media, including, but not limited to, all electronic, worldwide web, CD-ROM, electronic databases, archival and/or data retrieval systems, optical, digital and other electronic media whether now known or
hereafter created.

E. Reuse Rights
❏ Yes
❏ No
The right to publish and use the Work which appeared in the Publication in all of the Publisher's other
publications in consideration of a one (1) time additional fee equal to twenty-five (25%) percent of the
original compensation paid.

3. Author's Deliverables
Author agrees to provide manuscripts in final form and of
the agreed upon length, together with all source material
and backup material relating to the Work on or before the
Due Date. If the Publisher exercises the right to reject the

work and pay a kill fee, all ownership rights shall revert to the Author.

4. Publisher's Right to Edit
Author grants Publisher the right to edit, condense or alter the work as necessary for publication. The Author agrees to cooperate fully and expediently in the fact-checking, editing and revision process.

5. Payment Terms
Publisher agrees to process Author's invoice for payment within thirty (30) days of acceptance of the Work. Publisher agrees to process Author's invoice for expenses (which shall be accompanied by original receipts) within 15 days. Publisher agrees to pay a ten (10%) percent late penalty of the amount owed for each week payment is past due.

6. Author's Employment Status
Author agrees that he is an independent contractor and not an employee of the Publisher.

7. Agreement Changes
This Agreement represents the entire Agreement of the parties, and any change to this Agreement must be made in writing and signed by all parties. This Agreement shall be construed in accordance with the laws of the State of Georgia, the courts which shall have the exclusive jurisdiction and venue for the resolution of any disputes.

8. Agreement Signatures
This agreement is not binding on the Author until Author

receives a signed and completed copy of this Agreement from Publisher.

Publisher or Representative Signature

Publisher's Address

Publisher's Phone Number

Publisher's Fax Number

Publisher's Email Address

Date of Agreement

Peak Writing, LLC

By: _____
     David Taylor

Date: _____

WORK FOR HIRE AGREEMENT

This agreement is hereby made and entered into by _____
_____(the "Publisher") and David Taylor (the "Author") of Peak Writing, a Georgia limited-liability company located at 37 West Fairmont Avenue, Building 2, Suite 202, Savannah, Ga., 31406.

Publication _____

Manuscript title _____

Length _____

Due date _____

Compensation _____

Kill fee (%)_____

Expenses _____

Preferred style sheet _____

Projected publication date _____

Credit line in editorial use _____

The Author and the Publisher have agreed as follows regarding the Publisher's acquisition of the Author's written contribution (the "Work").

1. Author's Warrant
   Author represents and warrants that the Work is the Author's original work; that the Author has the right to sell the Work; that there has been no prior sale, publication or transfer of rights of the Work or any part of it; that publication of the Work will not infringe upon any other party's copyright; that publication of the Work will not violate the rights of pri-

vacy of others or their rights relative to defamation; and that Author has obtained all waivers of rights or releases which may be necessary.

Author agrees to cooperate in the defense of any legal action which may be brought against Publisher arising from the publication of the Work, and agrees to retain all notes, drafts and copies relating to the Work for three (3) years from publication.

2. Grant of License

Author acknowledges that Publisher has commissioned Author to create the Work, and that ownership of the Work is to be solely and exclusively vested in the Publisher. Author agrees that the Work is a work made for hire within the meaning of Copyright Law, and Publisher will be considered the owner of the Work for all purposes, including copyright. To the fullest extent permitted by law, Author hereby assigns his copyright in the Work to Publisher for the duration of the Copyright and any extensions thereof.

Author hereby appoints Publisher its attorney-in-fact to sign any documents necessary to transfer and assign Author's copyright to Publisher, and further, Author agrees to sign any other documents reasonably necessary to transfer and assign said copyright to Publisher, at such times as may be requested by Publisher. Author agrees that Publisher is the owner of the Work throughout the world.

Author agrees that all rights granted by this Agreement are applicable in all media, including, but not limited to, all electronic, worldwide web, CD-ROM, electronic databases, archival and/or data retrieval systems, optical, digital and other media whether now known or hereafter created.

3. Author's Deliverables

Author agrees to provide manuscripts in final form and of the agreed upon length, together with all source material and backup material relating to the Work on or before the Due Date. If the Publisher exercises the right to reject the work and pay a kill fee, all ownership rights shall revert to the Author.

4. Publisher's Right to Edit

Author grants Publisher the right to edit, condense or alter the work as necessary for publication. The Author agrees to cooperate fully and expediently in the fact-checking, editing and revision process.

5. Payment Terms

Publisher agrees to process Author's invoice for payment within thirty (30) days of acceptance of the Work. Publisher agrees to process Author's invoice for expenses (which shall be accompanied by original receipts) within 15 days. Publisher agrees to pay a ten (10%) percent late penalty of the amount owed for each week payment is past due.

6. Author's Employment Status

Author agrees that he is an independent contractor and not an employee of the Publisher.

7. Agreement Changes

This Agreement represents the entire Agreement of the parties, and any change to this Agreement must be made in writing and signed by all parties. This Agreement shall be construed in accordance with the laws of the State of Georgia, the courts which shall have the exclusive jurisdiction and venue for the resolution of any disputes.

8. Agreement Signatures

This agreement is not binding on the Author until Author receives a signed and completed copy of this Agreement from Publisher.

_____

Publisher or Representative Signature

_____

Publisher's Address

_____

Publisher's Phone Number

_____

Publisher's Fax Number

_____

Publisher's Email Address

_____

Date of Agreement

Peak Writing, LLC

By: _____
    David Taylor

Date: _____

*"The most original thing a writer can do
is write like himself.
It is also the most difficult."*
—Robertson Davies

 **APPENDIX V**

SAMPLE MODEL RELEASE

To download printable copies of these forms, go to: *www.peakwriting.com/sampleforms*

The author accepts no liability with respect to the proper completion of these forms or alterations made to them. The form begins on the following page.

TALENT/MODEL RELEASE

KIDS WANNA KNOW

37 Fairmont Ave., Savannah, GA 31406

Tel: (912) 921–1121 • Fax (912) 921–1065

Project Description: _____Date: _____

Your Legal Name: _____

Mailing Address: _____

Phones: _____

I hereby consent and grant you, your successors, assigns and licensees, the sole and exclusive right, but not the obligation, to use my name, voice, and/or any video or photographs taken by you of my acts, poses, plays, face, person, likeness and appearances of any and all kinds and/or any recordings of my voice (with the right to "dub" the voice of another in the place of mine), instrumental, musical and other sound effects produced by me, or any simulation thereof, as you see fit in the exercise of your sole discretion, in and with connection with the production, distribution, exhibition, advertising and marketing by any means whatsoever, forever and for use worldwide.

The rights granted hereunder should include without being limited to, the right to use video and photographs and in connection with commercial tie-ups and products related to any motion picture, book, article, television show or web site. I attest that I am acting on my own behalf and am not a member of any union or guild that would have any recourse for retroactive or future actions against the licensees. I am non-union and understand that this is a non-union project being produced by non-union signatories for broadcast and publication purposes.

This instrument shall endure to your benefit as well as to the benefit of your successors, assigns and licensees and is executed by me with full knowledge that you intend to rely and act pursuant to the consent herein above granted, and that you would not do so in the absence of this instrument.

X_____

SIGNATURE (Parent/Guardian signature if not of legal age)

_____

WITNESS   POSITION   DATE

"Writing is an exploration. You start from nothing and learn as you go."
—E L Doctorow

INDEX

Trupp, Phil, 114

U

U.S. Copyright Office, 183
University Microfilms, Inc., 124
University of Virginia, 65
User Interface Engineering, 205

W

Wallingford, Anne, 152
Wayman, Anne, 236
Web writing, 203–27
    career, 220–22
        resources, 223
    contracts
        resources
            National Writer's Union, 219
    e-rights, 212–19, *See also* E-rights
    hyperlinks, 208
        tips, 208–10
    improving, 211–13
    markets, 222–23
        resources
            Bacon's Internet Media Directory, 223
            freelancer online communities, 223
            job pages, 223
            Online Markets for Writers, 223
            Writer's Online Marketplace, 223
    print vs. web, 204–11
    publishing print simultaneously, 226–27
    reading speed, 206–7
        tips, 207–8
    resources, 219

scanning, 204–5
    tips, 205–6
simplicity, 210–11
travel writing, 223–25
    resources
        Travelwriter Marketletter, 226

W

Will, George, 115
Wise Owl Books, 265
Word, 14
Words That Sell: A Thesaurus to Help You Promote Your Products, Services and Ideas, Richard Bayan, 109
Workflow management, 30
Write the Perfect Book Proposal: 10 That Sold and Why, Jerr Herman, 236
Writer's block, 13, 54–66
    causes, 54–59
    tips for busting, 59–63
Writer's Digest, 138
Writer's Digest School, 21
Writer's Digest Guide to Literary Agents, 244
Writer's Guide to Book Editors, Publishers, and Literary Agents, 2003–2004: Who They Are! What They Want! and How to Win Them Over, 244
Writer's Guild East, 192
Writer's Market, 2, 14, 38, 119, 138, 154
Writer's Online Marketplace, Debbie Ridpath Ohi, 223
Writer's Relief, Inc., 247